Just War, Nonviolence, and Nuclear Deterrence

Ethics, Violence and Peace

Series Editor: Kenneth H. Klein

JUST WAR, NONVIOLENCE AND NUCLEAR DETERRENCE
Philosophers on War and Peace

Edited by

Duane L. Cady

and

Richard Werner

Longwood Academic
Wakefield, New Hampshire

Published in 1991 by Longwood Academic, a division of Hollowbrook Communications, Inc., Wakefield, New Hampshire 03872-0757.

Printed on acid-free paper.

Library of Congress Cataloging in Publication Data:

Just war, nonviolence, and nuclear deterrence : philosophers on war and peace / edited by Duane L. Cady and Richard Werner.
    p.   cm. -- (Ethics, violence and peace)
Includes index.
ISBN 0-89341-675-4 (alk. paper) — ISBN 0-89341-676-2 (pbk. : alk. paper)
    1. Just war doctrine. 2. War (Philosophy). 3. Nonviolence.
    4. Deterrence (Strategy)--Moral and ethical aspects. I. Cady, Duane L. II. Werner, Richard. III. Series.
B105.W3J86 1991
172'.42--dc20   91-27150
                                                  CIP

Dedicated to

George Hampsch

1927-1990

College of the Holy Cross

A Concerned Philosopher for Peace

CONTENTS

Part II: Nuclear Deterrence and Deterrence Discourse

Acknowledgments

The editors thank the following for their help in making this volume possible:

The University of Notre Dame and James Sterba for hosting the Third Annual Conference of Concerned Philosophers for Peace, October 1990, at which early versions of many of these papers were presented and discussed.

Hamilton College and Hamline University for financial support in the preparation of the manuscript.

Kenneth H. Klein, the series general editor, and Joseph C. Kunkel, Executive Secretary of Concerned Philosophers for Peace, for their encouragement and support.

William C. Gay, editor, *Concerned Philosophers for Peace Newsletter*, for permission to include the essays comprising the *Afterword* as well as for his Star Wars Bibliography included at the end of this volume.

Civia and Steven Liebman for their original artwork designed especially for the cover.

Adeel Hasan, Ahsan Janoo and Eric Werner for their assistance in the preparation of the manuscript.

Northern Wisconsin wilderness for therapeutic shelter from the storm.

Finally, we are beholden to our families for their support and patience and especially for helping us ignore the man behind the curtain.

D. L. C. & R. W.

Foreword

In this anthology, contemporary philosophers turn their attention to the issues of war and peace. Using their skills in ethical theory, critical analysis, social and political philosophy, they debate the applicability and viability of just war theory, the ethics and practicality of nonviolence, and the morality and rationality of nuclear deterrence. In an attempt to apply philosophy in a practical manner, the articles contained in the book minimize technical jargon and attempt to make the ideas accessible. A variety of perspectives and points of view are represented, including feminism, political realism, pacifism, and the just war tradition.

Most of the articles in this collection were presented at the Third Annual Conference of Concerned Philosophers for Peace held at the University of Notre Dame in September of 1990. The articles appear in print for the first time. Many of the contributors are well known for their previous books on the issues of war and peace.

In Part I, Just War and Nonviolence, the focus is upon moral issues which arise within the just war tradition and the concepts of nonviolence and pacifism. The articles are arranged along a spectrum beginning with a defense of traditional just war, continuing through critical reflections on just warism, to close with considerations of positive peacemaking. Actual cases discussed include incidents from World War II, recent democratization in Eastern Europe, the Persian Gulf War, and contemporary feminist peace politics.

In Part II, Nuclear Deterrence and Nuclear Language, the nine articles are arranged in three sets of triplets. The first set discusses issues relating to the morality and rationality of various deterrence strategies. The second set considers the topic of deterrence within the just war tradition while raising criticisms of just war theory. Set three addresses the language and metaphors in which deterrence discussion occurs and the implications these have for our understanding of nuclear deterrence policy.

The present volume is part of the Ethics, Violence and Peace series published by Longwood Academic. The next volume, to appear in fall 1992, will concentrate on the topic of Nationalism and Militarism in Regional Conflicts.

Part I

Just War
and Nonviolence

Introduction to Part I:
Just War and Nonviolence

Duane L. Cady

All of the essays collected under this heading are reflections on moral restraint concerning war and acts of war. The articles are arranged to reflect the increasing degrees of moral restraint required by the various philosophers represented. Readers will note the diversity of positions and approaches to moral appraisal of war along a broad spectrum from the just war tradition through considerations of varieties of pacifism to articulations of nonviolent commitment. These selections exemplify the range of current discussion in the field and further the conversation in this growing research area.

In the opening essay, "Moral Philosophy, International Law and the Deaths of Innocents," Sheldon Cohen examines the use (and misuse) of international law by philosophers writing on war and morality. Focusing initially on the notion of "bombardment of towns," and demonstrating the subtlety and complexity of distinctions in relevant legal documents, Cohen turns his attention to the broader concept of innocents in war and defends the view that both international law and moral tradition permit—and may sometimes require—the deaths of innocents in war.

Cohen's reasoning rests on the claim that the principles which are the primary source of protection for the innocent cannot themselves be enforced without putting innocent lives at risk. He develops and defends this claim by reference to specific military operations including WW II bombings of Caen and St. Lo during the Normandy campaign, the recent attempt by Kuwaiti troops to defend Kuwait City from Iraqi attack, and Romanian army resistance to government security forces in house-to-house fighting in Bucharest during the collapse of the Ceausescu regime. Cohen takes these to be examples of justifiable risk to innocents—both legally and morally. His point is that nations may justifiably prefer risk and even death of innocents to capitulation. All of this follows from an even broader observation: morally and legally, placing human lives at risk can be justified in view of other significant gains.

In "Double Effect and the Killing of Innocents," **Mark Vorobej** examines arguments crucial to Robert Holmes' defense of anti-war pacifism in *On War and Morality* (1989). Holmes' book is an important contribution to the philosophical literature on the morality of war and peace. Holmes' principal aim is to argue that war in the modern world cannot be morally justified. Rather than promote an extreme form of pacifism, Holmes proceeds from what he calls "moral personalism," the conviction that concern for the lives and well-being of persons (including ourselves) is the basis for valuing. This leads him to critique and ultimately reject the just war tradition on the grounds that it collapses into war realism by its endorsement of the principle of double effect. This principle allows such killing to be morally justified on the grounds that acts have both intended and unintended (hence "double") effects; the tradition takes all harm to innocents to be wrong, but excuses unintended harm. Holmes considers the principle to be theoretically intelligible but practically vacuous. As he puts it, "the morally artful can turn it to whatever purpose they want."

Vorobej challenges Holmes' claim that the presumption against killing innocent persons can never be defeated by undercutting Holmes reasons for rejecting double effect. Vorobej charges Holmes with inconsistency over the relevance of intention to moral appraisal, and he denies Holmes the grounds for claiming double effect to be inherently subject to capricious abuse. Admitting abuse and deception, including self-deception, in *describing* any actions as having had good intentions, Vorobej argues that such abuse is *not* inherent to the principle of double effect. The application of any moral principle may be misdescribed. Despite his defense of the principle of double effect against Holmes' criticisms, Vorobej admits that the principle itself may fail to justify killing innocents. If it does, he thinks it would be for reasons other than those provided by Holmes.

In "Reconciling Pacifists and Just War Theorists" **James Sterba** challenges the traditional representations of pacifism and just war theory as moral opposites. Working from within the just war tradition, Sterba argues that pacifism and just war theory, in their most morally defensible interpretations, can be substantially reconciled.

Sterba's argument begins with the traditional elements of just war: just cause and just means. His focus is on the just means requirements that harm to innocents not be intended and that war not cause more harm than would nonbelligerent means. He goes on to observe that these traditional conditions are not essentially about war; rather, they apply to a wide range of defensive actions including war. This allows him to consider reconciliation with anti-war pacifists, i.e., pacifists who oppose modern war on moral grounds but allow restricted use of lethal force (for example, in personal self-defense against an unprovoked violent attacker).

By creating several cases all falling short of massive lethal violence, Sterba challenges the anti-war pacifist to draw the line between clearly justifiable uses of small-scale defense and slightly larger-scale actions involving the killing of innocents to prevent greater harm. The distinction between consequences intended and those simply foreseen proves crucial to satisfying just war conditions. Sterba concludes that still larger-scale conflicts may proportionately resemble the cases examined and thus that anti-war pacifists are not justified in morally prohibiting every participation in war. He closes by asking just war theorists to make a comparable concession: that harm to innocents, not loss of liberties or other goods, must be the basis on which war is morally appraised.

Noting the centrality of the "domestic analogy" in just war thinking, Joseph Kunkel challenges its common use in defense of war. The domestic moral right of an individual to use even lethal force in self-defense against aggression is very widely accepted. Perhaps this is why it is so rarely questioned when it is used, by analogy, to justify nations engaged in war. Rather than question the strength of the analogy itself, Kunkel reviews the rational arguments which are used to justify killing in self-defense. He finds them so inconclusive that their use to justify war is undercut, not because war and interpersonal violence are disanalogous (though they may be) but because the justification for an individual killing another in self-defense is not the clear case it is often taken to be.

Four types of arguments used to justify killing an aggressor in private self-defense are examined: consequentialism (good ends outweigh evil means), forfeiture of rights (by committing acts of aggression people forfeit their right to moral treatment), deontology or nonconsequentialism (we are duty-bound to kill when necesssary to protect innocents), and double effect (intended versus merely foreseen killing). In each case Kunkel finds counterarguments sufficiently strong to undermine the arguments for killing in self-defense. The upshot is that being morally allowed to kill in order to avoid being killed is not at all self-evident; rather, it turns out to be quite problematic at best. Given this serious problem at the root of the domestic analogy, Kunkel concludes that justifying war may be a much heavier burden than is commonly thought.

In "Hobbes' Solution to the Problem of Power," **Bob Litke** examines dominating power as a central feature of civil life as he moves the discussion away from justifications for war and toward constructions of social peace. He takes us back to Hobbes, an early and articulate proponent of power as domination, to understand the concept, its problems and Hobbes' own attempts at solutions.

In Hobbes, Litke finds both the claim that humans naturally drift toward conflict *and* the suggestion that there is in our nature the means with which to control this drift. Having discovered the tension of opposing tendencies within human nature, Hobbes formulates a route to peace.

First, Hobbes states the potentially bleak consequences of our insatiable desire for power: competition, enmity and the war of each against all leading to lives which are "nasty, brutish and short." But next, rather than leave us hovering on the brink of chaos, Hobbes offers hope in that we learn the self-destructive dangers of acting as his account of power suggests we must. Focusing on Hobbes' fifth law of nature, which says that our ability to accommodate ourselves to others takes precedence over our restless desire for power after power, Litke sees Hobbes as suggesting that sustained and coordinated human activity presupposes substantial imaginative, perceptual and intellectual capacities as well as alertness to the consequences of specific destructive interactions. Put simply, our capacity for mutual accommodation enables us to create and maintain peaceful society.

This study closes with an examination of Hobbes' use of the sovereign to check the burgeoning problem of domination. It strikes Litke as unimaginative of Hobbes to solve the problem of domination with more domination. He speculates that Hobbes preferred consent as a check on domination, but that he could not see how we might learn from each other how best to coordinate with each other. Short of such knowledge to guarantee mutual accommodation, we "consent" not about what is good but to having an authority resolve such conflicts. Since Litke does not share Hobbes' pessimism about gaining the knowledge requisite for peaceful, consenting society, he calls us to pay more attention to the peace-seeking/society-making side of our nature rather than endorse the necessity of absolute sovereigns.

Jerald Richards explores the tensions between Gene Sharp's position on nonviolence and that of the Western moral tradition. Sharp, perhaps the leading proponent of pragmatic nonviolence in the current Anglo-American literature, objects to the Western moral tradition's treatment of nonviolence in several ways: he claims that the tradition denies the universal validity of the principle of nonviolence, that it does so on purely pragmatic grounds, that it accepts immoral actions which aim to defeat immoral actions and that it takes the moral and the practical to be opposed. Richards, using Alan Donagan's *Theory of Morality* (1977) as his standard, defends the Western moral tradition against Sharp's objections and attempts to reconcile the two.

According to Donagan, the fundamental principle of Western (or Hebrew-Christian) morality is love of one's neighbor. This is interpreted in Kantian terms: it is our duty to respect persons. Among the obligations derived from this principle is the duty of nonviolence. The principle is not absolute; those who use or threaten violence forfeit their immunity from violence. Self-defensive violence is permissible and sometimes obligatory.

Richards proposes a compromise between Sharp and the tradition, a view of the principle of nonviolence which would maintain its universality but deny its absoluteness, thus allowing it to be suspended for overriding moral reasons. By this distinction between universality and absoluteness, Richards argues that traditional moralists in fact hold an ethics of nonviolence. He finds it somewhat ironic that Sharp, known for his pragmatic nonviolence, turns out to hold to a principled nonviolence with absolute applicability.

Richards' point is that advocates of nonviolent action and advocates of just war may need to join together in implementing moral restraints on war leading eventually to the abolition of war. Despite his claim to pragmatic nonviolence, Sharp may not be willing to accept empirical testing in international conflict.

Richards concludes by calling for further dialogue between Sharp and the traditionalists on the nature of nonviolence.

The last three authors in this section take the discussion of nonviolence beyond comparison and compromise with traditional Western morality. R. Paul Churchill, Sara Ruddick and Robert Holmes all offer visions of nonviolence which challenge us to think past where the tradition has left us.

Focusing on Vaclav Havel's *The Power of the Powerless*, R. Paul Churchill challenges and stretches our thinking on nonviolence. Churchill ranks Havel's essay with classics from Tolstoy, Gandhi, Camus and Martin Luther King, Jr. Beyond its historical significance as the basic text for Czechoslovakia's "velvet revolution" in November of 1989, *The Power of the Powerless* presents Havel's empowering ideology. When this is understood together with several other themes from his short essays, Havel emerges as the most philosophical of the major writers on nonviolence.

Churchill confines his efforts to discussing Havel's notion that emancipation from oppression requires self-renewal and a quest for authentic existence based on reverence for truth. For Havel, as for Gandhi, violence and nonviolence must first be understood metaphysically before we can appreciate their political significance.

For Havel, the basic human burden is a search for meaning. This search is a permanent balancing act between the living experience of meaning and its unknowableness. We succeed only when our lives are infused with hope, wonder, humility and a spontaneous respect for the mystery of Being. Ultimately, human rationality is the source of meaning, but this must not be scientific/technological rationality which arrogantly rejects human responsibility as mere subjective illusion. Recognizing the significance of small, individual, subjective acts is radical because it exposes the small, ordinary acts of compliance which *are* the system. For Havel, violent revolution is not radical enough; reform comes from the fundamental reconstitution of people. We live within the truth by freeing ourselves from our private, internal exile and thus conform our public behavior to our genuine subjective selves. When this happens for enough people, political revolution is inevitable.

This existential revolution is not only a nonviolent political revolution against oppressive political regimes, but also an empowering ideology for reclaiming life against the meaninglessness of modernity. Because he holds that "consciousness precedes being," Havel sees the salvation of the world to lie "in the human heart, in the human power to reflect."

With "A Fierce and Human Peace," Sara Ruddick offers her feminist peace politics. Based on a feminist critique of war as well as a positive vision of peace derived from feminist reconstruction, Ruddick's peace politics is characterized by a sturdy, public suspicion of organized violence even in the best of causes. Its goals are to disrupt organized violence and develop effective nonviolent actions.

Just as she sees feminism as part critical deconstruction and part aspirational reconstruction, so Ruddick sees peace politics as part critical of war and part inventive of peace. Her essay is organized around just these parts.

Ruddick's feminist critique of war begins by acknowledging the widely-held notion that war is in some sense "masculine." She examines two aspects of military masculinity, both of which support the feminist suspicion of war. One is a distinctly misogynist and homophobic masculinist ethos invoked by some militarists in training and inspiring soldiers. War is genderized and a military femininity provides an androphiliac response to misogynist military masculinity. The result is a glorification of war, a masking of violence and a cooptation of women. The other aspect of military masculinity discussed is the psychosexual character of war. Ruddick exposes the "Man of Reason" as fantasizing just war via abstraction, euphemism, and binary opposition to conceal or sanitize the realities of war. The feminist critique reveals lost subjective and emotional experience, the pain and suffering of victims on all sides.

No matter how thoroughly war is criticized, the critique itself is not enough; people need alternative means to protect what they love and get what they need. Ruddick looks to women's ordinary lives for ordinary peace. Wary of overgeneralizing, she highlights recurring patterns in women's lives, e.g. the tendency to take up responsibilities and work of 'care'—of feeding, clothing, sheltering, nursing, tending children and the elderly and so on. In activities like these, especially in maternal work, Ruddick finds both a stark contrast to military thinking and hopeful elements of peace. Where militarists aim to dominate (often in the name of good causes), caregivers try to resist temptations to terrify, injure and humiliate, and so on. While it is not easy to translate maternal nonviolence into peace politics, Ruddick's project is hopeful and productive.

In "The Morality of Nonviolence," **Robert Holmes** aims to clarify the concept of nonviolence by describing the different ways in which it is understood. Beyond this, Holmes offers his reasons for choosing nonviolence as a moral position.

Within the philosophy of nonviolence Holmes sees both *normative* and *non-normative* forms. The former defends the adoption of nonviolence, while the latter is purely descriptive. When normative, nonviolence may be *personal*, that is, chosen for oneself without prescribing it to others, or *interpersonal*—a moral position meant for others as well as oneself. This is the form of nonviolence on which Holmes focuses.

Interpersonal nonviolence may be *principled* or *pragmatic*. The principled view is held on moral grounds, the pragmatic is not. *Absolute* nonviolence renounces violence in every conceivable circumstance, while *conditional* nonviolence does not. Since principled nonviolence may be absolute or conditional but pragmatic nonviolence must be conditional, conditional principled nonviolence and pragmatic nonviolence differ only by degree. Finally, principled interpersonal nonviolentists may expect us to *be* certain sorts of persons, or to *act* in certain sorts of ways, or both. That is, they may adopt nonviolence as an ethics of virtue or as an ethics of conduct or both.

Having mapped the territory, Holmes goes on to locate nonviolence in the broader context of ethical theory and to defend the plausibility of nonviolence in a world in which some people are nonviolent and others are not. He considers a variety of objections to nonviolence and defends a broad conception of nonviolence that recognizes subtlety and complexity, going beyond physical to psychological manifestations (e.g., sexism and racism).

As may be anticipated, a great deal turns on the defense of the innocent. While many people think it admirable—if a bit strange—to refrain from using violence even in self-defense, they find it contemptible that anyone would fail to defend innocent persons under attack. Holmes makes clear that nonviolentists do not stand by passively while innocents are made victims. Rather, they resist, albeit nonviolently. Holmes concedes that critics of nonviolence can create hypothetical cases in which *only* violence can save innocents; the problem is that such cases beg the question by stipulating all relevant factors. Actual cases always involve an open-ended set of conditions, not all of which can be known.

Holmes closes by defending conditional principled nonviolence. He believes that one ought always act nonviolently. Following Gandhi and King, Holmes underscores the recognition that any resort to violence presumes knowledge of willful wrongdoing that we may not have. Our aim must not be prevailing over an enemy but avoiding harm—harm to others as well as to ourselves, harm that is psychological as well as physical, harm to moral integrity as well as to life and property. We are invited to join in the creation of a nonviolent world where the capacities for good and moral growth are more important than divisions of race, gender, class, religion and nationality which divide us.

Hamline University

1 Moral Philosophy, International Law and the Deaths of Innocents

Sheldon Cohen

Philosophers writing on war and morality sometimes seek support for their views through citations of international law. When they do so, they are often on shaky ground in their interpretation of that law.

In this paper I discuss one such case in Section (I). In Section (II) I elaborate on the legal distinction at issue in (I). In (III) I argue that this legal distinction has some moral claim on us. If it does, a good deal of the philosophical literature on nuclear war and nuclear deterrence needs to be reexamined.

My general intention is to convince philosophers that the international law of war deserves more serious attention from them than it has hitherto received.

International Law and Indiscriminate Bombardments

In a 1987 article, "The Irrelevance of Countervalue,"[1] Douglas Lackey quoted Paragraph Three, Article XXIV, of the (unadopted) 1923 Hague Draft Rules of Aerial Warfare, as follows:

> (3) The bombardment of cities, towns, villages, dwellings, or buildings in the immediate neighborhood of the operations of land forces is prohibited.

Lackey then attempted to reconcile this with Paragraph 4:

> (4) In the immediate neighborhood of the operations of land forces, the bombardment of cities, towns, villages, dwellings, or buildings is legitimate provided that there exists a reasonable

---

[1] *The Monist*, Vol. LXX, No. 3 (July 1987).

presumption that the military concentration is sufficiently important to justify such bombardment, having regard to the danger thus caused to the civilian population.

These conflict: (3) forbids, without qualification, the bombardment of towns in the immediate neighborhood of the operations of land forces, while (4) allows such bombardments in order to attack a military concentration—subject only to a principle of proportionality. To reconcile the two Lackey supplies a function for (4) that will make it compatible with (3): "to prevent opponents from protecting their land forces by putting them in protected zones." The implication is that if A by choice places land forces near undefended towns or heavily populated areas, then if noncombatants or their property are injured in an attack, responsibility for the destruction lies more with A than with the attacker.[1]

But the seeming inconsistency between (3) and (4) is due only to a misquotation of (3), which does not read:

> (3) The bombardment of cities, towns, villages, dwellings, or buildings in the immediate neighborhood of the operations of land forces is prohibited.

It reads:

> The bombardment of cities, towns, villages, dwellings, or buildings *not* in the immediate neighborhood of the operations of land forces is prohibited.[2]

---

[1] *Ibid.*, p. 261.

[2] The entire Article reads as follows:

(1) Aerial bombardment is legitimate only when directed at a military objective, that is to say, an object of which the destruction or injury would constitute a distinct military advantage to the belligerent.

(2) Such bombardment is legitimate only when directed exclusively at the following objectives: military works, military establishments or depots, factories constituting well-known centers engaged in the

Once the *not* is reinstalled, (3) and (4) are compatible: (3) forbids the bombardment of towns remote from the battlefield; (4) allows the bombardment of towns in an area ground troops are contesting—subject to a principle of proportionality.

Thus the 1923 Draft Rules and the 1907 Fourth Hague Convention use different principles of division to decide the circumstances in which towns are subject to bombardment. The 1923 Draft Rules would have outlawed the general bombardment of any town remote from ground operations—whether the town is defended or not—while the Fourth Hague Convention forbids the bombardment of undefended towns (Article XXV), allowing the bombardment of defended towns, whether or not they are remote from ground operations.

The basic wording for the protection granted to undefended towns in the Hague Conventions was hammered out at the 1874 Brussels Conference on the laws of war. The minutes of that conference record an objection by a Danish representative, Colonel Brun, to the resulting paragraph, which said that attacks on undefended towns are forbidden: *"enonce l'avis qu'on pourrait supprimer le mot 'attaquees,' parce qu'on ne peut pas attaquer ce qui n'est defendu."*[1] An army cannot attack that which is not defended—it can merely damage or destroy it. Thus, both the 1923 Draft

---

manufacture of arms, ammunition, or distinctly military supplies; lines of communication or transportation used for military purposes.
(3) The bombardment of cities, towns, villages, dwellings, or buildings not in the immediate neighborhood of the operations of land forces is prohibited. In cases where the objectives specified in paragraph 2 are so situated that they cannot be bombarded without the indiscriminate bombardment of the civilian population, the aircraft must abstain from bombardment.
(4) In the immediate neighborhood of the operations of land forces, the bombardment of cities, towns, villages, dwellings, or buildings is legitimate provided that there exists a reasonable presumption that the military concentration is sufficiently important to justify such bombardment, having regard to the danger thus caused to the civilian population.
[1] *Actes de la Conference de Bruxelles de 1874 sur le Projet d'une Convention Internationale Concernant la Guerre* (Paris: A. Wittersheim & Cie., 1874), p. 41.

Rules and the 1907 Hague Rules allow the general bombardment of towns contested by ground troops.

To say this is, in a way, misleading, because there is room for uncertainty, and there has in fact been disagreement, about precisely what it is that renders a place defended according to 1907 Hague IV. The US Air Force, for example, has adopted an extremely broad interpretation, taking a "defended place" to be a place to which access is denied by enemy troops. On that interpretation any town behind enemy lines is a defended place. On the interpretation I favor, the place needs to have its own defensive capability. The mere fact that it is behind enemy lines would be irrelevant.

These differences of interpretation arise because the 1907 IV Hague Convention governs land warfare. It was not designed to apply to air war—in 1907 the newly-invented plane had not yet been used militarily. Yet the thought had occurred to people, and for this reason the article on bombardment in the 1899 Hague Conference was modified. The 1899 treaties had never been ratified, but the 1907 Hague Treaties, which were ratified, incorporated the provisions of 1899 Hague almost word for word. In the case of the article on bombardment, however, the invention of the airplane between 1899 and 1907 led to a significant modification: where the 1899 treaty forbids the bombardment of undefended towns, the 1907 treaty forbids the bombardment "by any means" of undefended towns. "By any means" was added in anticipation of the development of the warplane.

So there are some who say that though 1907 Hague IV is explicitly a convention on the rules for land warfare, its provisions on bombardment apply to every military arm. But the case isn't that simple (which is why the 1923 Conference was held), for in fact 1907 Hague has a convention, the Ninth—On Bombardment by Naval Forces in Time of War—and the Ninth Hague Convention doesn't follow the Fourth.

The Ninth Convention forbids naval general bombardment of undefended towns (Article 1), but unlike the Fourth Convention (for ground warfare) allows the bombardment of military works and installations in such towns (Article 2), with the naval commander incurring no responsibility for "unavoidable damage" the bombardment may cause the town, though he must take "due measures in order that the town may suffer as little harm as possible." Thus the Naval Rules allow the bombardment of military targets even in *undefended* towns, while the Land Rules do not.

The bombardment of undefended towns is prohibited to ground troops because they are free to enter and hold undefended towns, and there is no proper military advantage to destroying installations that are yours for the taking. The destruction would be wanton. A naval fleet, on the other hand, is not typically able to occupy and hold towns, though its guns may be able to destroy the town's military facilities. Consequently naval forces are allowed to destroy with gunfire targets that are forbidden to ground forces.[1] Since air fleets (and missiles) are in a similar position regarding their ability to occupy enemy towns and cities, we should perhaps imagine rules for air warfare along the lines of the naval rules, not the land rules.[2]

The principle incorporated in the Hague Conventions, then, is that wanton attacks on civilian areas are prohibited, not that attacks on civilian areas are prohibited. Defended towns and cities are subject to general or indiscriminate bombardments; even undefended towns are subject to the bombardment of their military works and industry.

Lackey's failure to notice the "not" in Paragraph Three is understandable given an assumption widely held by philosophers who write on war and morality. Richard Wasserstrom, for example, claimed that nuclear war is immoral because it would involve the "intentional or knowing" killing of innocents.[3] And it is the central contention of Robert L. Holmes in *On War and Morality*[4] that though there might be conceivable circumstances in which war might be morally justifiable, "war in the modern world is not morally justified . . . because modern war inevitably kills innocent persons."

---

[1] Naval commanders also have the right to order the town's civil authorities to destroy those military installations.

[2] 1907 Hague incorporates rules for land (Hague IV) and naval (Hague IX) bombardment, but not for air bombardment. This was the reason for the 1923 Hague Conference.

[3] Robert L. Holmes, "War, Nuclear War, and Nuclear Deterrence," *Ethics*, Vol. XCV (April 1985).

[4] Robert L. Holmes, *On War and Morality* (Princeton: Princeton University Press, Princeton, N.J., 1989), p. 211.

In any war, Holmes writes, at least one side must go to war
unjustly. Even so, those of its combatants who oppose the war
(who might "contribute to dissenting groups and even participate in
antiwar activities") are innocent. If the other side goes to war justly,
all of its combatants are innocents. Hence war involves the killing
of innocents and is not morally justifiable. A war would not involve
the deaths of innocents only if "both sides act unjustly and only
those responsible for the war participate in it."

On the standard view, war's victims are innocent if they are
innocent bystanders as opposed to participants. Holmes takes the
innocent to be those who either do not support or do not willingly
participate in an unjust war, and contrasts these with the guilty—
those who both support and initiate or participate in an unjust war.
He concludes that war can be morally justified only if both sides go
to war unjustly: were a nation to go to war justly, the very fact that
it had justly gone to war would make the war unjust.

We note, thus, some paradoxical reversals of just war theory:
on Holmes' version, (a) unjust cause is a necessary condition of the
just war, (b) a war can be just only if both sides act unjustly, and (c)
if either side acts justly, the war is unjust.

The paradoxical ring arises for two reasons. First, Holmes takes
any war in which one side is done an injustice to be an unjust war.
If Germany unjustifiably invades Denmark, and the Danes defend
themselves, the war is unjust because the German invasion is
unjust, and thus Denmark is participating in an unjust war.

Second, Holmes would have us believe that even Denmark acts
unjustly so long as the invading German army includes conscripts
who do not support the invasion. The special conception of
innocence at work here is unexpected, and I shall ignore it in the
subsequent discussion. I shall also ignore the claim that if one side's
participation in a war is unjust, then the war itself is unjust: the
Franco-Prussian War, I want to allow, might be just even if the
Prusso-Frankish War is unjust, just as the road from Athens to
Thebes is uphill while the road from Thebes to Athens is downhill.
We are left with a thesis something like the following: it is
immoral in war to take actions likely or certain to result in the
deaths of innocents.

Such actions are, however—as I have indicated—compatible
with the provisions of international law on bombardment of towns
and cities. Perhaps in this case the international law of war allows

what is immoral—it certainly does in some other cases. But I want to argue that this is not such a case.

I want to argue, in other words, that it is morally permissible in war to take actions likely or certain to result in the deaths of innocents. I am not arguing, however, that it is permissible to target innocents—to attack them per se. That, I think, is wrong.

International Law and Friendly Fire

Those who hold the opposing view must oppose the provisions of international law that allow such actions, and condemn military actions that are commonly regarded as well within the limits of permissibility. Let us consider some examples of two sorts of cases that would be permitted by both 1907 Hague IV and the 1923 Draft Rules: (1) a defended town is bombarded by enemy troops in preparation for an assault on the town; (2) troops fight in an inhabited town or city. Both of these are likely to result in civilian casualties; both are common occurrences in war. Are they immoral?

If (1) is immoral, the WWII bombardments of Caen and St. Lo during the Normandy campaign were immoral. The July 25, 1944 bombardment of St. Lo, for example, which led directly to the Allied breakout from Normandy, the heaviest bombardment of the war, involved 1,500 four-engined bombers, 380 two-engined bombers, 550 fighter-bombers, and 800 artillery pieces.

Yet few philosophers have condemned these operations as immoral. The condemnation of Allied policy in WWII for harming civilians has almost exclusively focused on attacks against cities that were not being contested by ground troops, with Hamburg, Dresden, Tokyo, Hiroshima, and Nagasaki being the major examples. These were attacks that would have been forbidden by the 1923 Draft Rules' provisions concerning bombardments directed against urban areas not contested by ground troops.

This suggests that there is a widespread but unrecognized moral acceptance of the sorts of considerations that have weighed heavily in the minds of the jurists, statesmen, and soldiers who molded the relevant international law: that we *do* somehow think that there is a moral difference between the bombardment of a city ground troops are trying to wrestle from the enemy and the bombardment of a city far to the rear, and between bombarding defended and undefended cities.

If (2) is immoral, the recent attempt by Kuwaiti troops to defend Kuwait City from its Iraqi attackers was immoral. Kuwaiti deaths in this action have been quoted as ranging between 200 and 700, and we can assume that some of these were innocents caught in the wrong place at the wrong time. Does this make the Kuwaiti resistance immoral?

Or consider the events of eight months earlier, when units of the regular Romanian army engaged government paramilitary security forces in house-to-house fighting in Bucharest—fighting in which many innocent civilian bystanders became casualties. Given that armed opposition to the security forces in downtown Bucharest was almost certain to result in civilian casualties, was it immoral for the the army to fight the security forces?

If so, naval battles at sea might be permissible, or tank battles in the Sinai Desert, but military actions in developed areas would not. Densely populated countries, like Singapore and the Netherlands, would have no morally justifiable way of defending themselves once enemy troops had entered their territory.

The bombardments of St. Lo and Caen bring to light another consideration. Elizabeth Anscombe once claimed that Allied area bombing in WWII was motivated by a "villainous hatred" of the enemy.[1] Surely this claim becomes implausible if we take as our example St. Lo or Caen instead of Dresden or Hiroshima. We may find them discomforting at times, but no one claims we hated the French. The Vichy government was not in the Allied camp, but the Allies looked at the French as temporarily fallen allies, and were concerned to minimize French civilian casualties, which ultimately reached into the tens of thousands.

To minimize French casualties in heavily populated areas, some missions were flown at low altitudes, permitting more accurate bombing but exposing aircrews to greater danger. These missions were flown by Free French volunteers. It was not felt that Allied aircrews were obligated to place themselves at greater risk to reduce French civilian casualties. Rather, the feeling was that these missions were supererogatory.

---

[1] "War and Murder," in *War and Morality*, ed. Richard A. Wasserstrom (Belmont, CA: Wadsworth, 1970), p. 50. "War and Murder" originally appeared in *Nuclear Weapons: A Catholic Response* ed. Walter Stein (New York: Sheed & Ward, 1961).

The surprising lesson is that we seem less inclined to criticize military operations that cause friendly civilian casualties than ones that cause enemy civilian casualties. In the Kuwaiti and Romanian cases, too, the civilians whose lives were at risk due to military action were friendly. International law does not address the distinction, in bombardments, between cities inhabited by friendly, neutral, and enemy civilians. Perhaps it is right not to do so—perhaps the implication is that they all must be treated on a par.

At any rate, if the law is morally justifiable here, then a nation at war is not obligated to conduct the war in such a manner as to guarantee that its civilian population is not placed at risk. A nation might prefer placing some of its civilians in harm's way to capitulation, if the price to the nation of capitulation is sufficiently high: the imposition of an alien government; the impoverishment of the population; enslavement; the loss of national sovereignty or self-determination; or the abandonment of an important domestic political right.

I said earlier that I am taking the innocent here to be innocent in the sense in which we speak of "innocent bystanders"—people who are not participating in the activities of war, but who merely happen to be where a war is going on. In this sense many high officials in the Nazi party in WW II were innocents. If we wish instead to use the term with a more direct moral significance, and say that those are innocent who are not supporting an unjust war, then I think it is still true that nations may put innocents at risk. Indeed, in this case the nation wrongfully attacked places its own innocent soldiers at risk when it sends them to resist the aggressors, and I see nothing blameworthy in that.

If, on the other hand, it is immoral to place innocent people at risk, then the building of the aqueducts that carried water to Rome, or of a subway line under the streets of New York, or a natural gas line in suburban London, is immoral. Either the construction or the very existence of these pose threats to innocent people, but we do not seem to feel that because natural gas is explosive, and natural gas explosions have killed innocent people, that it should be banned in inhabited areas. Rather, we seem to feel that somehow we can assess the risks, do what we can afford to minimize them, and then proceed if the gains seem to outweigh the dangers. We have not, for example, stopped mining coal, even though coal mines seem more hazardous than nuclear power plants. And we send criminals to jail, even though their innocent spouses and children may be suffering in consequence.

Placing innocent people at risk is not confined to war. It happened when we built the Brooklyn Bridge, and is a consequence of a great many human activities. In these cases we seem to think that, at least to some extent, the placing of human life at risk can be justified in view of other significant gains—greater ease of communication, for example, between Manhattan and Brooklyn.

Here our thinking certainly proceeds on utilitarian grounds. In others, it need not. Our 1991 intervention in the Persian Gulf has been defended on the grounds that who controls Kuwait's oil is a matter of vital national, or even supra-national, self-interest. Were that the only justification I would think the intervention at best ill-advised, and, more likely, downright immoral. For control of Kuwaiti oil could fall into Iraqi hands by other, more acceptable means, in which case we would have no right of intervention. Had Kuwait, for example, voluntarily sought union with Iraq, that would be a matter solely between the Iraqis and the Kuwaitis, no matter how adversely it affected the interests of the other nations of the world. (Iraq claims that Kuwait is a part of Iraq, but Kuwait has for decades been a sovereign state, treated as such even by Iraq.) Having deprived the Kuwaitis of their national sovereignty and right of self-determination, Iraq seemed to be in the process of dispersing the Kuwaiti population and replacing them with Iraqi homesteaders. If they were doing this, and succeeded, the Kuwaiti state and the Kuwaiti people would cease to exist, and there would have been nothing left for us to liberate except the oilfields.

Perhaps this assessment of Iraqi intentions is wrong, but let us assume that it is right. Shall we take refuge in the principle that it is better to allow people to be harmed than to do something that will harm people, no matter how egregious the harm that others are willing to do? Should we take that position, even if the majority of Kuwaitis would prefer our taking military action to having their fate left in the hands of Saddam Hussein—which seemed in fact to be their wish?

A great deal was at stake in the Gulf, but more than anything what is at stake are the principles of the Kellogg-Briand Pact and the U.N. Charter, and the extent to which, over decades to come, relations between weak nations and their powerful neighbors will be governed by those principles. Yet if the facts are as I have described them, we cannot enforce those principles that are the primary source of protection for the innocent in the international arena without ourselves putting innocent lives at risk.

It is my hope that these principles be enforced, by collective military action if necessary. And to go one further, I think it would be a better world if we could push this notion, and allow the use of collective international force even in conflicts that are not international in nature. Liberia in 1990 was in dire need of such intervention, and Cambodia certainly was a few years ago. Such humanitarian intervention is rarely attempted by nations unless their national interests are also involved, so this seems to me unlikely, but I think a world in which it were more likely would be a morally better place.

Perhaps we are seeing the birth of a world in which, under the aegis of the United Nations, military force, or its threat, will be used to make war inevitably unprofitable. St. Augustine once said that it is not a confusion to pray that God make His enemies freely love him. I do not think it a confusion if the community of nations uses force to make nations eschew force. I think this would be a fine thing. That it cannot be done without harming some innocent people shows that the design of the world is faulty, not that the project is immoral.

The University of Tennessee, Knoxville

2 Double Effect and the Killing of Innocents

Mark Vorobej

Analytical discussions of pacifism by contemporary Western philosophers are rare. Those that exist tend to be curt, uncharitable and uncomplimentary. Robert L. Holmes' recent sustained, mature and impassioned defense of a form of anti-war pacifism in his book *On War and Morality* thus constitutes a most welcome and important contribution to the philosophical literature on war and peace.[1] Although Holmes' discussion covers an exceptionally broad range of topics, this book is primarily a work in moral philosophy, the central thesis of which is that warfare in the modern world cannot be morally justified. In this paper I attempt to show that one of Holmes' principal lines of argumentation in support of this provocative thesis fails. It is worth stressing, however, that pacifism may yet be defensible in spite of any particular shortcomings of Holmes' discussion. A careful reading of *On War and Morality* compels one to continue to seriously consider pacifism as a live option. That is just one mark of the enduring value of this very stimulating work.

Holmes bases his moral outlook on the claim that it is presumptively wrong to do violence to innocent persons. Knowingly killing innocent persons is a form of violence and thus is presumptively wrong. If, as Holmes also claims, modern warfare inevitably involves the intentional or foreseeable killing of innocent persons,[2] then modern warfare is presumptively wrong as well. In his pivotal sixth chapter, Holmes argues at length that this presumption can never be overridden. It follows that modern warfare is in fact categorically wrong, i.e. wrong all things considered.[3]

---

[1] Robert L. Holmes, *On War and Morality* (Princeton: Princeton University Press, 1989).

[2] *Ibid.*, p. 188.

[3] Holmes concedes that there are logically conceivable, highly speculative scenarios within which it is possible for war to be

Is Holmes correct in claiming that the presumption against killing innocent persons can never be defeated? Attempts to justify the killing of innocents frequently invoke either the principle of double effect or principles of consequentialist reasoning. Holmes offers a number of apparently quite devastating criticisms of each of these two approaches. I will now attempt to show that, without exception, his criticisms of the principle of double effect fall well short of their mark. (I also disagree with Holmes' criticisms of consequentialism, but that is better left for another occasion.) Most of the ensuing overtly polemical discussion is concerned with fairly abstract problems in moral theory which have nothing in particular to do with the nature of war, though they are absolutely crucial to Holmes' defense of pacifism.

The principle of double effect is a complex moral principle, many components of which are not relevant to Holmes' discussion. What interests Holmes about this principle is its claim that good *intentions* may justify otherwise reprehensible actions. More specifically, according to the principle of double effect an act which kills innocent persons may be morally permissible provided that the actor's intention is to bring about some *other* effect which is good. The deaths of innocent persons may be a foreseeable evil consequence of the act in question, but must not be what the actor "aims at" or intends to bring about, either for its own sake or as a causal means to the production of the good effect.[1]

Holmes offers three criticisms of this principle. The first, harshest, and to my mind most novel criticism is that the principle is inconsistent. Moral judgments are universalizable. Part of what this means is that actions may receive different moral appraisals only if there are morally relevant differences between them. Holmes charges that "double effect allows virtually identical acts . . . to be judged differently."[2] To use a classic example, a pilot may bomb a

---

morally justified. Therefore, his version of pacifism is not absolutist. However, in his opinion, "the conditions that might theoretically justify war simply are not met in the actual world." *Ibid.*, p. 14.

[1] Double effect also typically requires that the act in question must not be intrinsically impermissible, and that the good and evil effects must be of roughly the same order of magnitude.

[2] *Ibid.*, p. 197.

munitions factory and foresee that his act will result in the deaths of innocent civilians. Holmes is troubled by the fact that, according to the principle of double effect, what this pilot does is permissible if the foreseeable deaths are not intended by the pilot. The act is impermissible, however, if they are intended. But what the pilot actually does in these respective cases is no different. One and the same act receives different moral appraisals. This violates universalizability.

Holmes concedes that this criticism fails if it could be established that acts include intentions as proper parts. For then the relevant acts would be different, since they incorporate different intentions. But this, Holmes says, flies in the face of "much of our common-sense understanding of acts"[1] since we can identify acts and know what someone did without knowing what their intention was. Indeed, the principle of double effect itself seems to presuppose that one and the same act may be performed with different intentions. Holmes therefore advocates what I will call a *narrow* description of acts according to which actions do not include intentions as parts.[2]

It is doubtful that there is some objective fact of the matter as to whether an intention is "part of" an action. Whether someone's intention is part of "what they did" will probably depend on why we are interested in what they did, and thus the identity conditions of actions are to some extent conventional. Holmes may in fact accept this, since at one point he claims that a narrow description of actions makes moral theory "less confusing."[3] For the sake of argument, therefore, I will grant the claim that in moral theory it is at least sometimes *useful* to describe actions narrowly.

This concession, however, in no way threatens the logical consistency of the principle of double effect. Holmes' argument falsely assumes that in order for two actions to consistently receive

---

[1]*Ibid..*

[2]A question naturally arises as to whether Holmes considers *consequences* to be part of actions. Presumably not, since on a common-sensical understanding of acts I can know what someone did — they pushed a button — without knowing the consequences of what they did. Indeed, one and the same act of pushing a button may have very different consequences. However, this line of reasoning would apparently commit Holmes to the unpalatable conclusion that consequentialism violates universalizability as well.

[3]*Ibid.,* p. 198n.

different moral appraisals, there must be some morally relevant difference which resides within the narrow description of those actions. But there is nothing formally inconsistent about the view that phenomena *associated* with some action, though not strictly speaking part of it in Holmes' sense, may be relevant to the moral appraisal of that action. Consider abortion, for example. Many people believe that a woman's health, age and socio-economic status may be relevant to the moral appraisal of an act of abortion. Yet presumably none of these features are captured within the narrow description of that act. I can know what a doctor did in performing an abortion without knowing the mother's annual income or how many children she already has. Universalizability has to do ultimately with the giving of reasons. If someone wants to say that one action is morally permissible and another is not, logic dictates that they have to be able to explain why by pointing to a relevant difference. But logic does not preclude them from appealing to factors, such as intentions or socio-economic status, which lie beyond an action's narrow description.

Of course, not everyone believes that economic considerations are morally relevant to the question of abortion. However, this is a substantive rather than a logical disagreement. Holmes' real worry with double effect, I suspect, may be of this nature and, if so, his first criticism of this principle eventually collapses into his second charge that "intentions are of questionable relevance to the moral assessment of acts."[1] However, this is simply an astonishing claim for Holmes to make, since elsewhere in the text he flatly contradicts himself.[2] Much of the first chapter of *On War and Morality* is devoted to a careful conceptual analysis of violence. One of Holmes' principal conclusions in that chapter is that primary physical violence, defined as "the use of force with the *intention* to harm or kill,"[3] is prima facie wrong. The concept of violence is hardly peripheral to Holmes' moral critique of war, yet here he is claiming that whether an act is violent (and hence prima facie wrong) may

---

[1] *Ibid.*, p. 198.
[2] There is also a tension, though not an outright contradiction, between this claim and his later remark that the moral appraisal of an action "depends to a considerable extent upon the character. . .and personality of those affected by it." *Ibid.*, p. 208.
[3] *Ibid.*, p. 34.

depend on the nature of an agent's intentions![1] Holmes cannot consistently make this claim and challenge the principle of double effect for allowing the moral character of an action to rest upon the presence or absence of certain relevant intentions.[2]

Holmes, however, backs up this second criticism with a further independent argument as to why intentions are irrelevant to the moral appraisal of actions. Again, the allegation is that there is some *logical* difficulty associated with this view. Holmes grants that intentions are relevant to the moral assessment of *persons* as good, bad, praiseworthy or blameworthy. He also rightly claims that we base our judgments about the moral character of persons partly upon their actions. Therefore, he claims, if intentions figured into our judgments about the moral rightness or wrongness of actions, "we could not without circularity cite a person's actions as a basis for our judgment of the person. In judging the act we would already have judged the person."[3]

This peculiar argument is difficult to understand, in part, I am sure, because of the brevity with which it is stated. Holmes appears to be claiming that there is some circularity in maintaining both that (A) acts are relevant to the moral appraisal of persons, and (B) intentions are relevant to the moral appraisal of both acts and persons. The argument, I think, runs as follows. Suppose that the principle of double effect, or something like it, is valid and that someone's intention is relevant to both the permissibility of their action and the appraisal of their moral character. Then presumably what this person does could not serve (as it must) as an *independent* ground for appraising their character. To suppose that it could would be to argue in a circle since the permissibility of the act is itself a function of the intention which on its own already provides a ground for appraising moral character. Any attempt to base a judgment of a

---

[1]The notion of foreseeability also plays a role in Holmes' analysis of violence, but this does not affect the point I am making in this paragraph.

[2]I am assuming throughout this paragraph that it would be implausible to claim that intentions are relevant to the prima facie rightness or wrongness of actions, but not relevant to their overall moral character.

[3]*Ibid.*, p. 198.

person's character on their actions would be redundant, which is absurd.

If this is Holmes' argument, it is fallacious since it overlooks at least two quite plausible possibilities. First of all, other features of an action *besides* the intention with which it is performed may be relevant to the moral appraisal of the agent's character. For example, it may be relevant to appeal to the manner in which the action is performed, the agent's mental state during and following the performance of the action, and the frequency with which she engages in actions of this type. According to double effect, a pilot who bombs an enemy target with the intention to kill innocent civilians acts wrongly. But our appraisal of her moral character may be affected by the fact that her bombing raids were carefully designed to minimize the suffering of those she killed, that she carried out her mission reluctantly and with remorse, that it was difficult for her to cultivate the intention to kill innocent persons, and that she turned down assignments of this sort at every possible opportunity. In these and countless other ways, what the pilot did is independently relevant to assessing what sort of a person she is. That she acted wrongly with such and such an intention falls far short of telling the whole story.

A second possibility overlooked by Holmes is that a person's intention may not be relevant to the moral appraisal of their action in *exactly the same way* as it is relevant to the moral appraisal of their character. If so, then two separate appeals to that intention may not be redundant. The principle of double effect is a fairly mechanical, bivalent principle according to which the mere presence or absence of an appropriate intention, along with certain other conditions, is sufficient to establish whether some action is permissible or impermissible. However, as evidenced in the last paragraph, appraisals of a person's character are considerably more nuanced than this. There is nothing remotely like a set of mechanical rules for generating a character appraisal from the existence of an intention, and the moral language of character appraisal is much richer and thicker than the bare skeletal deontic framework of permissibility and forbiddenness. Moral judgments play incredibly diverse roles in human affairs, and intentions may matter in different ways at different points along the moral spectrum. Holmes' charge that intentions are irrelevant to the moral assessment of actions is therefore unconvincing.

Holmes' third and final criticism of the principle of double effect is of a less theoretical nature. Holmes claims that the principle is "vacuous" from a practical standpoint in that

> it lends itself to the justification of virtually any action its user wants. On the assumption that we can 'direct' or 'aim' intentions as we please, any act whatever can be performed with a good intention or, at any rate, can be described as being performed with a good intention.[1]

Double effect is a principle prone to flagrant abuse.

A portion of this argument rests upon a false assumption or, at any rate, an assumption that Holmes cannot make use of without again contradicting himself. Commenting on St. Augustine's attempt to ground just war theory upon an appeal to purity of heart, Holmes writes that

> We cannot, in any event, choose our motives as we can our actions; at least not in the short run .... We cannot just decide to do something from a certain motive; or decide to do something and then decide which of several motives to do it from. When we decide to perform one action rather than another we are governed by one motive rather than another. But that is not within our control. For the most part we simply have the motives we do.[2]

Holmes cannot have it both ways. If his immediately preceding remarks are correct, as I believe they are, then the principle of double effect simply is not subject to the sort of capricious abuse that would result from aiming our intentions as we please, from one situation to the next, so as to rationalize the satisfaction of our antecedent desires.

This, however, is not to deny Holmes' other perfectly valid point that it is notoriously easy to erroneously *describe* virtually

---

[1] *Ibid.*, p. 199.
[2] *Ibid.*, p. 140.

any action as being performed with a good intention and, given the epistemological problems associated with verifying the existence and content of intentions, this opens the door to widespread abuse and deception (including self-deception). That a moral principle is subject to abuse is, of course, no trivial matter. But why a principle should be discredited or discarded simply because it is subject to abuse is far from clear. One fairly trivial point to make initially is that every moral principle is presumably subject to some sort of abuse or other, given the epistemological limitations and moral vices to which humans are prone. But this is not a reason to embrace moral nihilism.

Perhaps Holmes' worry is that abuse is more likely to occur, or is more difficult to detect, or will have more serious repercussions with a principle such as double effect. These points are certainly debatable.[1] But even if true, this may at most give us reason to believe that double effect should be used with caution (or perhaps ought not to be used at all) as a *decision procedure* for deliberating about morally right action. Double effect might fail a kind of publicity condition if there are good reasons why some (or all) agents should not directly (consciously) appeal to that principle in deciding what morality demands of them. Perhaps the risks of abuse in this process simply are too great (for certain agents). None of this, however, does anything to discredit double effect as a legitimate criterion of right action—a justified theoretical standard for identifying morally relevant features of the world and discriminating between morally right and morally wrong action. However, if double effect is defensible at this level, then it may continue to serve a useful practical purpose as a guide for the morally perplexed who are at the same time sincere in their commitment to determining what morality demands of them, and sensitive to the manner by which their thoughts on this matter may be distorted. This general line of reasoning may also provide all agents with reason to work towards the ameliorization of those conditions of our lives (including lack of self-knowledge) which

---

[1]Consequentialist principles of right action are subject to comparable abuse through miscalculation of future consequences, lack of imagination, prejudice, human tendencies to exaggerate the significance of one's own welfare, to discount or fail to appreciate the suffering of others, etc.

render the abuse of such principles as double effect such an attractive and accessible option.

Finally, I hasten to add in closing that for all that I have said in its defense in this paper, double effect may very well ultimately prove to be either a defective moral principle or one which is incapable of justifying the killing of innocents—but, if so on either count, it would not be for any of the reasons Holmes offers.

McMaster University

3 Reconciling Pacifists and Just War Theorists

James P. Sterba

Traditionally pacifism and just war theory have represented radically opposed responses to aggression. Pacifism has been interpreted to rule out any use of violence in response to aggression. Just war theory has been interpreted to permit a measured use of violence in response to aggression.[1] It has been thought that the two views might sometimes agree in particular cases, for example, that pacifists and just war theorists might unconditionally oppose nuclear war, but beyond that it has been generally held that the two views lead to radically opposed recommendations. In this paper, I hope to show that this is not the case. I will argue that pacifism and just war theory, in their most morally defensible interpretations, can be substantially reconciled both in theory and practice.

In traditional just war theory there are two basic elements: an account of just cause and an account of just means. Just cause is usually specified as follows:

1) There must be substantial aggression.
2) Nonbelligerent correctives must be either hopeless or too costly.
3) Belligerent correctives must be neither hopeless nor too costly.

Needless to say, the notion of substantial aggression is a bit fuzzy, but it is generally understood to be the type of aggression that violates people's most fundamental rights. To suggest some

*An earlier version of this paper was presented as the presidential address for 1990 National Meeting of Concerned Philosophers for Peace at which time I received many helpful suggestions. In particular, I would like to thank Timo Airaksinen, Joseph Boyle, Laurence Bove, Duane Cady, Sheldon Cohen, Barry Gan, Robert Holmes, Robert Johansen, Janet Kourany, Douglas Lackey, Robert Phillips, Ronald Santoni, Jonathan Schonsheck, Paula Smithka and Richard Werner.

[1] Some would say with too generous a measure.

specific examples of what is and is not substantial aggression, usually the taking of hostages is regarded as substantial aggression, while the nationalization of particular firms owned by foreigners is not so regarded. But even when substantial aggression occurs, frequently nonbelligerent correctives are neither hopeless nor too costly. And even when nonbelligerent correctives are either hopeless or too costly, in order for there to be a just cause, belligerent correctives must be neither hopeless nor too costly.

Traditional just war theory assumes, however, that there are just causes and goes on to specify just means as imposing two requirements:

1) Harm to innocents should not be directly intended as an end or a means.
2) The harm resulting from the belligerent means should not be disproportionate to the particular defensive objective to be attained.

While the just means conditions apply to each defensive action, the just cause conditions must be met by the conflict as a whole.

It is important to note that these requirements of just cause and just means are not essentially about war at all. Essentially, they constitute a theory of just defense that can apply to war but can also apply to a wide range of defensive actions short of war. Of course, what needs to be determined is whether these requirements can be justified. Since just war theory is usually opposed to pacifism, to secure a non-question-begging justification for the theory and its requirements we need to proceed as much as possible from premises that are common to pacifists and just war theorists alike. The difficulty here is that there is not just one form of pacifism, but many. So we need to determine which form of pacifism is most morally defensible.

Now, when most people think of pacifism they tend to identify it with a theory of nonviolence. We can call this view "nonviolent pacifism." It maintains that:

Any use of violence against other human beings is morally prohibited.

It has been plausibly argued, however, that this form of pacifism is incoherent. In a well-known article, Jan Narveson rejects nonviolent pacifism as incoherent because it recognizes a right to life yet rules out any use of force in defense of that right.[1] The view is incoherent, Narveson claims, because having a right entails the legitimacy of using force in defense of that right, at least on some occasions.

Given the cogency of objections of this sort, some have opted for a form of pacifism that does not rule out all violence, but only lethal violence. We can call this view "nonlethal pacifism." It maintains that:

Any lethal use of force against other human beings is morally prohibited.

In defense of nonlethal pacifism, Cheyney Ryan has argued that there is a substantial issue between the pacifist and the nonpacifist concerning whether we can or should create the necessary distance between ourselves and other human beings in order to make the act of killing possible.[2] To illustrate, Ryan cites George Orwell's reluctance to shoot at an enemy soldier who jumped out of a trench and ran along the top of a parapet half-dressed and holding up his trousers with both hands. Ryan contends that what kept Orwell from shooting was that he couldn't think of the soldier as a thing rather than as a fellow human being.

However, it is not clear that Orwell's encounter supports nonlethal pacifism. For it may be that what kept Orwell from shooting the enemy soldier was not his inability to think of the soldier as a thing rather than as a fellow human being, but rather his inability to think of the soldier who was holding up his trousers with both hands as a threat or a combatant. Under this interpretation, Orwell's decision not to shoot would accord well with the requirements of just war theory.

Let us suppose, however, that someone is attempting to take your life. Why does that permit you, the defender of nonlethal

---

[1] Jan Narveson, "Pacifism: A Philosophical Analysis," *Ethics*, (1965), pp. 259-71.

[2] Cheyney Ryan, "Self-Defense, Pacifism and the Possibility of Killing" *Ethics*, (1983), pp. 514-524. Also reprinted in James P. Sterba, *The Ethics of War and Nuclear Deterrence* (Belmont, CA: Wadsworth Publishing Co. 1985).

pacifism might ask, to kill the person making the attempt? The most cogent response, it seems to me, is that killing in such a case is not evil, or at least not morally evil, because anyone who is wrongfully engaged in an attempt upon your life has already forfeited his or her right to life by engaging in such aggression.[1] So, provided that you are reasonably certain that the aggressor is wrongfully engaged in an attempt upon your life, you would be morally justified in killing, assuming that it is the only way of saving your own life.

There is, however, a form of pacifism that remains untouched by the criticisms I have raised against both nonviolent pacifism and nonlethal pacifism. This form of pacifism neither prohibits all violence nor even all uses of lethal force. We can call the view "anti-war pacifism" because it holds that:

Any participation in the massive use of lethal force in warfare is morally prohibited.[2]

In defense of anti-war pacifism, it is undeniable that wars have brought enormous amounts of death and destruction in their wake and that many of those who have perished in them have been noncombatants or innocents. In fact, the tendency of modern wars has been to produce higher and higher proportions of noncombatant casualties, making it more and more difficult to justify participation in such wars. At the same time, strategies for nonbelligerent conflict resolution are rarely intensively developed and explored before nations choose to go to war, making it all but impossible to justify participation in such wars.[3]

To determine whether the requirements of just war theory can be reconciled with those of anti-war pacifism, however, we need to consider whether we should distinguish between harm intentionally

---

[1] Alternatively, one might concede that even in this case killing is morally evil, but still contend that it is morally justified because it is the lesser of two evils.

[2] For two challenging defenses of this view, see Duane L. Cady, *From Warism to Pacifism* (Philadelphia: Temple University Press, 1989) and Robert L. Holmes, *On War and Morality* (Princeton: Princeton University Press, 1989).

[3] See Cady, *op. cit.*, pp.51, 89ff; and Holmes, *op. cit.*, p. 278.

inflicted upon innocents and harm whose infliction on innocents is merely foreseen. On the one hand, we could favor a uniform restriction against the infliction of harm upon innocents that ignores the intended/foreseen distinction. On the other hand, we could favor a differential restriction which is more severe against the intentional infliction of harm upon innocents, but is less severe against the infliction of harm that is merely foreseen. What needs to be determined, therefore, is whether there is any rationale for favoring this differential restriction on harm over a uniform restriction. But this presupposes that we can, in practice, distinguish between what is foreseen and what is intended, and some have challenged whether this can be done. So first we need to address this challenge.

Now the practical test that is frequently appealed to in order to distinguish between foreseen and intended elements of an action is the Counterfactual Test. According to this test, two questions are relevant:

1) Would you have performed the action if only the good consequences would have resulted and not the evil consequences?
2) Would you have performed the action if only the evil consequences resulted and not the good consequences?

If an agent answers 'Yes' to the first question and 'No' to the second, some would conclude that (1) the action is an intended means to the good consequences, (2) the good consequences are an intended end, and (3) the evil consequences are merely foreseen.

But how well does this Counterfactual Test work? Douglas Lackey has argued that the test gives the wrong result in any case where the 'act that produces an evil effect produces a larger good effect'.[1] Lackey cites the bombing of Hiroshima as an example. That bombing is generally thought to have had two effects: the killing of Japanese civilians and the shortening of the war. Now suppose we were to ask:

---

[1] Douglas P. Lackey, 'The Moral Irrelevance of the Counterforce/Counter-value Distinction,' *The Monist* (1987), pp. 255-276. For a similar view, see Susan Levine, 'Does the "Counterfactual Test" Work for Distinguishing a Means from a Foreseen Concomitant?', *Journal of Value Inquiry* (1984), pp. 155-7.

(1) Would Truman have dropped the bomb if only the shortening of
the war would have resulted but not the killing of the Japanese
civilians?

(2) Would Truman have dropped the bomb if only the Japanese
civilians would have been killed and the war not shortened?

And suppose that the answer to the first question is that Truman
would have dropped the bomb if only the shortening of the war
would have resulted but not the killing of the Japanese civilians, and
that the answer to the second question is that Truman would not
have dropped the bomb if only the Japanese civilians would have
been killed and the war not shortened. Lackey concludes from this
that the killing of civilians at Hiroshima, self-evidently a means for
shortening the war, is by the Counterfactual Test classified not as a
means but as a mere foreseen consequence. On these grounds,
Lackey rejects the Counterfactual Test as an effective device for
distinguishing between the foreseen and the intended consequences of
an action.

Unfortunately, this is to reject the Counterfactual Test only
because one expects too much from it. It is to expect the test to
determine all of the following:

(1) Whether the action is an intended means to the good
consequences;
(2) Whether the good consequences are an intended end of the
action;
(3) Whether the evil consequences are simply foreseen
consequences.

In fact, this test is only capable of meeting the first two of these
expectations. And the test clearly succeeds in doing this for Lackey's
own example, where the test shows the bombing of Hiroshima to
be an intended means to shortening the war, and shortening the war
an intended consequence of the action.

To determine whether the evil consequences are simply foreseen
consequences, however, an additional test is needed, which I shall
call the Nonexplanation Test. According to this test, the relevant
question is:

Does the bringing about of the evil consequences help explain why the agent undertook the action as a means to the good consequences?

If the answer is 'No,' that is, if the bringing about of the evil consequences does not help explain why the agent undertook the action as a means to the good consequences, the evil consequences are merely foreseen. But if the answer is 'Yes,' the evil consequences are an intended means to the good consequences.

Of course, there is no guaranteed procedure for arriving at an answer to the Nonexplanation Test. Nevertheless, when we are in doubt concerning whether the evil consequences of an act are simply foreseen, seeking an answer to the Nonexplanation Test will tend to be the best way of reasonably resolving that doubt. For example, applied to Lackey's example, the Nonexplanation Test comes up with a 'Yes,' since the evil consequences in this example do help explain why the bombing was undertaken to shorten the war. For according to the usual account, Truman ordered the bombing to bring about civilian deaths which by their impact upon Japanese morale were expected to shorten the war. So, by the Nonexplanation Test, the civilian deaths were an intended means to the good consequences of shortening the war.[1]

---

[1] This Nonexplanation Test also solves a related problem of distinguishing foreseen from intended consequences, as noted by Charles Fried. (Charles Fried, *Right and Wrong* [Cambridge, MA: Harvard University Press, 1978], pp. 23-4) Fried was concerned with the following example, first discussed by Philippa Foot (Philippa Foot, 'The Problem of Abortion and the Doctrine of Double Effect,' *Oxford Review* 5 [1967], pp. 5-15): 'Imagine that a fat person who is leading a party of spelunkers gets herself stuck in the mouth of a cave in which flood waters are rising. The trapped party of spelunkers just happens to have a stick of dynamite with which they can blast the fat person out of the mouth of the cave; either they use the dynamite or they all drown, the fat person with them.' Now suppose someone made the claim that using the dynamite was simply a means of freeing the party of spelunkers and that the death of the fat person was just a foreseen side-effect. Fried's problem is that while he rejects this account of the action, he can find no way of successfully challenging it. What he clearly needs is the Nonexplanation Test. For suppose we employ the test and ask whether the death of the fat person helps explain why the dynamite

Assuming, then, that we can distinguish in practice between harm intentionally inflicted upon innocents and harm whose infliction on innocents is merely foreseen, we need to determine whether there is any rationale for favoring a differential restriction that is more severe against the intentional infliction of harm upon innocents but is less severe against the infliction of harm that is merely foreseen over a uniform restriction against the infliction of harm upon innocents that ignores the intended/foreseen distinction.

Let us first examine the question from the perspective of those suffering the harm. Initially, it might appear to matter little whether the harm would be intended or just foreseen by those who cause it. From the perspective of those suffering harm, it might appear that what matters is simply that the overall amount of harm be restricted irrespective of whether it is foreseen or intended. But consider: Don't those who suffer harm have more reason to protest when the harm is done to them by agents who are directly engaged in causing harm to them than when the harm is done incidentally by agents whose ends and means are good? Don't we have more reason to protest when we are being used by others than when we are affected by them only incidentally?

Moreover, if we examine the question from the perspective of those causing harm, additional support for this line of reasoning can be found. For it would seem that we have more reason to protest a restriction against foreseen harm than we have reason to protest a comparable restriction against intended harm. This is because a restriction against foreseen harm limits our actions when our ends and means are good, whereas a restriction against intended harm only limits our actions when our ends or means are evil or harmful, and it would seem that we have greater grounds for acting when both our ends and means are good than when they are not. Consequently, because we have more reason to protest when we are being used by others than when we are being affected by them only incidentally,

---

was used to free the spelunkers from the cave; the answer we get is clearly 'Yes.' For how else could the use of the dynamite free the party of spelunkers from the cave except by removing the fat person from the mouth of the cave in such a way as to cause her death? It follows, according to the Nonexplanation Test, that the death of the fat person is a means intended for freeing the party of spelunkers and not merely a foreseen consequence of the use of the dynamite.

and because we have more reason to act when both our ends and means are good than when they are not, we should favor the foreseen/intended distinction that is incorporated into just means.

It might be objected, however, that at least sometimes we could produce greater good overall by violating the foreseen/intended distinction of just means and acting with the evil means of intentionally harming innocents. On this account, it might be argued that it should be permissible at least sometimes to intentionally harm innocents in order to achieve greater good overall.

Now, it seems to me that this objection is well-taken insofar as it is directed against an absolute restriction upon intentional harm to innocents. It seems clear that there are exceptions to such a restriction when intentional harm to innocents is:

1) trivial (e.g., as in the case of stepping on someone's foot to get out of a crowded subway),
2) easily reparable (e.g., as in the case of lying to a temporarily depressed friend to keep her from committing suicide), or
3) greatly outweighed by the consequences of the action, especially to innocent people (e.g., as in the case of shooting one of two hundred civilian hostages to prevent in the only way possible the execution of all two hundred).

Yet while we need to recognize these exceptions to an absolute restriction upon intentional harm to innocents, there is good reason not to permit simply maximizing good consequences overall, because that would place unacceptable burdens upon particular individuals. More specifically, it would be an unacceptable burden on innocents to allow them to be intentionally harmed in cases other than the exceptions we have just enumerated. And, allowing for these exceptions, we would still have reason to favor a differential restriction against harming innocents that is more severe against the intentional infliction of harm upon innocents but is less severe against the infliction of harm upon innocents that is merely foreseen. Again, the main grounds for this preference are that we would have more reason to protest when we are being used by others than when we are being affected by them only incidentally, and more reason to act when both our ends and means are good than when they are not.

So far, I have argued that there are grounds for favoring a differential restriction on harm to innocents that is more severe against intended harm and less severe against foreseen harm. I have further argued that this restriction is not absolute so that when the evil intended is trivial, easily reparable or greatly outweighed by the consequences, intentional harm to innocents can be justified. Moreover, there is no reason to think that anti-war pacifists would reject either of these conclusions. Anti-war pacifists are opposed to any participation in the massive use of lethal force in warfare, yet this need not conflict with the commitment of just war theorists to a differential but nonabsolute restriction on harm to innocents as a requirement of just means. [1] Where just war theory goes wrong, according to anti-war pacifists, is not in its restriction on harming innocents but rather in its failure to adequately determine when belligerent correctives are too costly to constitute a just cause or lacking in the proportionality required by just means. According to anti-war pacifists, just war theory provides insufficient restraint in both of these areas. Now to evaluate this criticism, we need to consider the following cases:

Case (1) where only the intentional or foreseen killing of an unjust aggressor would prevent one's own death.[2]
Case (2) where only the intentional or foreseen killing of an unjust aggressor and the foreseen killing of one innocent bystander would prevent one's own death and that of five other innocent people.
Case (3) where only the intentional or foreseen killing of an unjust aggressor and the foreseen killing of one innocent bystander would prevent the death of five innocent people.
Case (4) where only the intentional or foreseen killing of an unjust aggressor and the foreseen killing of five innocent people would prevent the death of two innocent people.
Case (5) where only the intentional or foreseen killing of an unjust aggressor and the foreseen killing of five innocent people would

---

[1] This is because the just means restrictions protect innocents quite well against the infliction of intentional harm.
[2] By an "unjust aggressor" I mean someone who the defender is reasonably certain is wrongfully engaged in an attempt upon her life or the lives of other innocent people.

prevent the death of two innocent people and ensure certain liberties or other values for a larger group of people.

Let us discuss each of these cases in turn.

Case (1) seems to present no problems. In the first place, anti-war pacifists have adopted their view because they are convinced that there are instances of justified killing. And, in this case, the only person killed is an unjust aggressor. So surely anti-war pacifists would have to agree with just war theorists that one can justifiably kill an unjust aggressor if it is the only way to save one's life

Case (2). Here we do have the foreseen killing of an innocent person as well as the killing of the unjust aggressor, but since it is the only way to save one's own life and the lives of five other innocent people, anti-war pacifists and just war theorists alike would have reason to judge it morally permissible. In this case, the intended life-saving benefits to six innocent people surely would outweigh the foreseen death of one innocent person.

Case (3). In this case, despite the fact that we lack the justification of self-defense, saving the lives of five innocent people in the only way possible should still provide anti-war pacifists and just war theorists with sufficient grounds for granting the moral permissibility of killing an unjust aggressor, even when the killing of an innocent person is a foreseen consequence. In this case, the intended life-saving benefits to five innocent people would still outweigh the foreseen death of one innocent person.

Case (4). In this case, neither anti-war pacifists nor just war theorists would find the cost and proportionality requirements of just war theory to be met. Too many innocent people would have to be killed to save too few. Here the fact that the deaths of the innocents would be merely foreseen does not outweigh the fact that we would have to accept the deaths of five innocents in order to be able to save two.

Case (5). The interpretation of this case is crucial. Up to this point in previous cases, we have simply been counting the number of innocent deaths involved in each case and opting for the solution that minimizes the loss of innocent lives that would result. In this case, we are asked to sanction a greater loss of innocent lives in order to preserve certain liberties or other values for a larger group of people.

Now, some just war theorists have accepted the legitimacy of trade-offs of just this sort, thereby giving credence to the charge that their theory provides insufficient restraints on just cause and just means.[1] These just war theorists have argued that when interpreting the cost and proportionality requirements of just war theory, we cannot simply do some type of utilitarian calculation weighing lives against lives, presumably not even weighing innocent lives against innocent lives, but that moral values such as liberty and the preferability of certain ways of life must also be taken into account.

But it is unclear how this argument is supposed to go. Surely we might argue that in order to preserve certain freedoms or values in our own society, we are justified in taking defensive actions that have as their foreseen consequence a lessening of freedom in the aggressor's society. For example, our resistance might cause a crackdown on dissidents in the aggressor's society. But it is a further step to justify taking defensive actions that have as their foreseen consequence the greater loss of innocent lives in the aggressor's society than any loss of innocent lives that would thereby be prevented in one's own society. Such trade-offs would not be acceptable even if failure to take such defensive actions would also result in the loss of important liberties in our own society. Thus, for example, even if Lithuania could effectively free itself from the Soviet Union by infiltrating into Moscow several bands of saboteurs who would then attack several military and government installations in Moscow, causing an enormous loss of innocent lives, such trade-offs would not be justified. If the cost and proportionality requirements of just cause and just means are to be met, we must save more innocent lives than we cause to be lost, we must preserve more liberty and other goods than we cause to be destroyed, and we must not kill innocents, even indirectly, simply to preserve important liberties.[2]

---

[1] See, for example, William V. O'Brien, *The Conduct of Just and Limited War* (Praeger Publishers, 1981) and John Courtney Murray, *Morality and Modern War*, Council on Religion and International Affairs, 1959.

[2] Of course, we would not be causing innocent lives to be lost or goods to be destroyed in the relevant sense with respect to those who knowingly have choosen to sacrifice their lives and goods in defense of a just cause. Thus, it is always possible for people to say "Give

Of course, sometimes our lives and liberties are threatened together. Or better, if we are unwilling to give up our liberties then our lives might be threatened as well. Nevertheless, if we are justified in our use of lethal force to defend ourselves in cases that will indirectly kill innocents, it is because our lives are also threatened, not simply our liberties. And the same holds for when we are defending others.

What this shows is that the constraints imposed by just war theory on the use of belligerent correctives are actually much more severe than anti-war pacifists have tended to recognize.[1] In determining when belligerent correctives are too costly to constitute a just cause or are lacking in the proportionality required by just means, just war theory under its most morally defensible interpretation 1) allows the use of belligerent means only when they minimize the loss of innocent lives overall, and 2) allows innocent lives to be threatened only to prevent the loss of innocent lives, not simply to prevent the loss of liberties or other goods.

Now, it might be objected that all that I have shown through the analysis of the above five cases is that killing in defense of oneself or others is morally permissible, not that it is morally required or morally obligatory. That is true. I have not established any obligation to respond to aggression with lethal force in these cases, but only that it is morally permissible to do so. For one thing, it is difficult to ground an obligation to use lethal force on self-defense alone, as would be required in Case 1. Obligations to oneself appear to have an optional quality that is absent from obligations to others. In Cases 2 and 3, however, the use of lethal force would save the lives of others, and here I contend it would be morally obligatory if either the proposed use of lethal force required only a relatively small personal sacrifice from us or if we were fairly bound by convention or a mutual defense agreement to come to the aid of those whose lives we could save. In such cases, I think we can justifiably speak of a moral obligation to kill in defense of others.

---

me liberty or give me death." What we cannot do, however, is make this choice for other people.

[1] And more severe than some just war theorists have tended to recognize.

Another aspect of cases 1-3 to which someone might object is that it is the wrongful actions of others that put us into situations where I am claiming that we are morally justified in killing.[1] But for the actions of unjust aggressors, we would not be in situations where I am claiming that we are morally permitted or required to kill. Yet doesn't something like this happen in a wide range of cases when wrongful actions are performed? Suppose I am on the way to the bank to deposit money from a fundraiser, and someone accosts me and threatens to shoot if I don't hand over the money. If I do hand over the money, I would be forced to do something I don't want to do, something that involves a loss to myself and others. But surely it is morally permissible for me to hand over the money in this case. And it may even be morally required for me to do so if resistance would lead to the shooting of others in addition to myself. So it does seem that bad people, by altering the consequences of our actions, can alter our obligations as well. What our obligations are under nonideal conditions are different from what they would be under ideal conditions. If a group of thugs comes into this room and makes it very clear that they intend to shoot me if each of you doesn't give them one dollar, I think, and I would hope that you would also think, that each of you now has an obligation to give the thugs one dollar, when before you had no such obligation. Likewise, I think that the actions of unjust aggressors can put us into situations where it is morally permissible or even morally required for us to kill when before it was not.

Now it might be contended that anti-war pacifists would concede the moral permissibility of cases 1-3, but still maintain that any participation in the massive use of lethal force in warfare is morally prohibited. The scale of the conflict, anti-war pacifists might contend, makes all the difference. Of course, if this simply means that many large-scale conflicts will have effects that bear no resemblance to cases 1-3, this can hardly be denied. Still, it is possible for some large-scale conflicts to bear a proportionate resemblance to the above cases. For example, it can plausibly be argued that India's military action against Pakistan in Bangladesh and the Tanzanian incursion into Uganda during the rule of Idi Amin resemble case 3 in their effects upon innocents. What this shows is

---

[1] See Holmes, *op. cit.*, pp. 208-211.

that anti-war pacifists are not justified in regarding every participation in the massive use of lethal force in warfare as morally prohibited. Instead, anti-war pacifists must allow that at least in some real-life cases, wars and other large-scale military operations both have been and will be morally permissible.

This concession from anti-war pacifists, however, needs to be matched by a comparable concession from just war theorists themselves, because too frequently they have interpreted their theory in morally indefensible ways. I have argued that when just war theory is given a morally defensible interpretation, the theory favors a strong just means prohibition against intentionally harming innocents. I have also argued that the theory favors the use of belligerent means only when such means 1) minimize the loss of innocent lives overall, and 2) threaten innocent lives only to prevent the loss of innocent lives, not simply to prevent the loss of liberties or other goods. Obviously, just war theory, so understood, is going to place severe restrictions on the use of belligerent means in warfare. In fact, most of the actual uses of belligerent means in warfare that have occurred turn out to be unjustified. For example, the U.S. involvement in Nicaragua, El Salvador and Panama, Soviet involvement in Afghanistan, Israeli involvement in the West Bank and the Gaza Strip all violate the just cause and just means provisions of just war theory as I have defended them. Even the recent U.S.-led war against Iraq violated the both the just cause and just means provisions of just war theory.[1] In fact, one strains to find examples of justified applications of just war theory in recent history. Two examples I have already referred to are India's military action against Pakistan in Bangladesh and the Tanzanian incursion into Uganda during the rule of Idi Amin. But after mentioning these two examples it is difficult to go on. What this shows is that when

---

[1] The just cause provision was violated because the extremely effective economic sanctions were not given enough time to work. It was estimated that when compared to past economic blockades, the blockade against Iraq had a near 100% chance of success if given about a year to work. (See *New York Times,* January 14, 1991) The just means provision was violated because the number of combatant and noncombatant deaths were disproportionate. As many as 150,000 Iraqi soldiers were killed according to U.S. intelligence sources.

just war theory and anti-war pacifism are given their most morally defensible interpretations, both views can be reconciled. In this reconciliation, the few wars and large-scale conflicts that meet the stringent requirements of just war theory are the only wars and large-scale conflicts to which anti-war pacifists cannot justifiably object. We can call the view that emerges from this reconciliation "just war pacifism."[1] It is the view which claims that due to the stringent requirements of just war theory, only very rarely will participation in a massive use of lethal force in warfare be morally justified. It is the view on which I rest my case for the reconciliation of pacifism and just war theory.[2]

The University of Notre Dame

---

[1] For another use of this term, see Kenneth H. Wenker, "Just War Pacifism," *Proceedings of the American Catholic Philosophical Association* (1983), pp. 135-141. For a defense of a similar view to my own, which is considered by the author to be a defense of pacifism, see Richard Norman, "The Case for Pacifism," *Journal of Applied Philosophy* (1988), pp. 197-210.

[2] Of course, more needs to be done to specify the requirements of just war pacifism. One fruitful way to further specify these requirements is to appeal to a hypothetical social contract decision procedure as has been done with respect to other practical problems. Here I have simply tried to establish the defensibility of just war pacifism without appealing to any such procedure. Yet once the defensibility of just war pacifism has been established, such a decision procedure will prove quite useful in working out its particular requirements.

4 Challenging the Domestic Analogy:
A Critique of Killing in Self-Defense

Joseph Kunkel

Introduction

Killing an aggressor in private self-defense is often claimed intuitively to be morally justified. Michael Walzer, for instance, uses the self-evidence of this domestic norm as grounds for approving wars fought against aggressors. "Individual rights (to life and liberty)," he says, "underlie the most important judgments that we make about war."[1] By contrast, morally restraining oneself from killing, in a case of self-defense, has been subjected to extensive ethical criticism.

With this context in mind, I set out to review the rational arguments favoring killing an aggressor in private self-defense. To my surprise I found the arguments generally inconclusive. If the argumentation is indeed weak, then those who wish to justify war based upon this domestic analogy need to find another moral presupposition to bolster their position.

In this paper I review and critique these arguments. I have limited the question to killing in private self-defense. Public self-defense—for example, capital punishment, war, and police activity— introduces additional issues that would best be taken up only after reviewing the clearer private case. Critiquing the arguments in support of killing in private self-defense is not the same as arguing that such killing is wrong; still, as I will show, it does shift the strength of moral force in that direction.

I shall begin by anticipating a few potential ambiguities. Violence has frequently been equated with force. 'Force', however, applies to geophysical as well as to human phenomena. For

---

[1]Michael Walzer, *Just and Unjust Wars: A Moral Argument With Historical Illustrations* (New York: Basic Books, 1977), p. 54. See also Jeffrie Murphy, "The Killing of the Innocent," *The Monist* Vol. 57 (1973), p. 535.

example, electricity, the wind, flowing waters, and earth tremors are called forces. By contrast, as Newton Garver has shown, 'violence' stems from the same root as 'violation.'[1] Violence or a violation is more than a simple demonstration of force, like gravity; violence carries a connotation of destructiveness. Accordingly, high winds are sometimes called 'violent,' but in a geophysical sense. When I use 'violence' here I mean it in a moral sense, a violation of one person by purposive, destructive harm to another. For instance, a surgeon's forced entry into another person's body may do physical harm, but if the surgeon's purpose is healing, and the patient tacitly consents, there is no moral violence.

Self-defense is first and foremost a defense. Defending oneself is natural and moral. An ethical dilemma arises only when one uses violence to defend against violence. The difficulty comes in returning violence for violence when doing violence is considered wrong. The classic ethical case of returning violence for violence is killing in self-defense when the defensive killing is not purely accidental.

This paper addresses the justification for killing in response to a violent threat to life; I do not address justifications for forms of self-defense short of killing the attacker. The paradigm case is an encounter in which a human aggressor threatens the life of a victim. The emphasis is on the aggressor's *threat to kill* the victim. Without violent response to this threat, the result may be the victim's death. The victim, however, is not certain that her death will occur, but is certain that her life is genuinely threatened. In response to this life-threatening provocation the victim, or a third-party bystander, kills the aggressor in self-defense. The question for us is whether this killing in private self-defense is morally justified.

There are four types of arguments given to justify killing an aggressor in private self-defense: consequentialism, forfeiture of rights, deontology, and double effect. Each form of argument is examined and counterargued below. With one restricted exception, the arguments are found insufficient to justify killing in private self-defense. In the process of counterarguing I maintain that a

---

[1]Newton Garver, "What Violence Is," *Philosophy for A New Generation* Eds. A. Bierman and J. Gould (New York: Macmillen, 4th ed., 1981), pp. 217-228. The article is here revised from its original appearance in *The Nation* (June 24, 1968), pp. 817-822.

satisfactory argument must be sufficiently precise so as only to include the victim's killing of the aggressor and not also to justify the aggressor's killing of the victim. I begin with the consequentialist arguments.

Consequentialism

The utilitarian justification for killing in self-defense over killing in general is vague. This stems in part from the conceptual difficulty utilitarians encounter in formulating what has traditionally been called the human right to life, or the right not to be killed. Utilitarians tend to view human life as equivalent to biological life, something humans share naturally with plants and animals. When life is restricted to conscious life, plants but not animals are excluded. Life is thus significant, in classical utilitarianism, for the pleasures and pains that accrue. In this sense ceasing to live, as in being instantaneously killed, does not constitute an additional pain but rather a cessation of pleasures and pains.

A person killed enters into the utility calculus only when one either looks at the total view or counts up the side-effects. Under the total view, killing in a torturously painful manner would be wrong. However, killing an unhappy person quickly adds to the maximization of pleasure in the universe, and killing a happy person subtracts from that maximization. Killing the aggressor in self-defense, accordingly, would be justified only if the original victim were happy and the aggressor unhappy. Among side-effects may be listed effects on family and friends, loss to the community of contributions from the deceased, hatred aroused, and the undermining of the sense of security of others.[1] But these side-effects cut both ways, affecting the victim who kills in self-defense as well as the aggressor who is killed. Both may have had family and friends, and the one killed may have made a larger contribution to society if still alive. So killing in self-defense under classical utilitarian criteria does not automatically favor the victim.

With serial killers and with deranged individuals who open fire on crowds of people or on children at play, the situation changes. Results favor the killing of such attackers by the threatened victims

---

[1] Jonathan Glover, *Causing Death and Saving Lives* (New York: Penguin Books, 1977), p. 114.

or by others. In these instances it is the multiple murders that weight the consequences toward defense of the victims. Such examples, however, cannot serve as models for evaluating single aggressor-victim situations.

Another consequentialist approach is found in what Peter Singer and others call preference utilitarianism.[1] The preference refers to the person's desire to go on living. The position maintains that killing a self-conscious being is worse than killing a conscious being, and among self-conscious beings killing a person with a preference for continued life is worse than killing a person having no such preference. So, all side-effects being equal, persons can be killed justifiably if they do not desire to go on living. In cases of self-defense, however, the situation is less clear. The act of aggression with a deadly weapon does not in itself display the aggressor's own preference for living or not living. Thus preference utilitarianism, like classical utilitarianism, does not always favor killing the aggressor over the victim in cases of private self-defense. Some cases appear to favor killing the aggressor, and others the victim.

Philip Montague shifts away from preferences to behaviors, and defends a utilitarian rule called forced choice.[2] With behaviorism as his starting point, he first broadens the self-defensive descriptors to include innocent aggressors and self-preservation situations. He then claims, "[W]hen faced with a forced choice between lives, it is sometimes permissible to kill some number of persons in order to save the lives of others."[3] In particular, Montague is attempting to distinguish people who are innocent victims from those displaying "threatening and aggressive behavior." The difficulty is the ensuing ambiguity as soon as the victim moves to defend herself. Does not the victim then behave in a threatening and aggressive manner toward the original aggressor? If so, is not the aggressor also forced to choose between lives as soon as the victim behaviorally creates a

[1] Peter Singer, "Killing Humans and Killing Animals," *Inquiry*, Vol. 22 (1979), pp. 145-56, and *Practical Ethics* (Cambridge: Cambridge University Press, 1979), pp. 72-84.
[2] Philip Montaque, "Self-Defense and Choosing Between Lives," *Philosophical Studies*, Vol. 40 (1981), pp. 207-219.
[3] Montague, *op. cit.*, p. 211. The remaining quotes from Montague are from this same page.

life-threatening situation for the aggressor? Would not the aggressor-become-victim be justified, according to the same forced choice rule, in killing the victim-become-aggressor? Forced choice thus resembles "the fastest gun" in the Old West.

Montague tries to circumvent this difficulty by distinguishing provoked from unprovoked behavior. Provoked behavior he calls "*culpable*" behavior." The aggressor is thus viewed as culpable, the victim as innocent. Such designations, however, are highly subjective. They ignore previous events, personal histories, undisclosed intentions. In one-to-one encounters they encourage each participant to be what John Yoder calls a "judge, prosecutor, and executioner in one's own case."[1] Self-righteousness may be allowed to supersede judicious balance.

An analogous difficulty has plagued the justification of wars fought in defense of the innocent. This is partly offset by use of functional descriptors to separate those who are culpable and "combatants" from those who are innocent and "noncombatants."[2] Still, such a differentiation does not settle who are the aggressors and who are the non-aggressors.

No terms similar to 'combatants' and 'noncombatants' have yet been found applicable for private encounters. Whose behavior, for example, is culpable when two people fight in a barroom, when family members feud in an apartment, when householders keep revolvers on their nightstands, or when pharmacists place loaded guns under the counter? Is the innocent person the one who draws second but shoots first? Unless such descriptors are made available, the distinction between culpable and innocent behavior is practically meaningless for situations of private self-defense.

Cheyney Ryan takes another tack in differentiating between the aggressor and the victim.[3] Ryan suggests that the asymmetry of roles between the aggressor and the victim can best be brought out by the notion of responsibility. "When Aggressor threatens Victim," Ryan says, "his actions have created a situation in which

---

[1] John Yoder, "'What Would You Do If. . . ?' An Exercise in Situation Ethics," *The Journal of Religious Ethics,* Vol. 2.2 (Fall, 1974), p. 85.

[2] See, for example: Jeffrie Murphy, *op, cit.,* pp. 527-536.

[3] Cheyney Ryan, "Self-Defense, Pacifism, and the Possibility of Killing," *Ethics,* Vol. 93, (1982-1983), pp. 515-520.

someone's life will be lost (he hopes Victim's)." The aggressor is thus responsible for the situation, while the victim only determines *"whose* life will be lost." By appealing to self-defense, then, a person is saying that the aggressor is the one responsible for the loss of life. However, Ryan's analysis only works if there is a necessary connection between the aggressor's opening thrust and the boomeranging lethal ending. Yoder shows there are other options, including natural disruptions of the sequence, interventions, talking downs, disarmings, and even unsuccessful killings.[1] Options short of killing the aggressor are thus sufficiently available to indicate that the self-defending victim normally has more responsibility for the result than merely choosing "whose life will be lost."

Forfeiture of Rights

The second kind of argumentation involves forfeiture of rights. This argument goes back at least to John Locke. Locke maintains a view that natural rights, including the right not to be killed, are inherently part of being human. Natural rights are inalienable, unconditional, and universally applicable. But when these rights are violated, Locke says, the violator is placed outside the state of nature, forfeiting his natural rights and falling into a state of war. An aggressor who threatens the life of a victim is thus portrayed as an "outlaw," a person outside the natural constraints of morality and the constitutional bounds of law.

There is an obvious difficulty with this view. Since natural rights are said to be based on nature, how can they be forfeited? Surely they can be grossly violated, but that does not establish a natural basis for loss of possession. Based on a natural foundation for rights Locke's forfeiture claim runs counter to the inherent inalienability: if rights are natural and inalienable, how can an individual forfeit them?

A way around this problem is to ground rights not on nature but on a social contract, which can be broken. Many contractarians, like Locke, build the social contract on a basis of natural rights, and then the problem remains. But if, as in Hobbes, the contract is the foundation for morality, then moral rights are lost whenever the contract or moral promise is broken. Accordingly, if one attacks

---

[1]Yoder, *op. cit.*, pp. 90-94.

another person one ceases to be protected by moral restraints. This loss of moral restraints, of course, would appear to cut both ways, in that one who has forfeited moral rights may *ipso facto* no longer be obligated to respect the rights of others with whom she is no longer under moral contract. For example, if a woman aggressor loses her right to life, does she not also lose her duty to preserve life? May she then not kill amorally with impunity? This, ironically, would also impact on the case of the serial killer.

Additional troubling questions arise for the theory of forfeiture.[1] Does a violation of any right constitute sufficient grounds for the forfeiture of all rights? Locke, for instance, lists robbery as sufficient grounds. Or are some rights more fundamental than others? If fundamental rights are forfeited by aggressors, are all rights and consequent duties forfeited? If an aggressor physically harms a victim, does the aggressor forfeit his right not to be tortured or maimed? If in abusing the victim he unfairly violates a criminal statute, does he as an outlaw forfeit his right to be treated fairly under the law? Are aggressors presumed guilty until proven innocent? Are rights, laws, and morality only for the virtuous, with immoral-ity and unlawfulness the standard for the non-virtuous? If the aggressor is immobilized in the process of an unsuccessful act of aggression, can the victim nevertheless at will kill the defenseless aggressor that has forfeited the right not to be killed? If not, why not? How long does the forfeiture last? Does the attacker reacquire forfeited rights upon immobilization, after police arrival, or only after repudiation of the bad intention? In cases of capital punishment, does the newly convicted criminal again forfeit his right to life after having reacquired that right while preparing for trial? Then, too, most of the above questions repeat themselves as the condemned prisoner awaits execution. Some of these questions are disposed of in a practical way by legislatures, judges, and juries; however, from a theoretical standpoint the forfeiture claim adds more

---

[1] For these questions I am especially indebted to Hugo Bedau, "Capital Punishment," *Matters of Life and Death*, Ed. Tom Regan, (New York: Random House, 2nd ed., 1986), pp. 177-181, and to Judith Thomson, "Self-Defense and Rights," *The Lindley Lecture*, (U. of Kansas, April 5, 1976), pp. 3-6. See also Ryan, *op. cit.*, pp. 510-512, and George Fletcher, "The Right to Life," *The Monist*, Vol. 63, (1980), pp. 142-145.

problems than it solves, and thus would not seem adequate as an argument favoring killing in private self-defense.

Deontology

The third type of argumentatior flows out of the Kantian tradition. The common interpretation is that killing in self-defense, private or public, is moral. The argument is that killing an aggressor who is threatening the life of an innocent victim is in accord with the Kantian principle of respecting other human beings as equal.[1] What does this imply? At the very least it implies that the duty not to kill or the right not to be killed is not absolute. The reason, some say, is that there is a prior duty to preserve life. In this instance, however, by killing an assailant one is not preserving all lives.

Perhaps the prior duty is to self-defense. Or better, maybe W. D. Ross is correct in arguing that all rights and duties are prima facie rather than absolute.[2] Ross argues that in morally conflictive situations multiple duties are incumbent on us because of the complex relationships we have with one another. In conflictive situations, therefore, one right may be overridden by another right that is said to be more stringent than the first. In situations of self-defense, the argument claims, the aggressor has a right not to be killed, but this is overridden by the more stringent right (or duty) of the victim to be defended. To use more compelling terminology, the victim's or a third-party bystander's duty or obligation not to kill is overridden by the more stringent duty to defend the life of the victim. The issue is not any defense of the life of the victim, but defense with a deadly force. The claim is being made that the duty to kill in self-defense is more stringent than the duty not to kill.

If this is true, at least two troubling conclusions result. First, if it is a duty to kill in self-defense, then not killing, as in the case of radical pacifism, is immoral. Therefore those who universalize the maxim "Do not kill" in a supererogatory manner are violating a more stringent duty to kill in self-defense, unless, of course, there is

---

[1] See, for example, Alan Donagan, *The Theory of Morality* (Chicago: U. of Chicago Press, 1977), pp. 72-74.

[2] W.D. Ross, *The Right and The Good* (Oxford: Clarendon Press, 1930), pp. 19-20ff.

another (as yet unnamed) principle that overrides self-defense. Secondly, if preserving one's life overrides the obligation not to kill, the aggressor becomes duty-bound to kill the victim-become-aggressor and the victim becomes duty-bound to kill the aggressor. In other words, as soon as the victim or a third-party bystander moves to kill the aggressor, the aggressor becomes obligated to defend her own life. Thus victim, bystander, and aggressor-become-victim are all acting to defend human lives. A society founded on such a principle would have all defenders and no aggressors, and Hobbes's nightmarish natural condition of humanity would become a sanctioned reality. In response, most ethicists modify the situational context in which the right to life is overridden, by requiring the obligation not to kill to be less stringent only when the self-defending victim is innocent and the aggressor culpable. Such a modification, however, requires further explication either through reasons of innocence or forfeiture, two arguments previously discussed and found wanting, or through specification, an argument we shall presently address.

Specification purports to justify killing in private self-defense by delimiting or specifying the right not to be killed.[1] What supporters of specification say is that no one has a right not to be killed; instead one has a right not to be murdered, that is, a right not to be killed unjustly. What this amounts to saying is that killing is only wrong when one kills unjustly. Accordingly, victim may kill aggressor whenever it is not unjust to do so. Why? Because it is not unjust. When? Whenever what Judith Thomson calls the "factual specification" permits. But when does the factual specification permit killing?[2] When, for instance, the aggressor is trying to kill the victim who, in turn, can preserve his life only by killing the aggressor. Or when the aggressor is innocent, demented, and displaying behavior that seems deadly to others. Or when a deadly threat is posed by someone's culpable recklessness or negligence. Or sometimes in the case of rape or mugging. The list goes on and on, complicating rather than simplifying. Moreover, specifying factors does not entail the justification of the specifications that make killing permissible. In fact, the factors are

---

[1]For this argument and counter-argument I am especially indebted to Judith Thomson. See Thomson, *op. cit.*, p. 6-12.
[2]Thomson, *op. cit.*, p. 7.

justified by a principle that is itself established by recourse to the
same factors. But such circular reasoning is not the only problem.
The whole purpose of introducing duties as a foundation for
morality is defeated when duties are made contingent upon right or
just factual specifications, as opposed to wrong or unjust ones.
What are duties, for example, if we have duties only not to be
tortured unjustly, not to be held in slavery unjustly, not to be
discriminated against unjustly, or not to steal unjustly? Under such
specifications duties derived from more basic principles cease to be
the determinants of morality. So specification, like forfeiture, turns
out to be an unsatisfactory way of discriminating the innocent from
the guilty.

Double Effect

The final form of argumentation used to justify killing in
private self-defense is the principle of double effect as embodied in
natural law ethics. Natural law proponents admit killing is evil.
However, under the principle of double effect a single act with
double—good and evil—effects is permitted, provided four
conditions are simultaneously met. The conditions are: (1) The act,
exclusive of the evil effect, must be good; (2) The person acting
must have a right intention; (3) The evil effect may not be the
means to the good effect; and (4) There must be a proportionate
grave reason for acting.

As applied to situations of private self-defense the first
condition requires that preserving one's life in a threatening situation
not be evil for other reasons, which in the victim's case under
consideration it is not. The second condition strives to introduce
harmony into a threatening situation, and is met in preserving one's
life, provided some effort at mediating differences is undertaken.
The fourth condition, proportionate grave reason, is met by the
threat to one's life. The third condition, however, is not as readily
met. If the victim preserves her life by killing her assailant, then
killing her assailant becomes the means for saving her life, and
condition three is violated. Admittedly there are a few instances in
which the killing is purely accidental, as when an assailant who is
pushed to the ground hits his head and dies of a concussion. But the
usual case involves a lethal wounding by the victim that is not

accidental; such a killing, in turn, seems to be the direct means to the intended end.

Some authors circumvent this assessment by arguing that in cases of self-defense the death of the aggressor is foreseen but not intended. Only when the killing is *intended* as the means to the end, they say, is Condition Three violated. Their argument rests on the meaning of intention as applied to situations of self-defense.[1] They follow St. Thomas Aquinas in arguing that "moral acts take their species according to what is intended and not according to what is beside the intention. . . ."[2] Therefore, if only self-defense is intended then self-defense alone figures in the morality of the act. Killing may be foreseen, but unless it is actually intended it is not morally culpable. In this way the third condition is rewritten as:

(3a) The evil effect may not be intended as the means to the good effect.

If we grant this to be a plausible interpretation of double effect, preserving one's life becomes the acceptable intended act, and killing the aggressor is said to be foreseen, but not intended. Killing in private self-defense could therefore be justified by this interpretation of double effect.

The argument, however, has two drawbacks. The first drawback is that once self-defense is stressed as a personal intention—independent of the universal duty we discussed previously—any person, victim or aggressor, can claim the intention for self-defense over killing in situations of private lethal conflict. Either the victim-become-defender or the aggressor-become-defender could foresee the killing of the other person, while supposedly not intending it. In response to this criticism proponents of double effect can refer to the necessity of meeting all four conditions as a

---

[1]See, for example, Germain Grisez, "Toward a Consistent Natural-Law Ethics of Killing," *The American Journal of Jurisprudence*, Vol. 15 (1970), pp. 73-96, and Joseph M. Boyle, Jr, "Toward Understanding the Principle of Double Effect," *Ethics*, Vol. 90 (1979-1980), pp. 527-538.

[2]St. Thomas Aquinas, *The Summa Theologica*, Trans. Fathers of English Dominican Province (New York: Benziger Brothers, 1948). Vol. II-II, Quest. 64, Art 7.

precondition for the justification of an action. Thus an aggressor-become-defender also needs to have a right intention, to be performing an action that is not in itself evil, and to have a proportionately grave reason for acting in order for his action to be moral. In the paradigm case we are examining, if the aggressor intends to threaten the life of a victim, then the other three conditions cannot be met. However, if the threat is merely behavioral, as in displaying a gun during a robbery but with no intention of using it, or perhaps with only an intention to shoot over people's heads, then it is possible that a subsequent self-defensive reaction by the aggressor-become-defender could meet all four conditions for a moral action. For example, a robber with a gun may be committing an evil act in entering a pharmacy, but the evil act is robbery, or robbery with a lethal weapon, not murder. If the pharmacist reacts by pulling a gun and firing, the robber is then placed in an entirely different situation, one of self-defense. At that point the robber-become-victim could intend preservation of life and fulfill all four conditions of double effect. So in some instances double effect does not work, because it exonerates the aggressor-become-victim as well as the victim-become-defender.

The second drawback revolves around how intentions that are morally acceptable can be objectively distinguished from those that are not. For example, if the victim-become-defender shoots the aggressor in the head, chest, or back, and claims an intention only for self-defense, how can this intention be objectively supported against what might appear to others as an intended killing? In a few cases, such as when a person is first securely restrained and then killed, the murderous intention appears obvious, unless, of course, the murderer is judged mentally insane. But if the victim regularly carries a concealed weapon, or keeps a loaded revolver near the cash register, and shoots the aggressor with no warning, it is not clear whether the intention is preservation of life, or preservation of one's property and/or protection of one's turf. The latter intentions run counter to having a proportionate grave reason for killing. In other cases, such as when the shooting is preceded by a fight, or when the victim is challenging the aggressor to "make my day," a question can be raised about the right intention of the victim. On the other hand, if the aggressor puts herself in the same conflictive situation several times, as in the case of a serial killer, the objectivity of the intention becomes obvious. Applying double effect, therefore, turns out to be more complicated than was immediately evident. With four conditions needing to be met, killing in private self-defense is sometimes justified and sometimes not justified by one interpretation of the principle of double effect.

Conclusion

I have argued that, with this one carefully construed exception, killing in private self-defense is not justified by the arguments given in its support. Have I therefore proven that such killing is for the most part unjustifiable? Ryan says no. He claims that negating the arguments that purport to justify private self-defense only establishes "that we do not *know* if killing is justified or not."[1] He says that until arguments are given in support of the right not to be killed, skepticism reigns and individuals are free to choose either principle.

Is Ryan correct? Do the counterarguments lead only to moral skepticism regarding killing or not killing? Hardly. Rather, a moral obligation remains, but what it is follows upon one's ethical orientation. Under consequentialism, for instance, if the rules for forced choice and culpable behavior do not hold, the system reverts to calculating the costs and benefits accruing to the victim and aggressor in each instance. Such a method does not provide a solid basis for arguing that killing in self-defense is usually justified. Neither does it justify an individual in choosing either killing or not killing. Moral obligation, under consequentialism, always depends upon the results, not the individual's choice. Under forfeiture of rights, when the forfeiture argument is negated the case for not killing is bolstered. If there are no sufficient grounds for arguing that the right not to be killed can be forfeited, then the right not to be killed remains pervasively in force. Under deontology, if specification muddies the reasoning, we are left to search for another principle to decide the issue of killing or not killing. But if the overrider or stringency claims are countered, killing in private self-defense is not justified, and the duty not to kill remains in force. Under the principle of double effect, killing is admitted to be evil. The evil, however, is allowed when four conditions are met; when all four conditions are not met, the evil act is disallowed. So right

---

[1] Ryan, *op. cit.*, p. 520.

or wrong depends upon the particular intentions formed and the specific circumstances involved.

To sum up, almost all the arguments given in support of killing in private self-defense are unsatisfactory. This conclusion does not necessitate that every killing in self-defense is therefore immoral. To make the latter claim requires proof that private killings are not justified, and that type of argument too appears not to be forthcoming. At present there is no definitive moral argument for or against killing in private self-defense.

The suggestion that individuals can therefore choose to kill or not to kill in self-defense is indefensible. What happens morally depends upon one's ethical orientation. Some orientations do not allow killing in self-defense. Others do, but under restrictive circumstances. What is clear is that being allowed to kill in order to avoid being killed is not morally self-evident.

The morality of going to war is also affected by the lack of a definitive argument for killing in private self-defense. To the extent the domestic analogy is a prerequisite for proving that war against aggressors is justified, then going to war in self-defense may not be justified. Those wishing to justify war, therefore, must either settle for a highly restrictive set of satisfying conditions—more restrictive than the elastic set of just-war conditions now in vogue—or develop an alternate moral foundation for approving war. A third option would be to present a definitive argument for killing in private self-defense. To ignore these issues is to revert to an amoral, Hobbesian powerplay.

University of Dayton

5 Gene Sharp, Nonviolence, and the Western Moral Tradition

Jerald Richards

Introduction

Gene Sharp is one of the most important and creative contemporary proponents of nonviolent action as an alternative to violence in resolving conflicts between political groups and nations. The article or book is yet to appear which does justice to the breadth, complexity, and profundity of his thinking.[1] This paper is not, and is not intended to be, that commendable work. My purpose here is much more modest, and of both a critical and a constructive nature. I propose (1) to provide a critique of Sharp's criticism of the Western moral tradition's qualified acceptance of violence in conflict situations, and (2) to offer some thoughts on a possible compromise position between Sharp and the traditionalists.

To provide a framework for Sharp's criticism and my discussion of the Western moral tradition, I will rely upon Alan Donagan's exposition of this tradition.[2] For Donagan, there is one

---

[1]Sharp's most important works are the following: *The Politics of Nonviolent Action* (Boston: Porter Sargent Publishers, 1973); *Gandhi as a Political Strategist* (Boston: Porter Sargent Publishers, 1979); *Making the Abolition of War a Realistic Goal* (Chicago: Institute for World Order, 1980); *Social Power and Political Freedom* (Boston: Porter Sargent Publishers, 1980); *National Security Through Civilian-Based Defense* (Omaha: Association for Transarmament Studies, 1985); and *Making Europe Unconquerable: The Potential of Civilian-Based Deterrence and Defence* (Cambridge: Ballinger Publishing Company, 1985). For bibliographical references, copies of papers by Sharp and by others about Sharp, and copies of reviews of Sharp's works, I gratefully acknowledge my indebtedness to the following persons: Robert A. Irwin, Susan Abrams, Kendra McCleskey, and Ralph Summy.
[2]Alan Donagan *The Theory of Morality* (Chicago: University of Chicago Press, 1977).

fundamental principle of Western (or Hebrew-Christian) morality, from which all other principles are derived. This is the principle of neighbor-love ("you should love your neighbor as you love yourself") which Donagan interprets in Kantian terms: Act always so that you respect human beings, including yourself, as rational creatures.[1] To act in this way is to treat human beings as ends in themselves, and not to use or exploit them as means for egoistic, ulterior ends. Principles derived from this fundamental principle fall into three categories: obligations to oneself, obligations to other persons, and obligations to institutions one participates in.[2] Main obligations to oneself are the obligations not to harm oneself and to promote one's own well-being.[3] Main obligations to others are the duties of nonviolence, beneficence, and veracity.

The duty of nonviolence is set forth in the general prohibition that "it is impermissible for anyone at will to use force upon another,"[4] from which are derived the prohibitions against killing, inflicting bodily harm, and slavery.[5] On Donagan's interpretation, the duty of nonviolence is not absolute. Human beings who use or threaten the use of violence to further their own ends forfeit their right to immunity from violence. Thus, the general prohibition against violence is complemented by the precept, "It is permissible for any human being to use force upon another in such measure as may be necessary to defend rational creatures from the other's violence."[6]

In some situations, the duty to promote the well-being of others is conditional upon the duty not to stand idly by when innocent persons can be protected from violence. In these situations, the permissibility to use force to protect others from violence becomes a duty. Of course, the force used should be no more than necessary. However, says Donagan, "if it is reasonably believed necessary to kill the attacker in order to save the victim, the attacker not only may be killed but ought to be."[7]

---

[1] *Ibid.*, p. 65.
[2] See *ibid.*, p. 75.
[3] See *ibid.*, pp. 70-80.
[4] *Ibid.*, p. 82.
[5] *Ibid.*, p. 83.
[6] *Ibid.*, p. 85.
[7] *Ibid.*, p. 87. See also pp. 86, 156.

There are a number of precepts related to participation in civil society, among them being the obligation to obey the law, with the attendant rights (and perhaps even obligations) to disobey unjust laws and to rebel against unjust systems.[1] Part of the obligation to obey the law is the obligation to participate in defense of one's country against unjustifiable attack. This obligation includes the possibility of military service.[2]

Cases in which there are apparent conflicts between principles or in which the only options appear to be wrong in themselves are governed by ordering principles integral to and derivable from the fundamental principle of respect for persons. Among these are the principle that one should not do evil that good may come of it, and the principle that one should always do the least evil in situations where some evil may result. One application of the latter principle requires, in choosing between goods, choosing the good that involves the least loss. The principle of least evil applies also to cases of moral perplexity *secundum quid*, cases in which, no matter what one does (including not acting at all), some evil will be done. These situations result from the fact that, in the past, moral principles have been broken and moral wrongs have been committed, so that persons become enmeshed in conditions in which another principle or other principles must be broken.[3]

This brief summary of what is essentially Donagan's interpretation of Hebrew-Christian morality, with a focus upon those principles related to the possible use of violence, fairly well represents what I take to be the majority position that has emerged historically over the long centuries of the growth and development of Western morality. I will not argue this point in this paper, but assume its correctness in the discussion that follows.

I am assuming the correctness of both Donagan's identification of the principle of neighbor-love as the fundamental principle of Hebrew-Christian morality and his deontological interpretation of this tradition. Although other adherents of this tradition might disagree with Donagan on what its fundamental principle is, they would be in substantial agreement with him on what the most important principles of this system of morality are. This would be

---

[1]See *ibid.*, pp. 93-109.
[2]*Ibid.*, p. 110.
[3]On ordering principles, see *ibid.*, pp. 85-86, 144-145, 149-156.

true of both those who take a consequentialist (e.g., utilitarian) rather than a deontological, approach to the tradition, and those who are secularists rather than theists. These different interpreters tend to agree on the place and significance of the principle of nonviolence and related principles. Given this agreement, and given the fact that Sharp himself does not distinguish among the different interpretations, his criticism of the tradition can be taken to apply to the various interpretations.

Sharp's Criticism of Traditional Morality

There are a number of claims Sharp makes about the Western moral tradition's thinking on nonviolence. (1) Sharp claims that nonbelievers in the "ethics of nonviolence"—that is, persons who are not committed to the principle of nonviolence as an absolute principle (allowing for no exceptions)—are in effect denying the universal validity of the principle.[1] (2) Thus, it follows for Sharp that these "nonbelievers" believe in the necessity of engaging in immoral actions in order to defeat immoral actions.[2] (3) Sharp also holds that the reason for denying the universal validity of the principle of nonviolence is pragmatic. Its universal validity is denied because it does not "work," or is not practicable. On the traditional view, as Sharp expounds it, the ethical and the practical are opposed to one another or, to put the point in another way, the prescribed ethical course of action is not identical with the practical course of action.[3]

For Sharp, a moral principle is universal if, and only if, it is an absolute principle. A principle is absolute, for Sharp, if it does not permit any possible exceptions under any conceivable conditions. Thus, those who would allow possible exceptions to the principle of nonviolence ("it is impermissible for anybody at will to use force upon another") are denying its universal validity.

An alternative understanding of the nature of universal moral principles will enable us to preserve the importance of the principle of nonviolence and, at the same time, to avoid charging traditional moralists with denying its universality and importance. On this

---

[1] See Sharp op. cit. (1979), p. 300.
[2] See ibid., p. 293.
[3] See ibid., pp. 255-257, 300.

quite familiar alternative understanding, the first principle of one's system of morality is universal in an absolute sense. All the other principles of the system are universal in a qualified sense. In this qualified sense, moral principles are universal in that they are applicable to and obligatory for all human beings in all conceivable situations. But they are not absolute. They may be suspended (overridden) in specific situations, but only (1) in situations in which there is a conflict of moral principles and not all of them can be obeyed, and (2) if moral justification can be provided for the suspension by showing that the principle obeyed has "greater moral weight" in the specific situation than the principle(s) suspended. The principle which has "greater moral weight" is the one that best protects the persons and rights of all individuals involved, and which does not violate the ordering principles of "the least wrong."

Nonviolence as a Universal Principle

On this alternative understanding of universal principles, the principle of nonviolence is a universal principle applicable to all human beings in all conceivable situations, but it is not an absolute principle, since the use of violence may be justifiable in specific contexts.

In traditional Western morality, the principle of nonviolence is one of the most important principles derivable from the fundamental principle of respect for persons. Thus, it is not morally justifiable to use force against others except in situations where force may (or must) be used to protect oneself or others from violence. Sometimes a person is permitted, even obligated, to resist violence by force, including physical force. Obviously, to do what is morally permissible, or morally obligatory, is not to act immorally; it is to do that which is ethical in that situation. Since, in general, one ought not to cause harm to others, the force should be used only as a last resort after all other means to resolve the conflict have been tried and have not been successful, and the force used must be the minimum necessary to keep the attacker from causing serious harm.

Summary Critique of Sharp

Thus far, I have arrived at a number of conclusions regarding Sharp's criticism of traditional Western morality.

(1) To hold that the principle of nonviolence is not an absolute principle is not to deny its universal validity. A principle has universal validity if it is applicable to all persons in all possible relevant situations, and can be suspended only for stronger moral reasons and under the control of ordering principles.

(2) It is misleading to characterize those committed to traditional morality as nonbelievers in "the ethics of nonviolence." According to the tradition, the principle of nonviolence is a major principle derivable from the fundamental principle of respect for persons and must be honored except in cases where overriding moral reasons intervene.

(3) It is incorrect to say that traditionalists believe in the necessity of immoral actions when they resort to violent actions. The only cases in which this terminology might be correct are cases of moral perplexity *secundum quid*. Only in these cases must one do something which is evil (with doing nothing at all itself resulting in evil). But what one does in these cases, although of necessity evil, is considered to be obligatory and thus moral. In all other cases, actions involving the justifiable use of force are considered to be moral actions that do not entail evil.

(4) It is incorrect to hold, as Sharp does, that the traditionalist rejects the absoluteness of the principle of nonviolence on pragmatic grounds. On purely pragmatic grounds, neither violence nor nonviolence will "work" in some situations. That is, neither will result in the desired end or goal of the action undertaken. Traditionalists reject the absoluteness of the principle because they believe the honoring of the principle in some situations violates the fundamental principle of respect for persons.

(5) It is incorrect to maintain that the traditionalist believes the ethical and the practical are opposed to one another, and that a proposed ethical course of action is not a practical course of action. Granted, many persons who give lip service to the tradition, including some advocates of realpolitik, talk and write in this way. But the problem with them is just that they give lip service to the tradition but are not really committed to it. Or they are committed to it, but fail to understand it adequately. How one responds to Sharp's charge depends to a large extent upon what is meant by the term 'practical.' Assuming that "practical" means the effective achievement of justifiable goals, Sharp's charge is unfounded. If the

ethical is defined in terms of the "philosophy of nonviolence," and the practical is defined as the successful resolution of international conflict, then the traditionalist might find the two opposed to one another in specific situations. But to define the ethical in this way begs the question, assuming that the ethical rules out any justifiable use of violence.

Sharp's Pragmatic Approach to Nonviolence

In view of Sharp's criticism that traditional Western morality rejects the absoluteness of the principle of nonviolence on pragmatic grounds, it is of considerable interest to note that Sharp himself takes what he calls a pragmatic approach to the defense of nonviolent actions. Essentially, he argues that nonviolent actions "work" better than violent actions in conflict situations. By this he means that nonviolent actions are more effective than their alternatives in achieving the goals of the actions—thwarting attack, defeating an enemy, working one's will over one's opponent, etc. In taking this approach, Sharp claims he is appealing neither to questions of right and wrong, nor to belief systems in which nonviolence is a fundamental principle.[1] In this vein of thinking, he indicates a willingness to submit nonviolent action to empirical testing in international conflict resolution. He writes, for example, "Civilian-based defense (as an alternative to military defense) may ultimately prove to be a major contribution to the solution of the problem of war. Upon investigation, it may also prove to be a dead end."[2] Sharp seems to be saying that if nonviolent action works in international conflict resolution, i.e., if it enables nations to achieve their morally justifiable goals in conflict situations, then it should and would be accepted by all nations, but if it does not enable nations to achieve their morally justifiable goals, then it will not and should not be accepted by them.

A Possible Compromise Position

In this discussion, it is important not to lose sight of two related things that hold a significant place in traditional Western

---

[1]See Sharp, *op. cit.* (1973), pp. v-vii, and, *op. cit.* (1980b), p. 379.
[2]Sharp, *op. cit.* (1980b), p. 255.

morality. One is the commitment, in principle, to nonviolence, and the other is the fundamental claim that any use of violence against persons is, in general, immoral, with possible exceptions requiring moral justification.

Also, it is important not to lose sight of the positive benefits of nonviolent action. Nonviolent action is usually a less coercive type of influence than violent action. It usually tends to lessen the resentment of opponents, since those who practice nonviolence usually suffer more than their opponents. It usually disarms opponents who might think of themselves as the only ones concerned with peace and order. And it usually increases the chances of bringing about a constructive resolution of differences once the conflict is ended. As even the "realist" Reinhold Niebuhr writes,

> Nonviolent coercion and resistance . . . is a type of coercion which offers the largest opportunities for a harmonious relationship with the moral and rational factors in social life. . . It preserves moral, rational, and co-operative attitudes within an area of conflict and thus augments the moral forces without destroying them.[1]

Although the ideal, in conflicts among nations, is to resolve these conflicts through nonviolent means, given the current status of armed conflict in the modern world in the minds and hearts of political leaders and citizens alike, the only feasible thing to do at present is to get these armed conflicts under control, regulated by justified war morality and the laws of war. This is not only the realistic and practical thing to do. But also, it may well be the morally obligatory thing to do. Michael Walzer sums up this kind of position, writing:

> . . . the transformation of war into a political struggle has as its prior condition the restraint of war as a military struggle. If we are to aim at the transformation, as we should, we must begin by insisting upon the rules of war and by holding

---

[1]Reinhold Niebuhr, *Moral Man and Immoral Society* (New York: Charles Scribner's Sons, 1960), pp. 250-251. See also pp. 248-256.

soldiers rigidly to the norms they set.   The
restraint of war is the beginning of peace.[1]

What is needed, then, is to call persons back to the tradition
they presumably are committed to, and to reintroduce the restraints
upon the use of violence that are embedded in the tradition. To do
this is to insist upon the application of moral principles to concrete
conflict situations.

Advocates of nonviolent action may need to compromise with
advocates of justified war morality in advocating and implementing
the bringing of restraints to bear upon war, with the hope that the
exercise of these restraints will eventually lead to the abolition of
war itself.

If one is advocating a pragmatic approach to nonviolence, then
this compromise should be possible.   No moral principle would
seem to be violated by the compromise.   But Sharp seems to be
unwilling to support this kind of compromise.   To what can we
attribute this unwillingness?   One possible explanation might be to
hold that Sharp and traditional Western moralists subscribe to two
different moralities.   But this is implausible.   Both Sharp and the
traditionalists are committed to the Western or Hebrew-Christian
moral tradition as interpreted in this paper and, thus, are committed
to the worth and respect of persons, and to all the precepts and
principles derivable from this fundamental principle.   Sharp's
unwillingness to support this compromise is more likely due to the
fact that, in spite of his insistence that he is advocating practical
nonviolence, he is actually advocating principled nonviolence and
the absolute applicability of this principle.

Sharp's approach, then, is not a consistently pragmatic
approach.   Sharp himself is personally committed to "principled
nonviolence" and a nonviolent philosophy of life.[2]   What he is
actually doing in promoting the pragmatic approach is tentatively
and temporarily suspending belief in the commitment to principled
nonviolence in an effort to convince nonbelievers in principled
nonviolence to adopt nonviolent alternatives in conflict resolution.
Given his commitment, it seems unlikely he would give it up as a

---

[1]Michael Walzer, *Just and Unjust Wars* (New York: Basic Books,
Inc., 1977), p. 335.
[2]See Sharp, *op. cit.* (1979), p. 252.

result of unsuccessful efforts to resolve international conflicts by nonviolent means. It is more likely he would argue that the efforts (or experiments) were inadequate in one or more ways, and he would call for more experiments. If he is committed to principled nonviolence, then no amount of apparent failures would lead him to reject his commitment, because his commitment is not grounded in successes but in other values. These values revolve around his beliefs about the worth of human beings and how human beings should be treated. In addition to being committed to "principled nonviolence," Sharp believes that the consistent application of nonviolent techniques will always ultimately result in successful conflict resolution and that the consequences of violent action will always be worse than the consequences of alternative nonviolent action.[1] Sharp covertly appeals to his belief system in which nonviolence is a fundamental principle as well as to questions of right and wrong in promoting what he calls the pragmatic approach to nonviolence. Given his commitments and beliefs, Sharp cannot adopt the proposed compromise.

It is probably also the case that many traditionalists are not in a position to adopt the proposed compromise, not on principle, but because they have not really honored, and are not about to honor, the principle of nonviolence and the stringent conditions that must be met if a violent response to others is to be justified. These are the persons who, under the aegis of just war morality, have attempted to justify almost every violent conflict they have engaged in and almost every violent action they have committed during these conflicts.[2]

---

[1] See Sharp's discussion of his belief in the ultimate identity of practical nonviolence and the requirements of morality in op. cit. (1979), pp. 293-296. See also op. cit. (1980b), pp. 333-338.

[2] This failure to honor the principle and the conditions for its justifiable suspension undoubtedly has been a major factor contributing to the formation of Sharp's belief that the consequences of violent action will always be worse than the consequences of alternative nonviolent action. The movement from the failure to the belief is probably mediated, in part, by a domino theory of violence, by which it is held that violent actions tend to increase in terms of the numbers of persons and nations involved, the destructiveness of the violent actions engaged in, and the use (and attempted justification) of other and new types of violence. For Sharp, the

Concluding Remarks

Throughout this paper, I have drawn a number of conclusions and made several suggestions. I will not repeat those conclusions and suggestions here, but will only comment upon what I take to be the crucial difference between Sharp and the traditionalists. This is the difference between those who believe that killing in self-defense is permissible, and those who believe that killing another human being is clearly incompatible with respecting human beings as rational creatures. The disagreement on this issue arises because some persons within the tradition, upon deeper reflection, claim it is intuitively evident that violent physical force is clearly incompatible with the fundamental principle. These persons would claim, even though it is an established doctrine in the Hebrew-Christian moral tradition that the use of violent physical force is permissible as an extension of the precept that one has an obligation to protect the innocent from attack, that the significance of a feature or features of this kind of action has/have been overlooked by the tradition.[1]

At this point, it would be possible for the disputants to engage in dialog in an attempt to determine just what these significant features are and whether deeper reflection upon them would lead the adherents of the use of violent physical force to change their minds. Perhaps they would change their minds, but perhaps they would not. If they would not, it could be for one of at least a couple of reasons. One, they might not see the significance of a feature of violent physical force that their opponent sees. Two, they might maintain that a significant feature of this kind of action in specific situations that led to the adoption of the established doctrine is not being given proper weight by their opponent. Such a stalemate would not necessarily mean an end to the dialog. For both could engage in

---

logic of war leads to a continual increase in the levels of violence and to the violation of all restraints on its use. That Sharp holds these views may help to explain why, in the entire corpus of his writings, he does not give serious attention to the tradition of justified war morality, not even by way of a critique of this tradition.
[1] On the difficulties associated with deriving specific principles from the basic principle of respect for persons, see Donagan, op. cit., pp. 30-31, 60-74, 134, 143.

even deeper reflection on the meaning of the fundamental principle, the various features of the use of violent physical force in specific situations, and other precepts that might be relevant to deciding the case. As a result of this further reflection, the disagreement might well be resolved. I see no other way in which to attempt to resolve the differences between Sharp and the traditionalists.

Northern Kentucky University

$\textrm{6}$ Hobbes' Solution
to the Problem of Power

Bob Litke

In its most general sense, "power" simply means the ability to act. Because there are endless ways of acting there must be innumerable kinds of power. We often forget this. Contexts focus us on specific capabilities and obscure from us the full range of our possibilities. In the political context, for example, "power" is typically used to mean the ability to control or dominate. Morgenthau's definition in *The Politics of Nations* is a good example:

> Power may comprise anything that establishes and maintains the control of man over man. Thus power covers all social relationships which serve that end, from physical violence to the most subtle psychological ties by which one mind controls another. Power covers the domination of man by man, both when it is disciplined by moral ends and controlled by constitutional safeguards as in Western democracies, and when it is that untamed and barbaric force which finds its laws in nothing but its own strength and its sole justification in its aggrandizement.[1]

It is worth noting, moreover, that this usage is well-established, both historically and in contemporary practice. C.B. Macpherson summarizes the matter in a convenient way:

> Most of the literature of modern political science, from its beginnings with Machiavelli and Hobbes to its twentieth-century empirical exponents, has

---

[1]H. J. Morgenthau, *Politics Among Nations* (New York: Alfred A. Knopf, 1973), p. 9.

to do with power, understood broadly as men's
ability to get what they want by controlling
others. Hobbes put it succinctly in 1640. . . . The
reduction of power to power over others had
become even more explicit by the nineteenth
century. The high point was reached in the
propositions James Mill announced in 1820. . . .
When we move on to the twentieth-century
empirical political theorists we find the same
assumption that the only significant power in any
political view is one man's or one group's power
over others.[1]

It is rather unlikely that such long-standing and widespread
usage is a complete mistake. Power as domination is surely a
central fact of our foreseeable political and social life. It is, however,
not the only fact. Nor is it the only type of power. It may be a
mistake for us to remain narrowly focused on domination as the
only significant form of power and to insist on looking for
solutions to all our problems within the perspective it affords.

Indeed our best efforts at domination can make us worse off.
Certainly the recent arms race between the superpowers appears this
way, as do various serious environmental problems. I think our
assumptions about domination should be scrutinized. In this paper I
shall examine Hobbes' account of power. We will see why he
thought dominating power was a central feature of civil life, why he
thought it was problematic and where he thought solutions to such
problems would lie. Perhaps Hobbes' account can throw light on
some of our current problems.

This is an essay in philosophical psychology. As is well
known, Hobbes proposed his political philosophy in the context
provided by views he had about human nature. I shall focus on the
assumptions he was making about our psychological possibilities
when he formulated the first law of nature in the *Leviathan*. In this
law we are enjoined to seek peace and, when that fails, to defend

---

[1]C.B. Macpherson, *Democratic Theory* (Oxford: Oxford University
Press, 1975), p. 42-45.

ourselves by seeking war.[1] Since laws of nature are held to be
immutable and eternal features of the human condition,[2] Hobbes is
committed to the view that woven into our nature are the
dispositions and abilities necessary for compliance with them. In
the case at hand he seems to be supposing a kind of symmetry of
opposing sides to human nature. On the one hand, there is in
human nature a natural drift towards conflict and war. Hobbes'
detailed discussion of power is his account of this. On the other
hand, there is in our nature the means with which to control for this
drift. By drawing on the dispositions and abilities which make up
our peace-seeking side we can often avoid destructive conflict; we
can create and maintain a more or less peaceful society. It was
Hobbes' genius to have discovered this tension of opposing
tendencies within human nature rather than between groups of
people. I will now turn to the details of his account.

For Hobbes the fundamental assumption is that things in the
natural world are in constant motion.[3] Human beings are no
exception: we are constantly moved by our desires (appetites and
aversions). Consider Hobbes' conclusion of Chapter VI of the
Leviathan, a chapter in which he demonstrates that voluntary
behavior is the result of deliberation about our appetites and
aversions:

> For there is no such thing as perpetual Tranquility
> of mind, while we live here; because Life itself is
> but Motion, and can never be without Desire, nor
> without Fear, no more than without Sense.[4]

---

[1]Thomas Hobbes, Leviathan Ed. C.B. Macpherson. (New York:
Penguin Books, (1980), p. 190.
[2]Hobbes, op. cit., p. 215.
[3]Macpherson suggests that Hobbes was obsessed with the idea and
planned to write a systematic philosophy of motion embracing
physics, psychology and politics. See p. 19 of Macpherson's
Introduction to the Penguin edition . See Also Hobbes' remarks in
Elements of Philosophy Concerning the Body which are available
in: Thomas Hobbes, Metaphysical Writings, Ed. M. Whiton Calkins
(LaSalle, Illinois: Open Court, 1989), p. 72. See also Hobbes' remark
in the Leviathan that our body is in continual mutation. Hobbes, op.
cit., p. 120.
[4]Hobbes, op. cit., p. 129-30.

The implication of this is that so long as we are alive we are
never satisfied, in any final and lasting way. Unmet desires are
continuously arising within us. And this is because of the nature of
things, in Hobbes' view, not because of some moral or material
failing on our part. Moreover, it should be noted that this perpetual
non-satisfaction is amplified by our ability to imagine a future, a
matter he focuses on in Ch. XI of the *Leviathan*. For example in
the following passage he reiterates the point just noted—that our
desires are endless—and adds the dimension of the future:

> Nor can a man any more live, whose Desires are
> at an end, than he, whose Senses and Imaginations
> are at a stand. Felicity is a continual progress of
> the desire, from one object to another;   the
> attaining of the former, being still but the way to
> the later. The cause whereof is, that the object of
> man's desire, is not to enjoy once only, and for
> one instant of time; but to assure for ever, the
> way of his future desire.[1]

I take Hobbes' point to be this. Not only do we have a range of
desires which could, in principle, be satisfied in the present. In
addition to these, we are always subject to a set of second-order
desires having to do with *future* satisfaction. (Consider, for
example, loyalty, fidelity and security.) It follows that our inability
to be satisfied in any final and lasting way is guaranteed not only by
scarce resources, but also by our having an imaginable future. This
has two consequences for Hobbes: the concept of power becomes
integral to his account at exactly this conceptual juncture, and power
is discovered to be inevitably contentious.
    Looking back to Chapter X of the *Leviathan*, we can see that
Hobbes had introduced the concept of power in a way which
anticipated this focus on the future: "The Power *of a Man*, (to take
it Universally,) is his present means, to obtain some future apparent
Good."[2]   Since "good/evil" simply means "the object of some

---

[1]*Ibid.*, p. 160-61.
[2]*Ibid.*, p. 150.

appetite/aversion,"[1] it is evident that power is, in his view, always in the service of our appetites and aversions. And being instrumental in nature, it is always in the service of satisfactions we have yet to enjoy. It follows, therefore, that our desire for power must also be insatiable. He makes this point quite explicit in Ch. XI:

> I put for a general inclination of all mankind, a perpetual and restless desire of Power after power, that ceaseth only in Death. And the cause of this, is not always that a man hopes for a more intensive delight, than he has already attained to; or that he cannot be content with a moderate power: but because he cannot assure the power and means to live well, which he hath at present, without the acquisition of more.[2]

We see, therefore, that just as our ability to imagine a future prevents any complete satisfaction, so also it is the source of a desire for power which can never be satisfied in any final and lasting way. It remains to be seen that such power is inevitably contentious.

It turns out that our inability to be fully satisfied by any current amount of power is exacerbated by the condition of competition which naturally arises in any society. According to Hobbes, the substance of our power lies in our bodily and mental capacities in the first place, and in what further powers we acquire by these in the way of riches, reputation, friends, etc.[3] These are the means by which we can control our situation, now, and in the future, so as to obtain satisfaction. However the efficacy of our power is determined not merely by the substance but also according to the degree to which our control of the situation (so that it serves our ends) can override the control which others have (so that it serves their ends). Hobbes understood that our appetites and aversions may conflict with those of others. Power, in such cases, is the ability to prevail. In the *Leviathan* he compressed all these considerations into a single word. There he defines power as the *eminence* of one's bodily and

---

[1] *Ibid.*, p. 120.
[2] *Ibid.*, p. 161.
[3] *Ibid.*, p. 150.

mental capacities compared with those of others.[1] Macpherson points out that Hobbes made the same point much more explicit in the *Elements of Law*, Part I, Ch. 8, sec. 4:

> after defining a man's power as his ability to produce some desired effect, and hence as his faculties of body and mind and such further powers as by them are acquired, he concluded: `And because the power of one man resisteth and hindereth the effects of the power of another: power simply is no more, but the excess of the power of one above that of another.'[2]

And so it falls out that we find ourselves in inevitable competition with each other because each of us has an insatiable desire for more power over the other.

Characteristically, Hobbes does not flinch from stating the potentially very bleak consequences of this for society, namely the complete dissolution of social life into the chaos and destruction of civil war:

> Competition of Riches, Honour, Command, or other power, enclineth to Contention, Enmity, and War: Because the way of one Competitor, to the attaining of his desire, is to kill, subdue, supplant, or repel the other.[3]

It is worth noting that this tendency towards socially destructive behavior is quite independent of childhood experiences, personality traits, and difficult economic/social conditions. Because each of us is a potential competitor for increased control over our situation we all are disposed to contribute to the decline of social life into destructive conflict. According to Hobbes we are this way simply because of human nature and the nature of power. Let me summarize the steps by which he arrived at this unhappy prospect:

---

[1]*Ibid.*
[2]Macpherson, *op. cit.*, p.   42.
[3]Hobbes, *op. cit.*, p. 161.

(1) To be alive is to have endless desires.

(2) To have an imaginable future is to have an insatiable desire for more power (to satisfy the above desires).

(3) To be in society is to have an insatiable desire for more power over others.

This, according to Hobbes, is the genesis of dominating power. As we saw, Macpherson points out that this view of power has been reiterated many times since Hobbes put it forward in the mid-sixteen hundreds. What I wish to emphasize is that this account of power cannot be the whole story, for as Hobbes indicates in the passage just quoted, it would leave us hovering at the edge of an abyss (of the dissolution of society and culture) with nothing to prevent us from falling in. Indeed, it would be an account of a human nature which was necessarily inclined towards self-destruction. But how exactly does this problem arise and how does Hobbes propose to avoid it?

To get greater clarity on this it may be useful to reflect on the precise antithesis of what Hobbes has described. To this end let us consider Morgenthau's summary of the essential features of social homeostasis or social equilibrium:

> it is the purpose of all such equilibriums to maintain the stability of the system without destroying the multiplicity of the elements composing it. If the goal were stability alone, it could be achieved by allowing one element to destroy or overwhelm the others and take their place. Since the goal is stability plus the preservation of all the elements of the system, the equilibrium must aim at preventing any element from gaining ascendency over the others. The means employed to maintain the equilibrium consist in allowing the different elements to pursue their opposing tendencies up to the point where the tendency of one is not so strong as to overcome the tendency of the others, but strong

enough to prevent others from overcoming its own.[1]

Evidently the stability of such a system is dynamic like that of a mobile. Substantial shifts and changes may occur in the relationships among various elements without destabilizing the system as a whole. Indeed stability is preserved so long as the autonomy of each element is not diminished or eliminated by others.

Now Hobbes' discussion of power is an account, not of conditions which make such an equilibrium possible, but of conditions which promise to make it impossible, conditions which would cause any system of social relationships to self-destruct. If, as Hobbes suggests, each element is inevitably disposed to seek increasing power over every other element in the system (as a means to enhancing its control over its situation) it follows that each element is disposed to bring about the destruction of the social system itself. Though this is not its aim it is a more or less likely collateral effect of its seeking increasing power over others. And if enough elements in a system are inevitably inclined towards destroying the system itself this can only be a matter of time and material means. Hobbes' description of the complete breakdown of social equilibrium is given in Chapter XIII: the war of every man against every man.

But precisely why does such a breakdown always threaten to occur? I would suggest that several factors are involved. First, as Hobbes appreciated, the pursuit and exercise of dominating power has no inherent limitations. Not only do we never have enough power but our desire for more power is fuelled by desires which themselves are unlimited. But also there is the stubborn fact that things never turn out exactly as we planned. We are never completely in control. Sometimes this is for the good. Sometimes it is not. Thus we often find ourselves having to deal with counter-productive side effects.[2] Moreover, if we are not alert to these side

---

[1]Morgenthau, *op. cit.*, p. 169.

[2]In discussing Zeno's paradoxes, J.A. Benardete makes the following remarks which pertain to the matter at hand:

> There is always sludge that frustrates our efforts to implement the ideal in practice, not only in the present case

effects and make skillful adjustments for them we eventually find ourselves engaged in behavior which is not merely counter-productive but which is self-defeating in behavior as well. The problem is that there is nothing within the psychological dynamic of dominating power which can prevent this drift towards self-destruction, for dominating power is as blind as it is unlimited. In the case of civil society it is blindness to the socially destructive effects of unlimited competition for more power over each other.[1] Obviously, the point of obtaining such power is the promise of increased satisfaction of our desires. But it is almost as obvious that the end result of its unlimited exercise is the destruction of the society which is necessary for most of the satisfactions we seek. My conjecture is that we proceed towards our own frustration in this way to the extent that we are blind to the negative collateral effects of our unlimited activity. Hobbes' account of power details this natural drift towards self-destruction for the case of civil society. I believe, however, that the same problem arises in other cases of dominating power.[2]

---

but on all occasions. Sludge! It is what the Yankee calls the 'sheer cussedness' of things, that unruly, refractory element in the world that, assuming the form of mechanical friction in one case, renders the perpetual motion machine impossible and that, assuming the form of Godel's theorem in another, renders the consistency of mathematics incapable of proof. Sludge is everywhere, it cannot be escaped, not only in the physical world but even in the realm of pure ideas.... This principle of recalcitrance is familiar to all....

J.A. Benardete, *Infinity* (Oxford: Oxford University Press,1964), p. 252-53.

[1] A society can contain only limited amounts of adversarial activity. Like a symphony concert, it must be continuously woven together by the cooperative activity of its members. If they are always at odds with each other in all the relevant ways there can be no music — the society must tear apart.

[2] Perhaps the most obvious case would be the field of international politics. Morgenthau, who credits Hobbes with giving us 'the classic' analysis of our unlimited desire for power, discusses the matter under the topic of imperialism:

Consider the domain of parent-child relations. When children are very young they must be controlled for their own sake and it is relatively easy to control them. But things change. Children grow in strength and sophistication. They become more and more capable of resisting parental domination. If parents' only response to increasing recalcitrance is increased domination, they run the risk of damaging their relationship with the child, destroying the family system and even damaging or destroying the child itself. And the fact that the destruction will be done for the sake of the child does nothing to forestall the potential harm. Moreover, if the parents are too much focussed on the narrow issue of maintaining or increasing control, this very focus will tend to blind them to these collateral destructive risks. Put in general terms, this is essentially the same problem as the one discovered by Hobbes: the single-minded pursuit of increased domination in response to growing recalcitrance tends to blind us to the very self-destructive consequences which are collateral to such a pursuit.

And is this not a fair description of our recent experience with nuclear arms racing? Thinking that they could satisfy their legitimate desire for national security by unilaterally increasing their ability to dominate through military alliances and through the continuous development of increasingly destructive weaponry, two sub-groups of the human race devoted many of their best minds and trillions of dollars to the undertaking. Although the destructive capability of the respective armed forces has increased dramatically during the last forty years, it is widely recognized that this has made us worse off. It has produced a net loss of security for everyone

---

The outstanding historic examples of unlimited imperialism are the expansionist policies of Alexander the Great, Rome, the Arabs in the seventh and eighth centuries, Napoleon I, and Hitler. They all have in common an urge toward expansion which knows no rational limits, feeds on its own successes and, if not stopped by a superior force, will go on to the confines of the political world. This urge will not be satisfied so long as there remains anywhere a possible object of domination .... It is, as we shall see, exactly the lack of moderation, the aspiration to conquer all that lends itself to conquest, characteristic of unlimited imperialism, which in the past has been the undoing of the imperialistic policies of this kind. Morgenthau, *op. cit.*, p. 56-57.

concerned. A double paradox highlights two of the factors involved: (1) our unlimited pursuit of security through domination eventually began destroying all prospects for it; (2) those who knew the most about the arms race (military and strategic experts) tended to be the last ones to see it as self-destructive. The collateral effects were such that the solution to our security problem had to become the much worse problem of potential omnicide before a consensus emerged as to the irrationality of the pursuit. Fortunately, we have stopped ignoring the spectacular negative collateral effects of nuclear arms racing. We have learned, I take it, that it is dangerous to act as Hobbes' account of power seems to suggest we must.

In the case of environmental problems, we have sought without due regard for negative collateral effects to increasingly dominate certain elements in nature as a means to satisfying our endless desires. Almost daily new examples come to our attention. I hope that one example of transparently self-destructive behavior will suffice.

The following is taken from a discussion of the effects which current farming practices are having on the soil:

> In their natural state, soils reach an equilibrium with respect to soil organic matter. Plants grow in the soil, utilizing nutrients held in the organic matter. . . When soils are cleared, plowed and tilled, they begin to lose organic matter as the natural balance is upset. Removal of crop residues through harvesting interrupts the cycle of renewal. . . . Loss of organic matter is of concern because it is such an important component in maintaining agricultural productivity. A significant decline in the organic matter content increases the susceptibility of the soil to compaction and to erosion by water or wind. Furthermore, the organic matter is a major source of nitrogen and micronutrients and it increases moisture retention. . . . The loss of soil organic matter is a widespread problem in Canada. . . . For example, while Prairie soils are naturally high in organic matter content, they have lost nearly 45% of their original content since cultivation began there at

the turn of the century. . . . In Ontario and
Quebec, frequent and excessive tillage are seen as
being responsible for the decline in soil organic
matter content of as much as 50%.[1]

As in the arms racing example, the details about how the
system has us drifting towards our own destruction are enormously
complicated and not even fully understood. Nevertheless it is
becoming more widely accepted that we cannot continue current
farming practices much longer without disaster. Certainly we have
much less than another hundred years before our farmlands become
wastelands. (Desertification is already a substantial problem in
North America.) We see the irony of unlimited behavior leading to
self-defeat here as well: current food production practices promise to
lead to our starvation. Whether farmers and other agricultural
experts will insist on being the last to appreciate the problem
remains to be seen.

I conclude, therefore, that there is something fundamentally
mistaken about the single-minded attempt to satisfy our insatiable
desire for more and more dominating power without rich regard for
the collateral implications of such a pursuit. Apparently the world
is such that it is often self-destructive to act in this way. Hobbes'
bleak prognosis was essentially correct, not only for civil society
but for other domains as well. What does he offer as a solution to
this problem?

It is when our pursuit and exercise of dominating power is both
blind and unlimited that problems of self-defeat arise. This suggests
that solutions would stem from that which enables us to *see* which
limits to impose. I take this to be what Hobbes is touching on in
the fifth law of nature, where he mentions our ability to be
responsive and cooperative with each other so as to make society
possible. He refers to it as "mutual accommodation."[2] Hobbes
makes it clear in his very brief discussion that our ability to
accommodate ourselves to others is the expression of our peace-

---

[1]H.O. Sparrow, *Soil at Risk* A report of the *Standing Senate
Committee on Agriculture, Fisheries and Forestry* (Ottawa: The Senate
of Canada, 1984), p. 112-13.
[2]Hobbes, *op. cit.*, p. 209.

seeking side when he explicitly refers the reader back to his formulation of the first law of nature.

To get a fuller sense of what Hobbes is talking about here we can begin by considering what is lost when society dissolves into war. In Chapter XIII he mentions agriculture, transportation, the construction industry, knowledge, the arts and literature in this regard.[1] Roughly, Hobbes has listed the main ingredients of civilized life. But consider what it is that makes these things possible. To create them it seems that we must have the use of a range of social/cultural institutions and arrangements. I'm thinking of such things as various languages and notational systems, all the sciences, a variety of other disciplines and practices, together with various social, economic and political structures. Reflecting further on the matter, it seems that this entire range of cultural phenomena is spun out of our ability to coordinate ourselves with each other in a variety of complicated and sustained ways. And in every case such coordination is possible only if we adhere to rather complex self-imposed limits on our behavior. Evidently the creation of and participation in such forms of coordinated activity presupposes substantial imaginative, perceptual, and intellectual capacities on our part and the preservation of them requires considerable sensitivity and alertness to the consequences of specific interactions. I take what Hobbes refers to as "mutual accommodation" to presuppose this entire complex of human abilities which makes sustained coordination possible, coordination with each other in the first place and, by extension, with nature. It is the matrix of human abilities which is the source of our cultural life: it enables us to create and maintain society; it is how we seek peace.

Recall that in a general sense "power" simply means the ability to act. If this brief analysis of our capacity for "mutual accommodation" is correct, we can begin appreciating the symmetry of Hobbes' psychological perspective. Our ability to dominate is counterbalanced, on his view, by our capacity for mutual accommodation. Power of the war-seeking kind can be held in check by power of the society-making/peace-seeking kind.[2] This, I

---

[1] *Ibid.*, p. 186.

[2] It is interesting to note that Hannah Arendt explicates roughly this second sense of power: *Power* corresponds to the human ability not just to act but to act in concert. Power is never the property of an

believe, is his general solution to the problem of power as domination. Mutual accommodation presupposes the ability to properly limit our behavior so that sustained coordination with others is possible. It is precisely the exercise of some of the above-mentioned component abilities which would enable us to see the destructive collateral effects which domination is likely to generate in some field of endeavor, and it is the exercise of others which would enable us to arrange ways of pursuing our interests which avoid such effects.

It must be admitted that Hobbes does not explicitly present this symmetry of counterbalancing powers in the *Leviathan*. For my analysis of "mutual accommodation" I have had to read between his lines somewhat and expanded on what I have found. Nevertheless, Hobbes' particular solution to the problem of dominating power in civil society does fit with the account I have offered.

As noted above, Hobbes argues in Ch. XIII of the *Leviathan* that the unlimited pursuit and exercise of dominating power among people would lead to a war of every man against every man. It is imperative, therefore, that we impose limits on this perfectly natural human tendency. In Ch. X he claims that the power to limit our inevitable pursuit and exercise of more dominating power derives from our "consent" to be limited in this way by a political authority: he calls this "the power of a Commonwealth."[1] And in Ch. XIV his discussion of the particulars of the social contract is designed to show that such self-limiting behavior is rational. But what is it that enables us to see that such self-limitation by consent is necessary and rational in the political sphere? And what enables us to to create and preserve the specific social, legal, and political arrangements which could actually achieve this end for us in satisfactory ways? I submit that it is precisely the kinds of abilities

---

individual; it belongs to a group and remains in existence only so long as the group keeps together. ....What makes a man a political being is his faculty of action; it enables him to get together with his peers, to act in concert, and to reach out for goals and enterprises that would never enter his mind, let alone the desires of his heart, had he not been given this gift — to embark on something new.
Hannah Arendt, *On Violence* (New York: Harcourt, Brace & World, Inc., 1970), p. 44-82.
[1]Hobbes, *op. cit.*, p. 120.

which I have claimed are presupposed by Hobbes' term "mutual accommodation." I conclude , therefore, that Hobbes is committed to some version of the view, hinted at in his formulation of the first law of nature, that humans have within them these two counterbalancing powers—peace-seeking (society-making) and war-seeking.

Of course, the ways in which humans can, through self-limitation, coordinate themselves with each other are multifarious. Consider again for a moment the languages and notational systems, the various sciences, disciplines and practices, and the numerous economic, political and social arrangements being used in the world today. Even within the political domain there is a vast spectrum of possibilities, some of which have been described by political science, history and anthropology. The last question I shall address is this: What led Hobbes to choose the simplest, the most harsh and the least imaginative form of self-limitation—a sovereign with absolute dominating power over its subjects? I say "the least imaginative" because his solution to the problem of domination is more domination: he advocates a system in which the dominating power of individual members is to be dominated by the governor of the system. This question intrigues me, because it is only on rare occasions that we resort to such a heavy-handed solution to the many problems of human coordination with which we deal every day.

As noted, Hobbes believed that our ability to accommodate ourselves to each other was an eternal feature of the human condition. He was, however, far from believing that this ability alone could enable us to establish and maintain a society. His view was that the contributions which this capacity could make towards creating and preserving a society were seriously curtailed by a kind of epistemological anarchy which prevails in the field of social judgment. His argument goes back to his fundamental assumption of things being in constant motion:

> And because the constitution of a man's Body, is
> in continual mutation; it is impossible that all the
> same things should always cause in him the same
> Appetites, and Aversions; much less can all men

> consent, in the Desire of almost any one and the
> same Object.[1]

It is worth noting that Hobbes uses the notion of consent at
this juncture, for that is what his considerations turn on. The point
he wishes to establish is this: there is no reliable body of agreement
among people as to what is desirable which could serve as a basis
for mutual consent to self-limitation. This becomes more evident
in the next paragraph of his account. After stating that "good"
means "the object of one's appetite" and "evil," means "the object of
one's aversion," he offers the following:

> For these words of Good, Evil, and Contemptible,
> are ever used with relation to the person that useth
> them: There being nothing simply and absolutely
> so; nor any common Rule of Good and Evil, to be
> taken from the nature of the objects themselves.[2]

What Hobbes is claiming, then, is that our inability to agree on
what is desirable precludes our agreeing on what is good and evil.
In turn, this means that we could not agree with each other about
some general rules of good and evil which we could use to place the
socially necessary limits on our behavior. The upshot of this is
that we cannot learn from each other how best to coordinate
ourselves with each other. Such knowledge is simply not
obtainable, according to Hobbes. His conclusion is this: as a
consequence of being unable to "consent" on the matter of what is
desirable and good, we are forced to "consent" to having an authority
set up who can *dictate* the rules of good and evil to us.[3] Later, in
Ch. XX, Hobbes explicitly describes this authority: "He is Judge of
what is necessary for Peace; . . . He is Sole Legislator."[4] Hobbes
also explicitly mentions the epistemic role which the sovereign
must play on our behalf, namely, he must "prescribe the Rules of
discerning *Good* and *Evil*: which Rules are Laws; and therefore in

---

[1]*Ibid.*
[2]*Ibid.*, p. 120.
[3]*Ibid.*, p. 120-21.
[4]*Ibid.*, p. 252.

him is the Legislative Power."[1]   We see, therefore, that it was
Hobbes' pessimism about the possibility of obtaining a body of
agreed-upon social judgments which could enable us to evolve and
fine-tune ways of coordinating ourselves with each other which led
him to argue that we must consent to an authoritarian solution.[2] I
consider this a type of epistemic domination: we must rely on the
imaginative, perceptual, and intellectual capabilities of the sovereign
to discover the appropriate rules of self-limitation and mutual
accommodation by means of which a society can be created and
maintained, because our own capacities, when brought into contact
with each other, would prove epistemically anarchical. Because we
cannot learn much from each other about how best to coordinate
ourselves with each other, we must obtain this knowledge from
some sovereign authority.

The other problem is that of motivation. How can we ensure
that people will acquiesce to the sovereign's dictates about how to
limit and coordinate their behavior? Hobbes' solution is in terms of
coercive power. His worry is that political anarchy (a war of
everyone against their neighbor) is always waiting in the wings of
society. To forestall its destructive emergence he insists that
"Sovereign Power ought in all Commonwealths to be absolute."[3]
Thus sovereign power must be indivisible—not subject to challenge
by any other source of power from within the system over which it
governs.[4] The sovereign must be beyond reproach—subject to
neither criticism nor punishment. Also, the sovereign must be the
"Supreme Judge of Controversies. . . [and the ultimate determiner
of] Rewards and Punishments."[5] We see, therefore, that the
sovereign has ultimate control over the lives of its subjects.
Hobbes' response to his worry about political anarchy is to institute
a sovereign authority with enough power to dominate the

---

[1]*Ibid.*, p. 258.

[2]Hobbes is consistent on the matter. In Ch. XIX, when discussing the
advantages of a monarchy over aristocratic and democratic forms of
sovereign authority, he specifically notes the difficulties caused by
divergent interests and judgments. See, Hobbes, *op. cit.*, pp. 242-43.

[3]Hobbes, *op. cit.*, p. 260.

[4]*Ibid.*, p. 240.

[5]*Ibid..*, p. 252.

dominating power of all its subjects — a regime of complete political domination.

For Hobbes the only reliable kind of human motivation is fear in general and fear of death in particular.[1] By consenting to give the sovereign absolute power over their lives the subjects put into the sovereign's hands control over this fundamental source of their motivation—an elegant and grim solution to the problem of motivation. He makes this explicit at the beginning of Ch. XXXVIII:

> The maintenance of Civil Society, depending on
> Justice; and Justice on the power of Life and
> Death, and other lesser Rewards and Punishments,
> residing in them that have the Sovereignty of the
> Commonwealth; It is impossible a Common-
> wealth should stand, where any other than the
> Soveraign, hath a power of giving greater rewards
> than Life; and of inflicting greater punishments,
> than Death.[2]

Hobbes would insist that any social arrangement which was less able to dominate its constituent members (both epistemically and politically) will fail to withstand the centrifugal forces of the inevitable pursuit of more and more dominating power on the part of these members. It will eventually dissolve into anarchy, chaos and the destruction of civil war.

But Hobbes' harsh political solution to the problem of dominating power in civil society is reasonable only if one agrees with his views about the risks of epistemic and political anarchy and with his views about human motivation. I, for one, am considerably less pessimistic than he is. When I reflect on the vast spectrum of ways in which humans routinely limit themselves and successfully coordinate their behavior in the complete absence of any apparent absolute sovereign, I conclude that we are not as subject to anarchy as Hobbes feared. For example, we have been successfully speaking natural languages, accumulating knowledge, making music, and, in some parts of the world, farming, for

---

[1]*Ibid*.., p. 252-53.
[2]Cf. Hobbes, *Ibid*.., pp. 130, 188, 200, 251-52, 343.

thousands of years without the dictates of a supreme sovereign power. Nor have we fallen into an abyss of self-destruction because no such power coerces us to honor established forms of coordinated activity. Nor do I think that the relevant human motivation can so easily be reduced to the dismal matter of fear and fear of death. Surely we are moved to accommodate ourselves to each other by a broad range of interests, desires, affections and aversions in addition to being motivated by fear. I conclude, therefore, that there is considerably more to our capacity for mutual accommodation than Hobbes himself imagined. The fact that neither he nor most political theorists since his time have paid much attention to this peace-seeking/society-making side of our nature is no reason for us to remain narrowly focussed on domination as the only important form of social and political power. We can explore these possibilities which Hobbes pointed to with his reference to mutual accommodation. Given the urgency of some of the problems we face, it is surely important that we try to do so.[1]

Wilfrid Laurier University

---

[1] I would like to acknowledge the help I received from colleagues in the Philosophy Department at Wilfrid Laurier University, especially from Graham Solomon.

Vaclav Havel's *The Power of the Powerless*
and the Philosophy of Nonviolence

R. Paul Churchill

It is now generally recognized that Vaclav Havel's long essay, *The Power of the Powerless*, is one of the great contributions to the literature on nonviolent resistance and should be given honors comparable to Thoreau's classic essay on civil disobedience, Camus's *Neither Victims Nor Executioners*, Martin Luther King's "Letter from Birmingham Jail," and the best of Tolstoy's letters on Christian anarchism or of Gandhi's articles in *Young India*. Indeed, like the rest of this great seminal literature, Havel's *The Power of the Powerless* has exerted a crucial, formative influence on nonviolent social change. This essay, and especially its widely discussed "parable of the greengrocer" was regarded as the "basic text"[1] for Czechoslovakia's "velvet revolution" of November 1989. And because of the influence of his writings, as well as his role as an opposition leader, Havel himself became known as the "conscience of the nation."[2]

But, in addition to its historical significance as the basic text for an actual nonviolent revolution, *The Power of the Powerless* is a great work because of the universality of its message. Although Havel's essay was addressed first and foremost to alienated and powerless fellow citizens suffering under the "psychology of captivity" peculiar to bureaucratized totalitarian systems, his vision of authentic existence and empowerment can be generalized to contexts outside of Eastern Europe. Moreover, Havel makes it clear that the oppressiveness of totalitarianism is only the fullest expression, or avant garde, of immoral forces in modern civilization that are systematically brutalizing the lives of us all. Thus, Havel has much to say to all persons committed to nonviolence and the

---

[1]Amos Elon, "Prague Autumn," *The New Yorker* (January 23, 1990).
[2]Paul Wilson, "Introduction," Vaclav Havel, *Disturbing the Peace: A Conversation with Karel Hvizdala*, trans. by Paul Wilson (New York: Alfred A. Knopf, 1990), p. xiv.

formation of societies in which "living in dignity" and "living in truth" are genuine realities. Indeed, in the compass of a mere seventy-three pages, Havel covers so many important issues relating to the motivation of individual resistance to oppression—the possible effectiveness of powerless people against a regime with unlimited violence at its disposal and the necessity that successful resistance be nonviolent—that his text might be regarded as offering a catalogue of principles to be covered by a complete theory of nonviolent resistance.

The Power of the Powerless presents a number of intertwined arguments that together make up what I will call an "empowering ideology." In my judgment, this empowering ideology is best understood as consisting of six related but separable themes. These six can be summarized as follows: (1) an analysis of oppression that explores the psychology and mechanisms of domination and that relates oppression to moral and cultural crisis, (2) a theory of the individual's emancipation from oppression as involving self-renewal and a quest for authentic existence based on reverence for the truth, (3) an insistence on accepting responsibility for one's actions and an avowed willingness to make great personal sacrifices, (4) an emphasis on nonviolence as the only type of action consistent with reverence for the truth and the quest for authentic existence, (5) the rejection of the traditional means-ends dichotomy in politics and of consequentialist reasoning more generally, and (6) an account of the nonviolent transformation of society that explains how the formerly "powerless" can gain control by understanding the social reality of power and that identifies the crucial weak links of oppressive regimes against which nonviolent resistance should be directed.

Although it is unusual to find discussion of all six themes in a single text, each has been addressed previously by at least one other major writer on nonviolence, and often addressed with clarity, eloquence and power. Thus, even though Havel does not draw self-consciously on the traditions of pacifism or "non-resistance," and rarely refers to other seminal or analytical works on nonviolence, there are obvious points of comparison. For example, we can find strong similarities between Havel and the analysis of oppression in Adam Michnik's Letters From Prison.[1] Like Gandhi, Havel traces

---

[1] Letters From Prison and Other Essays, trans. by Maya Latynski (Berkeley: University of California Press, 1985).

the roots of political oppression to a moral crisis in Western civilization. Like Gene Sharp in *The Politics of Nonviolent Action*,[1] Havel's view of the effectiveness of nonviolent resistance is underwritten by a careful dissection of the phenomenon of power, by the identification of the crucial weak links in the system of domination and by attention to the ways in which resistors can, through a process akin to "political karate," apply pressure at these weak points. Havel's emphasis on "living in truth" in nonviolent struggle bears interesting similarities with Gandhi's reliance on Truth, or *Satya*, and his conception of *Satyagraha*. Finally, by renunciating narrow means-ends calculations, Havel joins company with a large number of activists who have embraced nonviolence on moral grounds.

It is obviously important to undertake a comparative study of Havel's text in relation to the other great, guiding literatures on nonviolent resistance. This would enable us to determine whether—despite the diverse political and cultural contexts from which they drew intellectual support—they share a common core of ethical principles or a converging social or political philosophy. Such a comparative analysis would provide a crucial foundation for a general philosophy of nonviolence. But it is also well beyond the scope of this short paper. Instead, in this paper I will explore another kind of "grounding" for our ideas and beliefs about nonviolent resistance: in particular, the way Havel's "empowering ideology" may be grounded in his broader and deeper philosophical perspective.

It just so happens that, in addition to *The Power of the Powerless*, Havel is the author of two influential philosophical essays, the open "Letter to Dr. Gustav Husak" and "Politics and Conscience," and the extended conversation recently published as *Disturbing the Peace*—all of which suggest interesting connections between nonviolent action and broader philosophical themes. Moreover, attention is now being given to the philosophical depth of Havel's long "meditations" written during the years of his imprisonment (1979-1982); these meditations were sent out of prison in his letters to his wife, and published as the collection called *Letters to Olga*. It is clear from these texts that Havel is the most philosophical of all the major writers on nonviolence and that,

---

[1](Boston: Porter Sargent Publishers, 1973).

drawing upon the thought of philosophers such as Hegel, Heidegger, Patocka, Levinas and Belohradsky, he already has done much to fashion a place for a philosophy of nonviolence within the currents of phenomenology and existen'ialism. So my objective in this paper will be to suggest, albeit briefly and tentatively, how Havel's "empowering ideology" might be grounded in the "worldview" and "metaphysical vision" of these other meditations. I shall confine my efforts to discussing the connection between these meditations and just one theme of *The Power of the Powerless:* the view that emancipation from oppression requires self-renewal and a quest for authentic existence based on reverence for the truth.

I choose to discuss this one of the six themes of Havel's "empowering ideology" because of its logical priority. In the case of Havel, as with Gandhi, one must first understand violence and nonviolence in their "spiritual" or metaphysical senses before one can fully appreciate the political significance of nonviolence. But even limited to the discussion of one theme, this is necessarily a speculative and treacherous undertaking: speculative because Havel does not claim to have developed a complete and self-consistent philosophy, and treacherous since there is the obvious danger of badly misrepresenting his thought. Despite all of this, I hope at least to be able to suggest the richness of Havel's philosophical meditations as a source for reflections about the philosophical grounds for nonviolence and to incite interest in the possibility of a philosophy of nonviolence.

Havel starts with a philosophical assumption similar to Hegel's (and Heidegger's) on the relationship between human consciousness and Being. Havel says, "for Being first had to call itself into question, through man, so that through his search for the 'meaning of life,' through its own manifestation in the world that surrounds him and ultimately through the encounter of one with the other, Being could return to itself and be fulfilled."[1] Havel characterizes the human as a "thrownness"; that is, as the creature that has "fallen out of Being and therefore continually reaches toward it. . . ."[2] At the center of our existence as humans, therefore, is the search for meaning: "man is 'questioning Being'. . . or rather the one through

---

[1]Vaclav Havel, *Letters to Olga: June 1979-September 1982,* trans. by Paul Wilson (New York: Henry Holt and Co., 1989), p. 265.
[2]*Ibid.,* p. 319.

whom Being can inquire after itself"[1] and "the meaning of Being itself, if it can be put that way, reaches out to us."[2]

But human consciousness and the "re-creation" of the world through consciousness is problematic from the outset, for Being manifests itself as two simultaneous but opposed tendencies. On the one hand, Being is manifest as the will toward contraction and homogeneity: the dissolving and blending together of all its particular expressions.[3] In this connection Havel speaks of the second law of thermodynamics and the tendency of the universe toward entropy. When it is manifest in human consciousness and intentionality, Havel refers to this tendency as the "order of death" because of its obsession with structure, order and uniformity as ends in themselves.

But Being simultaneously wills itself to be anti-entropic: to cultivate and strengthen the uniqueness of all its richly varied manifestations and to develop in the direction of ever higher forms. Havel refers to this movement toward transcendence as the "order of life." Its essential character, Havel says, is its movement "towards the fulfillment of its own freedom"[4] and he adds that "it refers not just to itself but beyond itself as well . . . by throwing open the question of its own meaning."[5] The presence of the order of life in individual consciousness is the "will to self," that is, "the will of a person to be what he is or wants to be, to be himself. And . . . to defend and enlarge the self."[6]

Havel makes no secret of his view that, as creatures uniquely "thrown out" by Being and as part of the biosphere, our allegiance should belong to the "order of life." He says that "[e]very attempt by man . . . to oppose that tendency is a negation of his own essence, a betrayal of consciousness and a destructive act of self-denial." [7] Moreover, he refers to the order of death as "diabolical" and as "the bastard son of Being, the offspring of indifference to the

---

[1]*Ibid.*, p. 226.
[2]*Ibid.*, p. 265.
[3]*Ibid.*, p. 301.
[4]Vaclav Havel, "The Power of the Powerless," *The Power of the Powerless*, ed. John Keane (London: Hutchinson Press, 1985), p. 29.
[5]Havel, *op. cit.* (1989), p. 198.
[6]*Ibid.*, p. 301.
[7]*Ibid.*, p. 189.

meaning of Being and vindictive fear of its mystery . . . ."[1]
Nevertheless, human consciousness is possessed by both tendencies
and the ever-present tension between them represents itself as what
Havel calls the "problem of identity."

The "will to self," the will to one's own identity as a distinct
self, requires both the expression of difference or uniqueness and the
integrity that comes from continuity and self-recognition. Identity
therefore requires finding stability and sameness within one's
diversity.[2] And hence, acquiring the sense of "wholeness" that
comes with identity requires, first, that even as we yearn for
transcendence, we acknowledge our own frailty and limitation—that
we find and respect the boundaries between the "I" and the "non-I,"
and second, that we relate to the "non-I" as the "background" against
which our efforts at transcendence have meaning, or as the "absolute
horizon" at which we aim: in effect, "as the originator, the bearer
and the giver of meaning . . . ."[3]

A life of integrity, wholeness and identity—in a word, authentic
human existence—is a project requiring the unceasing effort to
balance contrary tendencies in the soul and a project undertaken in
the presence of constant doubt. Havel says that it "is a kind of
permanent balancing act between the unattainability of Being and
succumbing to existence-in-the-world"[4] and "an endless tension
between the living experience of meaning on the one hand, and its
unknowableness on the other."[5] It is a project that can succeed only
when life is infused with hope, wonder, humility and a spontaneous
respect for the mystery of Being.[6] And it is always at risk of being
overwhelmed by the order of death. First through the "temptation to
Nothingness"—the abandonment of questioning, of the search for
meaning; and second, through the hubris involved in substituting
for the "absolute horizon" our human rationality as the source or
origin of meaning.

While the "temptation to Nothingness" has a constant lurking
presence in human experience, Havel believes that the rise of

---

[1]*Ibid.*, p. 186.
[2]*Ibid.*, p. 268 & 302.
[3]*Ibid.*, p. 152.
[4]*Ibid.*, p. 338.
[5]*Ibid.*, p. 152.
[6]*Ibid.*, p. 360.

modern civilization—with the advent of scientific rationality--
marked the historical beginning of domination by the "order of
death." The followers of Galileo and Machiavelli were the initiators
of politics as a rational technology of power. They "freed" human
reason from the constraints and realities of particular personal
experience and they insisted that, because science rises above
individual subjective "truths," it can replace them with a superior,
trans-subjective, trans-personal truth which is truly objective and
universal.[1] The consequences of this scientific and rational
"breakthrough" were two: those manifestations of human life that
make for diversity—including personal conscience—were decreed to
be subjective, wholly private and irrelevant, and were pushed into
internal "exile"; at the same time, by crashing through the boundary
of the natural world, humankind abolished its relationship with the
"absolute horizon" as the source of meaning and relegated the sense
of mystery, awe, and empathy with the natural into the same
dustbin of private irrelevance. As Havel says, "Man rejected his
responsibility as a 'subjective illusion'—and in place of it installed
what is now proving to be the most dangerous illusion of all: the
fiction of objectivity stripped of all that is concretely human, of a
rational understanding of the cosmos, and of an abstract schema of a
putative 'historical necessity'".[2]

Europe proceeded to force on most of the world all that today
has become the basis of this rational technology of power:
anonymity and depersonalization because of its reduction to a mere
technology of manipulation by managers, bureaucrats, and
apparatchiks; a priori innocence because it does not grow from a
world in which words like "guilt" and "innocence" retain their
meaning but is instead legitimized by science, cybernetics, ideology,
law, and abstraction—"that is, by everything except personal
responsibility to human beings as persons and neighbors"[3];
omnipotence because it is not constrained by human limits but
instead is "grounded in an omnipresent ideological fiction which can

---

[1]Vaclav Havel, "Politics and Conscience" in *Vaclav Havel, or Living
in Truth*, ed. by Jan Vladislav (London: Faber and Faber, 1990), p.
138..
[2]*Ibid.*, p. 142.
[3]*Ibid.*, p. 144.

rationalize anything without ever having to brush against the truth."[1]

Havel maintains that it is a grave error to believe that the growth of this anonymous, rationalized power serves the "universal welfare." The real consequence of this scientifically calculable and technologically achievable "universal welfare" is the capacity to do great evil with indifference: "that millions of people will be sacrificed to this illusion in scientifically directed concentration camps is not something that concerns our 'modern man'."[2] In the essay "Politics and Conscience" Havel argues that this anonymous, technological power is in the possession of no one; rather it has acquired a kind of "automatism" and we are being dragged along by its self-momentum. And in *The Power of the Powerless* Havel explains how power is exercised in the service of ideology, which in turn, legitimizes that same power. Havel says, "it is as though ideology had appropriated power . . . as though it had become dictator itself."[3] In fact, the inner aim of the totalitarian system—"the convex mirror of the inevitable consequences of rationalism"—is not the preservation of power in the hands of a ruling clique, but the social phenomenon of self-preservation—of a kind of automatism. Its essential characteristic is its "introversion"—a movement toward becoming ever more completely and unreservedly itself—that is, permanent, unchanging, and final. This automatism of power is the exact opposite of transcendence towards something beyond itself; indeed, it is in fact an objective manifestation—on the largest of social scales--of the "order of death."

But this autonomous power requires the continual suppression of the stirring in consciousness of the "order of life." Therefore, it must oppose absolutely every expression of individuality. It must require that reason and conscience be consigned to it as the higher authority. "The principle involved here," Havel says, "is that the center of power is identical with the center of truth . . . the highest secular authority is identical with the highest spiritual authority."[4] But because power does not serve genuine human needs, its movement toward auto-totality is not consistent with the truth and

---

[1]*Ibid.*, p. 146.
[2]*Ibid.*, p. 142.
[3]Havel, *op. cit.* (1985), p. 33.
[4]*Ibid.*, p. 25.

it is therefore necessary for power to cloak itself in deceit and hypocrisy. Ideology pretends that the requirements of the system derive from the requirements of life. "It is a world of appearances trying to pass for reality," Havel says, and adds, "It offers human beings the illusion of an identity, of dignity . . . while making it easier for them to part with them."[1]

For example, in his parable of the greengrocer Havel points out that the real meaning of the slogan the greengrocer displays in his shop window is not its trivial semantic content, "Workers of the World Unite," but a definite and subliminal message: "I am afraid and therefore unquestionably obedient." But because the sign, on its textual surface, suggests a level of disinterested conviction, it "helps the greengrocer to conceal from himself the low foundations of his obedience."[2] Moreover, the greengrocer thus declares his loyalty in the only way the system is capable of understanding—"that is, by accepting the prescribed ritual, by accepting appearances as reality, by accepting the given rules of the game."[3]

Of course, the greengrocer's displayed slogan makes only a small contribution to the general panorama of life, for similar slogans are everywhere: on lamp posts, walls, and in offices, other shops and apartment windows. And these slogans perform their functions as codes only because everyone is drawn into the illusion. "Metaphorically speaking," Havel says, "without the greengrocer's slogan the office worker's slogan could not exist, and vice versa. Each proposes to the other that something be repeated and each accepts the other's proposal . . . by exhibiting their slogans, each compels the other to accept the rules of the game."[4]

The greengrocer and his fellows are accomplices of the system and captives of its lies and falsifications. Havel notes that it does not really matter that individuals do not believe in these mystifications, as long as they behave as though they did. And this is what Havel calls "living within a lie." As he says, "It is enough for them to have accepted their life with it and in it. For by this

---

[1]*Ibid.*, p. 29.
[2]*Ibid.*, p. 28.
[3]*Ibid.*, p. 31.
[4]*Ibid.*, p. 36.

very fact, individuals confirm the system, fulfill the system, make the system, are the system."[1]

It is just because victims are also accomplices that the oppression of autonomous power cannot be ended by traditional political means. Havel asserts that the idea of violent revolution is not radical enough; reform cannot result from the victory of any traditional political conception. It will have to derive from the fundamental reconstitution of people: from an "existential revolution." One must begin by destroying totalitarianism in the soul: by extricating the self from terrible involvement in the mechanisms of totality. "One day something in our greengrocer snaps . . . He rejects the ritual and breaks the rules of the game. He discovers once more his suppressed identity and dignity. He gives his freedom a concrete significance. His revolt is an attempt to live within the truth."[2]

For Havel, "living within the truth" begins with the attempt to set the fundamental dimensions of our humanity free from their private exile; it begins by redefining our basic values—trust, openness, responsibility, solidarity, and love—in terms of our concrete experiences and emotions—and by the effort to ensure conformity between these values and our public behaviors. One begins to say aloud what one thinks, to express solidarity with fellow citizens, to refuse to comply with demands that sacrifice dignity, and to regain control over one's sense of responsibility. These first steps lead to deeper transformations of the self: to trusting in the voice of conscience more than in any abstract speculation, to assertions of one's dignity as an irreplaceable human being, and even the willingness to sacrifice oneself for what makes life meaningful. Paradoxically, as Havel notes, without this attitude toward life, individuals cannot have the courage to oppose absolute public schemes that lead to the actual sacrifice of individual lives.[3]

Havel believes that when individuals seeking to live within the truth reach a critical mass in a society, then political revolution is inevitable. First, because a coterie of individuals, seeking to be true to their deepest sensibilities and refusing to compromise their dignity even to the point of death, present the only force that the

---

[1]*Ibid.*, p. 31.
[2]*Ibid.*, p. 39.
[3]Havel, *op. cit.* (1990) p. 152.

system of autonomous power—depending as it does on falsity and complicity—cannot destroy. Second, because of its very nature, the "order of life" cannot impose limits on itself: the aims of life ineluctably seek to expand the space available for them. Thus non-compliance based on commitment to human values must lead inevitably to civil disobedience and to the formation, via "citizen initiatives" of a "second society" and a "parallel *polis*."

But Havel also believes that, through the recovery of the expression of human values in our lives, we open ourselves once again to the transcendent. Indeed, it is especially in one's conscience that one is most attentive to the demands for self-identity and integrity, and it is therefore through the voice of conscience that Being once again begins to manifest itself as the "order of life." Thus by "living within the truth" we rediscover the boundaries between the "I" as questioner and the "non-I" as "absolute horizon." We experience again the awe and mystery of the "absolute horizon" and we accept that there is something in the order of Being which exceeds our competence. Thus "living within the truth" leads to the recovery of our essential activity as humans—the search for the meaning in life.

Thus the "existential revolution" set in motion by individuals seeking to live within the truth is a nonviolent revolution in two senses. First, it is a nonviolent political revolution against particular oppressive regimes dominated by autonomous power, just as the "velvet revolution" of Czechoslovakia in November, 1989. Second, it is a more general nonviolent revolution against the domination in modern civilization of the "order of death." And thus the "empowering ideology" of *The Power of the Powerless* which laid the groundwork for chartism in communist Czechoslovakia and for the looming revolution of 1989, and especially Havel's confidence in nonviolence, is based not alone on appeal to selected and abstracted moral principles, nor alone on empirical analyses of its effectiveness. Rather, both this "empowering ideology" and Havel's confidence arise out of his metaphysics. There is therefore an odd but wonderful parallel between Havel and Marx, for the beliefs of both in the practicality of revolution and social change are deeply rooted in their philosophies of human consciousness and ultimate reality. But if Marx had turned Hegel upside down, Havel attempts the restoration: speaking before the Congress of the United States and as President of Czechoslovakia, Havel declared:

"Consciousness precedes being, and not the other way around, as the Marxists claim. For this reason, the salvation of this human world lies nowhere else than in the human heart, in the human power to reflect . . . ."[1]

George Washington University

---

[1]*The Washington Post,* February 22, 1990, p. A28.

8 Fierce and Human Peace

Sara Ruddick

Peace the great meaning has not been defined.
When we say peace as a word, war
As a flare of fire leaps across our eyes.
We went to this school. Think war;
Cancel war, we were taught.
What is left is peace.
No, peace is not left, it is no cancelling
The fierce and human peace is our deep power
Born to us of wish and responsibility.

Muriel Rukeseyer

In this paper, I outline one version of feminist peace politics. The peace politics I imagine is not preoccupied with the question "When, if ever, is it right to kill?" Nor is it committed to the absolute renunciation of violence often associated with pacifism. Rather, this politics expresses a sturdy, public suspicion of organized violence even in the best of causes. Accordingly, it seeks to disrupt the plans of those who organize violence and to develop effective forms of nonviolent action. My claim is that feminist peace politics can contribute in distinctive ways to awakening a sturdy suspicion of violence and to inventing the myriad forms of nonviolent disruption, cooperation, respect, restraint and resistance that would make up "peace".

It is often said that feminist theory is a critical deconstructive project with reconstructive and sometimes explicitly utopian aspirations. Similarly, I have spoken of peace politics as both critical of war and inventive of peace. It would be misleading, however, to divide, or still worse, to rank critical and reconstructive efforts. In feminist theory, inventions depend upon the skeptical space created by critique. Conversely, "the very *meaning* of what the feminist [critique] apprehends is illuminated by the light of what ought to be";[1] often critique is constructed from an emerging standpoint that reconstructivists are trying to articulate. Similarly, many people begin to invent the institutions and practices of nonviolence after they have become suspicious not only of a particular "bad" war but of war-making itself. Yet unless they have imagined "peace" and have some confidence that nonviolentlent action is intrinsically rewarding and effective, they are unlikely to gaze steadily at and through war.

Cancel War: Feminist Critique

Both within the United States and throughout the world there are many feminisms, some of which are explicitly militarist. In the particular feminist critique I imagine, feminist and anti-militarist impulses are interwoven at the start. Take, as an exemplar of this weave, a letter Virginia Woolf wrote during the First World War:

> I became steadily more feminist, owing to the Times, which I read at breakfast and wonder how this preposterous masculine fiction [the war] keeps going a day longer—without some vigorous woman pulling us together and marching through it.[2]

Nearly everyone agrees that war is in some sense masculine. Throughout history and across the globe, whatever the 'race' or history of particular cultures, men have greatly predominated among the generals, chiefs of staff, and heads of cadre, tribe, nation or state who direct wars. In technologically developed states, men predominate among the business entrepreneurs who fund wars and among the defense intellectuals and philosophers who justify them. Still, today, men predominate among the soldiers who execute war strategies. But there is no ready conclusion to draw from war's masculinity. Many militarists celebrate and many civilians accept

---

[1] Sandra Bartky, "Toward a Phenomenology of Feminist Consciousness" in *Femininity and Domination* (New York: Routledge, 1990), p. 14.

[2] Virginia Woolf, *Collected Letters*, Volume Two, Letter #740 (New York: Harcourt, Brace, and Javanovich, 1976), p. 76.

the conjunction of war and manliness as a natural or necessary
component of war. Many feminists who perceive and heartily resent
war's masculinity challenge military practices in the hope of
securing for women a citizen's right to fight and to command
fighters. To be sure, because of war's masculinity, many women
define themselves as "outside" military aims and institutions and
therefore seem poised on the edge of anti-militarism. But the
exclusion of women, along with their (our) voluntary assumption of
outsider status, is part of most military scripts; women are supposed
to weep from the sidelines. Woolf urged women to refuse the
seductions of loyal marginality, to enact their outsider status rather
than passively accepting it or thrashing its limits. But, and this is
what I want to remember, when Woolf declared war masculine and
herself "outsider" she already believed that practices of war-making
were "preposterous."[1] Because she had a prior, rooted suspicion of
the wars that excluded her, war's masculinity could inspire a peace
politics that was feminist and a feminism that was essentially
critical of militarism and other interlocking violences.

While neither war's masculinity nor feminist critique in
themselves generate a sturdy suspicion of war-making, anti-
militarist feminism might foment and focus suspicion, especially
among women, in distinctive ways. Here I consider only two
aspects of feminist focus, both of which identify and account for
disturbing variants of military masculinity.

1. Militarists invoke various norms of masculinity in order to
train, shame, and inspire soldiers. Feminists have identified, among
these norms, a 'male'-defining misogyny and homophobia[2] that
threads through military speech and practice. The "monstrous male,
loud of voice, hard of fist" who goes off to war singing of the
"Persian pukes" he is ready to "nape," the faggot assholes he is
ready to sodomize, the dead and diseased whore he is ready to rape,

---

[1]Woolf remained suspicious of violence even in the best of causes —
in her life these best causes were armed resistance to Franco in the
Spanish Civil war and the war against Nazi Germany.
[2]While militarist misogyny seems culturally pervasive, it is not
always intertwined with homophobia as it is in the United States.
Plato, for example, imagined an army of gay men.

expresses even as he caricatures this common military attitude.[1] To
be sure, soldiers differ from one another; the relation of soldier/men
to women, to other men, and to men's sexual love for each other is
as various and unpredictable as the soldiers themselves. But
individual soldiers often cannot overcome—and in fact are overcome
by—a masculine ethos that is distinctly misogynist and
homophobic.

Military masculine ethos may be attributed to chromosomal or
biochemical characteristics of males. By contrast, feminists claim
that, whatever its roots in biological sexuality and procreation,
masculinity is socially created and can be changed. Certain North
American and European feminists have provided an account of the
acquisition, at least among dominant classes, of "normal" masculinity. In social groups where men hold the principal governing
posts and are responsible for hunting, war, or other 'legitimate'
aggression, and where women are responsible for childtending,
masculinity is highly valid, potentially aggressive, and fragile. In
order to ward off envy of female birthgiving and dangerous longing
for the care of mothering women, and at the same time to affirm
male privilege and assuage misgivings (if any) about aggression,
boys becoming "men" define themselves as non-female and better
than female. Accordingly, they tend to devalue bodilyness and
emotionality, both of which are evoked by physical vulnerability
and associated with the bodies and emotions of females whose care
they need, fear and long for.

Men's masculinity may never be so vaunted, fragile, and
incipiently misogynist as in war. Amidst war's brutality, soldiers
may well long for and idealize gentle women. But women represent
emotionality and vulnerability. In extraordinarily trying
circumstances soldiers must control ordinary emotions—most
notably fear, rage at being made to risk pain and death, and also,

---

[1]I am specifically citing here Virginia Woolf *Three Guineas* (New
York: Harvest/HBJ, 1966 [originally 1938]), p. 105 and Joan Smith's
compelling account of the lyrics of a U.S. song book in "Crawling
from the Wreckage" in her *Misogynies* (New York, Ballantine Books,
1990, *passim*). These are only two of the many critics who have
explored military misogyny. Especially noteworthy is Klaus
Theweleit's study, *Male Fantasies* (Minneapolis: University of
Minnesota Press, 1987, 1989).

often, homosexual desires evoked by homoerotic bonding but forbidden by homophobic military policies. As they ward off forbidden feeling, many soldiers may turn against women because of the emotionality they represent. More specifically, soldiers can blame women for their own love and longing which endangers them and their comrades by diverting them from soldierly duty. [1] Moreover, even good women are comprised by literal and psychological distance from "the front." Soldiers scorn—and are encouraged to scorn—women who have never known battle and cannot understand their stories. They also resent, but cannot admit envying, the relative safety afforded to females who, actually or in soldierly fantasy, cheer them into danger from a safe, ignorant, patriotic distance.[2]

In this strained emotional ambience of danger and separation, commanders encourage and legitimate "masculine" aggressive impulses. Given this encouragement and the pressures to which their "normal masculine" defenses are subject, it is not surprising if many soldiers imaginatively elaborate or actually perpetrate rape, assault, and mutilation of women. Many men also appear to project their own aggressive impulses onto women who thus become dirty, diseased, castrating, and murderous.

In the genderization of war, masculinity has its counterpart in military femininity. Acting out of feminine sensibility, women

---

[1]For an example of "good" war stories by a "good" soldier that nonetheless use women in this way see Tim O'Brien, *The Things They Carried* (Boston: Houghton Mifflin, 1990). Death is embodied in the death of a nine-year-old girl, thoughts of a sweetheart lead a man (as he sees it) to neglect his men, women don't answer letters, don't respond to men's wars. A dumb Cooze (middle aged woman of liberal sentiments) doesn't understand O'Brien's stories.
In an earlier article ["Pacifying the Forces: Drafting Women in the Interest of Peace," *Signs* (1983)] I considered — and rejected — the possibility that women's presence in armed forces, and especially in combat, would exercise a restraining effect on war practices. It may be possible to put the hypothesis to some sort of test by examining the increasingly sexually integrated U.S. military. However, short wars fought by vastly superior forces (Panama, Persian Gulf) cannot be simply compared to long and unsuccessful wars (Viet Nam).
[2]Klaus Theweleit reports on this sentiment and Tim O'Brien is one of many, many literary and real life soldiers who expresses it.

weep for the fighters they lose, and the suffering, especially the
sexual assault, they themselves endure. Bereaved women express
the human losses of war while sexually endangered women inspire
their men to protect them. More prosaically, women nurse the
wounded, arm the fighter, sexually desire endangered restrained
warriors, and preserve a safe haven to which soldiers return. This
feminine military sensibility is meant to provide an androphiliac
response to misogynist military masculinity. While fighting men
are encouraged to scorn and blame women, military loyalty requires
women to avert their eyes from misogyny and from sexual
subordination. While military masculinity excuses and expresses
easy destructiveness, military femininity eroticizes alternate models
of masculinity: the masculine "just warrior" protects women and
other vulnerable people. He is courageous, restrained, and self-
sacrificing. A masculine "hero" is a conqueror, dashing and well-
mounted (previously on horseback, now in tank, plane, or
paradigmatically, stealth bomber). He enacts the national
interest/glory in which loyally excited women participate and are
meant to celebrate. Both feminine ideals of masculinity mask
misogyny and brutal or callous violence which are attributed, then,
only to enemy soldiers.

Because masculinity is socially created, different constellations
within the family, community and state create different
masculinities. Different militaries, and different circumstances
within one military or one war, will produce different military
effects on these already differing masculinities. It may be, for
example, that in the lives of actual soldiers, especially those who
believe that they are fighting a good war, ideals of self-sacrificing or
heroic masculinity are as influential as ideals of swaggering
misogyny. All three ideals may combine with other conceptions of
masculinity ranging from eternal "boyishness" of competitive
jousters to the comradely victory lust of team players.[1] In
highlighting the norms and actions of repugnant masculinity, anti-
militarist feminists publicize one kind of militarist fantasy
expressed, for example, in chants and songs, the graffiti on bombs

---

[1] It also seems, if the *New York Times* May 1, 1991 report on
soldiers' attitudes toward aiding Kurdish refugees is to be believed,
that many soldiers would rather comfort than create the victims of
war.

and guns, and the gestures, bonding rituals, and 'boyish' boasts of soldiers returning from battles and bombing raids. Feminists do not mean to simplify the motives of men who kill. Rather, they aim to disrupt militarist *women's* fantasies of noble heroic masculine warriors and thus begin to replace feminine militarism's loyal androphilia with disgusted rejection of the violence many men and sometimes women bring themselves to plan and enact.

2. Revelations of war's sexual aggressive fantasies might undermine loyal military femininity. Nonetheless many women, like many men, support war, whatever its psycho-sexual character, for moral reasons. The cause is just, the state is in danger, evil enemies threaten; or, more invasively, the 'legitimate' interest and good of the state depends upon securing a resource, port, territory, or a peoples' submission.[1] 'Warism', "the belief that war is morally justified in principle and often justified in fact",[2] is both a dominant and majority ideology in most past and present societies and states. To arouse sturdy suspicion of war, it is necessary to undermine the kinds of thinking—the just war theories—that legitimate war-making as an institution and, within that institution, sanction particular wars. Just war theories are entrenched; undermining them will require many kinds of criticism, expressed in many different genres. Neither feminists nor women predominate among just war critics. Nonetheless, "different voice"[3] and feminist vantages provide one distinctive basis, and illuminate particular grounds for criticism.

---

[1] I am including within the language of just war theory what many theorists would take as amoral, realist causes of war. States' reasons are, however, often expressed in moral language. In the recent war, President Bush's **moral** language mixed the right and obligation to control resources with other more traditionally just causes (e.g. resistance to aggression). Hussein similarly described Iraq's right to resources in moral terms.

[2] I take this definition from Duane Cady, *From Warism to Pacifism* (Philadelphia, Temple University Press, 1989).

[3] I take the term "different voice" from Carol Gilligan's *In a Different Voice*, (Cambridge: Harvard University Press, 1982). I use the term to refer to any theorists who believe that, because of the lives women tend to lead, many women have developed distinctive epistemologies and moral orientations.

Just war theory takes seriously the reality of states and their boundaries, of uniformed soldiers, and of weapons that can be selectively aimed at and by soldiers. The "wars" of which just war theory speaks are temporally bounded events negotiated by diplomats and fought upon or above "battlefields".[1] Just war theorists judge these wars, their weapons and fighters, in terms of abstract rules of justice and legitimacy. I believe that recent feminist critiques of dominant Western conceptions of rationality can be brought to bear upon this kind of "warist" categorizing.

According to these feminist critiques,[2] prevailing ideals of reason reflect compulsive tendencies to defend, dissociate, and abstract. These tendencies are sometimes called "masculine" because they can be explained by the same social constellation of female caregiving, "legitimate" male aggression, and masculine privilege that give rise to military "masculinity". As military masculinities are shaped by particular military institutions and particular wars, so philosophical masculinity is shaped by particular academic and other intellectual institutions as well as by an ideological construction of certain kinds of thinking as "masculine." Individual thinkers, women or men, are governed, to various degrees, by these 'masculine' tendencies depending upon their familial history, institutional affiliations, and relative access, dependence upon, or attraction to, masculine privilege and aggression.

To the extent that "Men of Reason" are governed by these dominant Western ideals, they thrive on boundaries and definition, eschew ambiguity, and suspect particular attachments. They separate thought from feeling, mind from body. On the other hand, Men of Reason seem almost compulsively attached to detachment. To adapt a phrase from Klaus Theweleit, they thrive on a fantasy of transcendence based on a "tradition of freeing the thinking brain from the depths of the most pressing situations and sending it off to

---

[1] Any city, village, or 'territory' can, of course, be marked as a battlefield.

[2] Many feminists have contributed to these critiques. In addition to Theweleit see, especially, Evelyn Fox Keller, *Reflections on Gender and Science* (New Haven: Yale University Press, 1985) and Carol Cohn "Sex and Death in the Rational World of Defense Intellectuals," *Signs* (Summer 1987), Genevieve Lloyd, Man of Reason (Minneapolis: University of Minnesota Press, 1984).

some (fictive) summit for a panoramic overview."[1] Yet the discourses of reason barely conceal the emotions that permeate them—anxiety, defensiveness, addictive sexual assertion or fear of sexuality, distaste for and envy of female sexual and birthgiving bodies, and, at least in most circles of reason in the United States, frankly competitive aggression. These emotions are especially evident to those who have been trained to read around what purports to be argument, to listen for nuance and take seriously metaphor and style.

In Western philosophy ideals of reason have sometimes been created in specific connection with the ideals of war. As Plato put the point boldly, an education in reason "must not be useless to warlike men [or, women]"; rulers must prove themselves "best in philosophy and with respect to war."[2] Whatever their historical connection, war theorists, like other men of reason, resort to abstraction, euphemism, binary oppositions, and sharply bounded concepts to conceal or sanitize the bodily injuring and domination of spirit that is war's purpose and consequence. Although too attached to detachments, these war theorists, like their philosopher counterparts, reveal their anxieties, aggression, arrogance, and often even the sexual and procreative envies and desires, that are familiar from soldiers' stories.

The "different voice and vision," often discovered by women who listen to or read women, challenges the bounded realities and rule-governed seriousness of just war stories.[3] This "different"

---

[1]Klaus Theweleit, *op. cit.*, Vol. 1., p. 364.

[2]Plato, *Republic*, 543a, 521d. See also, Genevieve Lloyd, "Selfhood, War and Masculinity" in *Feminist Challenges*, edited by Carole Pateman and Elisabeth Grosz, (Boston: Northeastern University Press, 1987).

[3]It has been claimed, notoriously, that this 'different' voice has been heard more frequently in women than in men, that it pervades African and African-American women's thinking, and that its values arise from a strong identification and engagement with mothering and caregiving and with community survival and resistance to oppression. (As Margaret Urban Walker pointed out, many people have been so preoccupied with deciding who speaks in a different voice and why that they have barely attended to what the different voice is saying.) I claim here that whoever speaks in the 'different voice' will find it difficult to speak just war theory.

perspective is grounded in attention to concrete particulars, expresses itself in open-ended narration, and tests its findings in the context of collective discussions that are respectful of distinctive experience.[1] Different voice theorists can, for example, be as attentive as just war theorists to the history of boundary making as it cuts across nationalist pasts, and as aware as their principled brothers of the complex and fervid meanings that a Fatherland can acquire for women and men. Certainly a voice that reflects the responsibilities of caregiving will respect the stability that a secure border is meant to provide as well as the need for resources on which care depends. But different voice theorists might also be less able to feel and less willing to carry the conceptual/emotional weight of diplomatic division that follows upon armed conquest and competitive negotiation. They might look across and through borders for ways of re-allocating resources to meet a peoples' or region's needs. When a border is unjustly breached or rules unjustly broken, they might accept workable compromises at the cost of abstract justice in order to preserve, for future negotiation, their homes and lives.

Generally, skeptical of attempts to conceal and control through rule-governed fairness, these different voice theorists would less likely isolate, "for the sake of argument" conducted in a style they find alien, the soldier from his or her community, family and friendships. Nor would they separate the uniformed killer from the people s/he fights among, or the targeted bomb from the civilians it unintentionally kills. Indeed "different voice" critics can appear disturbingly uninterested in the rules of war which are meant to constrain battle and whose violation is often an anguished focus of war memoirs. It is not that these critics are unable to distinguish between the destructiveness of rifle shot and napalm, of smart bomb and random Scud. Nor do they assimilate killing in battle with the bombing of soldiers in retreat or the ill-treatment of prisoners.

---

[1] I am drawing here, especially, on Margaret Urban Walker, "Alternative Epistemologies for Feminist Ethics" forthcoming from Indiana University Press in *Explorations in Feminist Ethics*, edited by Eve Browning Cole and Susan Coltrap McQuinn. Walker gives a perspicuous overview of various feminist writers including Carol Gilligan and Nel Noddings. Walker's account seems to me substantiated in Patricia Hill Collins, *Social Construction of Black Feminist Thought* (Boston: South End Press, 1990).

Rather they reject the categories and conventions through which war is seen and, in so doing, undermine the fiction of controlled and cordoned combat that is used to sanitize and legitimate violence.

Feminist just war critics may also challenge the fundamental concept of "war" as a discrete phenomenon that is arranged by diplomats and takes place on battlefields. There is, of course, a sense in which wars are temporally bounded events whose beginnings and endings have clear consequences. Multiple parties are sorted into "forces", weapons already deployed and aimed are detonated and new weapons are rushed into place, planned injuries are perpetrated and suffered until, in the "end" all "sides" have been destroyed by nuclear or "near-nuclear" weapons or else one "side" is prepared to sacrifice ideology, interests, or territory, rather than to endure further suffering.[1] Few see so "differently" that they deny the existence of "war" or the relief of peace. But wars rarely have the "neat" endings envisioned in dreams of victory. Moreover, the rewards even of neat victory are often compromised or reversed in decades, if not in months. For victors and losers, the psychic injuries, emotional losses, physical damages and socio-ecological destructions of battle have consequences long after surrender.

Nor does war begin only on the day of invasion. There is a thematic tradition in feminism that underlies the connections between interlocking systems of violence—intimate, social, economic, civic, and military. In this tradition discrete episodes of public and legitimate violence are predictable consequences of war-making institutions and ways of living. One vision of interlocking violences—intimate, social, civic, and military—is epitomized in Virginia Woolf's *Three Guineas*, written in the fascist thirties and still resonant for anti-militarist feminists.

According to Woolf, "the public and private worlds are inseparably connected; the tyrannies and servilities of one are the tyrannies and servilities of the other." Looking at the patriarchal (her word) family, and particularly at education and professional life in England, Woolf saw an ethos of military domination in the making. Now, as in Woolf's time, people are taught "not to hate force but to use it" in order to keep their possessions and defend

---

[1] I take this deliberately reductive account of war from Elaine Scarry, *The Body in Pain* (Oxford: Oxford University Press, 1985).

their grandeur and power, through varieties of economic, racial and sexual violences.[1] A contemporary feminist, Cynthia Enloe, has looked with equal suspicion at the connection, particularly as wrought by the United States, of militarism, international corporate capitalism, racism, sexism, and assaults against the poor. In *Bananas, Beaches and Bases*, Enloe reveals an economic and military war *system*, that allows the United States to initiate, fund, fight, or avoid discrete "wars". In this system a military ethos, sustained by military spending, prepares for and exploits racial and masculine domination despite, and partly because of, the fact that armed service appears to provide minority and female citizens, especially those who are poor, material advantages and symbolic status otherwise unavailable to them. To further the system, war planners manipulate allegedly private and sharply genderized relationships, playing upon class interests, racial fears, and sexual norms in order to recruit women's bodies, services and labor for military affairs.[2]

Feminist critiques such as Enloe's and Woolf's tend to undermine the reality of "war" and the loyalties, excitement and nostalgia that the discrete, exciting war horror evokes. Positively, these analyses of a concealed and deceptive war system encourage

---

[1]Virginia Woolf, *op. cit.*, 1966, p. 142

> Do they [the facts of history] not prove that education....does not teach people to hate force but to use it? Do they not prove that education makes [the educated]....so anxious to keep their possessions, that "grandeur and power" of which the poet speaks, that they will use not force but much subtler methods than force when they are asked to share them? And are not force and possessiveness very closely connected with war? (p. 29) ....The facts....seem to prove that the professions have an undeniable effect upon the professors. They make the people who practice them possessive, jealous of any infringements of their rights, and highly combative if anyone dares dispute them....And do not such qualities lead to war? (p. 66).

[2]Cynthia Enloe, *Bananas, Beaches and Bases* (Berkeley: University of California Press, 1990). In this connection, Duane Cady called to my attention G. Bush's celebration, during Black History month, of the military as an equal opportunity employer.

critics to ferret out the plans of leaders—and the histories of those plans—that both ordinary war talk and just war theory conceal. As the (then) East German writer Christa Wolf enjoined:

> You can tell when a war starts, but when does the pre-war start? If there are rules about that we should hand them on. Hand them down inscribed in clay, in stone. Do not let your own people deceive you.[1]

Of Wish and Responsibility: Feminist Reconstruction

The most clever unmasking of war does not give people alternative ways to protect what they love and get what they need. The most thorough unravelling of fears and fantasies that legitimate violence will only lead to despair without the inventions of new conceptions of peace making, new ways of cooperating and fighting.

As there is no sharp division between the violences of domestic, civic and military life, there is also no sharp division between the practices and thinking of private and public peace. Even in the midst of war, people cooperate, care for one another, anger and are angry without injuring. In the ordinary lives of women and men, including the lives of those who are frequently violent, there are almost always moments of cooperation and non-damaging conflict. One of the tasks of peacemaking is to transform this ordinary peacefulness which surrounds us into a self-respecting, articulate commitment to peace.

As war is associated with men, peace is associated with women and the "womanly". Understandably, then, many anti-militarist feminists, already partisans of women, look specifically to women's

---

[1]Christa Wolf, *Cassandra* (New York: Farrar, Strauss and Giroux, 1984), p. 66. While one should always suspect leaders, militaristic planning exacerbates grounds for distrust. Leaders act in secret, often deceptively, quieting dissent by appeals to selflessness and patriotism. While war may have always depended upon hierarchical institutions, elite access to information and hypocrisy, these anti-democratic virtues are evidently required by the massive mobilizations and high technology weaponry on which modern war depends.

ordinary lives for hints of ordinary peace. In earlier, more confident days some feminists argued that by dint of peacefulness, "feminine" women should enjoy political power and "feminine" values should inform government policies. It is now clear, however, that women's peacefulness has been entirely consonant with, and is indeed often expressed by, the tears and loyal marginality of military femininity. If in ordinary women's lives there are rudiments of "peacefulness," they will have to be transformed into instruments of public peace.

Women differ from each other as much as men do; there is no generic woman but only women with particular histories lived out in distinctive social locations. Nonetheless it might be possible to discover in women's lives recurring patterns, what Wittgenstein called "family resemblances" as opposed to essential commonalities. It may be possible, for example, to identify in women's lives a tendency to take up the responsibilities and work of "care"—of feeding, clothing, sheltering, nursing, maintaining kin and other social relations, tending children and the elderly. Many women reject caregiving work; more would do so if they could. Many men are committed, effective caregivers. Nonetheless, caregiving has been represented as, and has in fact been, primarily women's work. Caregivers—women and men—are wage earners, providers, sexual beings, and citizens or subjects of a state. None of these and other identities can be disconnected from that of the caregiver. Nonetheless, it may be possible to identify a kind of work of care threading through various social contexts and identities.

Drawing upon earlier feminist work, especially that of Nancy Hartsock[1], I have looked at the caregiving work for rudiments of the relationship and ways of knowing that might make up "peace". Caregivers appreciate material, especially bodily, realities and they respect the separate self-generated wills of vulnerable people. Whether mothers compare the quality of infant faeces in a Brazilian village or of diaper-rash in middle class North America, whether nurse-activists study the effect of lead on workers or the effect of a change of lighting in an intensive care unit, they are dealing with the *meaning* of material realities for themselves and those they care for; they must access material and bodily qualities in terms of needs

---

[1]Nancy Hartsock, *Money, Sex, and Power* (New York: Longman, 1983).

to which they are responding. Caregivers also work with vulnerable subjects who are dependent upon them and interpret and make use of the care they receive, often in ways that are frustrating and disappointing to the caregiver. Whether she counsels a six-year-old afraid of heights or a recently imprisoned convict, guides the wheel chair of a patient with advance multiple sclerosis or the shaking hand of an eighty-five-year-old trying to cope with a liquid meal, a caregiver depends upon a minimally respectful connection with the people she cares for and also, almost always, with the communities and institutions upon which both caregiver and person cared for depend. Ideally, caregivers set themselves to respect the self-generated wills and desires of people over whom they have considerable power and who might well, were they not committed to caring, provoke them to abuse.[1]

In the last several years, I have been looking at one kind of caring work—mothering[2]—with an eye to the ways mothers learn to interpret and respect material realities and the vulnerable wills of children. I have offered a "heuristic" representation of mothering that serves both to discover and to reveal the "peacemaking" elements of the practice and thinking I hope and believe to be there. Accordingly, my rendition of maternal thinking contrasts in detail and as a whole with military thinking. To cite only two examples: first, the attentive love of mothering requires concrete cognition, tolerance for ambivalence and ambiguity, receptiveness to change, and recognition of the limits of control. Secondly, mothers are apt to acquire a variegated concept of "nature" as at best beneficent and hospitable to goodness, at worst a respected negotiating partner. These and many other capacities and attitudes that I identify as "maternal" contrast with the abstractions and certainties of militarist thinking, and with the exploitative attitude toward human and non-

---

[1]I am drawing especially on Nancy Hartsock here, especially on the final chapter of *Money, Sex, and Power* (*ibid.*) that outlines a "feminist standpoint". I have also been affected by Nel Noddings, especially *Women and Evil* (University of California Press, 1990).
[2]Mothering is a potentially genderless work that has been largely delegated to, and undertaken by, women.

human nature that are characteristic of militarism and the instrumental technocracy on which it depends.[1]

Turning more explicitly to war, I identify an opposition between maternal and military responses to embodied willfulness. Central to militarism and militarized diplomacy is a readiness to impose one's will, by threatened or actual injuring, upon the embodied wills of others. By contrast, maternal aims, as I, in a heuristic mode, identify them, depend upon maintaining an actively nonviolent stance toward embodied willful life. Ideally, mothers protect, even treasure, the messy, unpredictable bodies they tend. They welcome bodily being as a locus of will and pleasure and therefore respect the bodily integrity and baffling, provocative willfulness of children who are at their mercy. This welcoming stance is not simply given to mothers. A violent stance toward embodied willfulness also arises plausibly from mothers' actual daily work under pressure amidst disturbingly willful, uncontrollable, vulnerable bodies. In the most malignant forms of maternal practice, terror-driven or wildly resentful mothers conceive of their children's willful, sexual, vulnerable bodies as the site and opportunity of sadism and domination. Less dramatically, more ordinary "good enough" mothers struggle against a compulsion for order and a drive to dominate unruly children through bodily discipline. Even the most benign mothers are sometimes likely to take their children's "nature", their willful embodied being, as an enemy to be conquered.

Peacemaking mothers are not, predictably, better people than militarists. Rather, they are engaged in a specific project: to create a child they *cannot* dominate, a child lively with her own desires and projects. To this end, they try to resist temptations to terrify, injure and humiliate even when their children are most provocative and mysterious. By contrast, militarists *aim* to dominate—often in the name of good causes. In the service of domination they arm and train themselves so that they can, if other means of domination fail, injure, terrify, humiliate, and finally defeat the will of opponents.

---

[1] I have developed the idea of an "heuristic" representation — along with the attendant notions of "diagnosis" and "transformation" in "From Maternal Thinking to Peace Politics" in Eve Browning Cole and Susan Coltrap McQuinn, *op. cit.*

Mothers are both powerful and powerless. For many years they can injure, terrify or humiliate their children. Yet they often feel powerless in the face of children's wills and are certainly powerless in the face of the accidents—illnesses, death of loved ones, for example—that "nature" visits upon them. Most mothers are also socially powerless, to varying and sometimes excruciating degrees, among the employers, judges, welfare workers, doctors, and other gate keepers and openers who control the resources on which their children depend. Even those mothers tightly connected to rulers and resources often have a fragile and derivative relationship to the power they employ.

When peacemaking mothers fight with their children or on their behalf, they cannot rely upon balances of power or "equal" strength and status to control aggression. From multiple positions of power and powerlessness, they have to invent nonviolent ways of fighting that will survive their anger at their children, children's anger at each other, and, often, their own and their children's rage when rulers and keepers cruelly or indifferently assault them. It is not surprising that even those mothers governed by ideals of nonviolence often fail to achieve the nonviolence to which they aspire. Since children are vulnerable and the vulnerable are subject to abuse and neglect, mothers may be more than usually overtaken by sadism, self-indulgent aggression, and self-protective indifference to the real needs of demanding children. Since many mothers see their children assaulted by racism, indifference, and poverty, they may be more than usually tempted to despair. It is a maternal *commitment* to care for children rather than neglecting them, to fight with children and on their behalf but without injuring them or others that I believe illuminates more public struggles for "peace".

Not all, perhaps not even most, mothers share this commitment to nonviolence. Individual mothers abuse their children without apparent remorse. In most cultures children suffer from accepted but abusive practices and some cultures appear to legitimate systematic maternal abuse. My hope—and belief—is that there are enough maternal practices that are sufficiently governed by principles of nonviolence to offer one model for nonviolent relationships.

Yet it is clear that domestic nonviolence does not translate easily into public peacemaking. Mothers themselves are often uninterested or unwilling to make such an extension. Given the current state of the world's governments, obedience is the handmaid of war, resistance the prerequisite of peace. Within their domestic practices nonviolent mothers often struggle against their own temptation to command obedience. They strive to make the work of training a work of conscience in which they develop and express their conscientiousness even as they foster authentic, reflective conscientiousness in their children.[1] But even these mothers may limit their own and their children's efforts of authentic reflection, delegating authority for decisions about collective defense and aggression to leaders and authorities. When mothers practiced in domestic nonviolence do take an active part in public deliberation, they cannot be counted on to articulate publicly, let alone to extend and act upon, their ways of understanding and resolving conflict. The discourses of diplomacy and militarism are culturally dominant and inimical to many variants of maternal thinking. Even mothers who experience a cognitive dissonance between maternal and political thinking may find that they cannot speak, and certainly cannot be heard, in a maternal voice.

Many mothers will find no dissonance between military and maternal commitments. Mothering begins in typically passionate loyalty to one's own children and the people they live among. Even as mothers have to learn to appreciate the sufferings and respect the provocative, uncontrolled willfulness of children, they also have to *learn* to respect the wills and minds and appreciate the suffering of adults outside and sometimes alien to their circle. In times of "peace", simple exhaustion or ignorance can prevent mothers from seeing, let alone responding to the needs, pain, even to the reality of distant or different stranger-mothers. Unless racism is identified and actively combatted, fairly benign maternal parochialism is transformed into bigotry by greed or fear. Moreover, mothers who worry over treating each child respectfully, without sacrificing the needs of one to the well being of another, have no compunction about accepting unjust divisions of resources that benefit all their children.

These ordinary liabilities of mothering in times of peace are magnified by real and advertised dangers of war. Government officials whose dictates are routinely accepted become Leaders and Defenders, bulwarks against fear. Violence is legitimated by and

---

[1]See my *Maternal Thinking, op. cit.*, Chapter 5.

fuels habits of racism. Greed and privilege on the one hand, bitter deprivation on the other, obscure the real sufferings and attachments of the other mothers. One person's children are set against another's. In particular, in most battles, late adolescent men (and sometimes women) of one's own country suffer an extended maternal protection—these are "our boys"—"we" love, arm, and support them. The soldier-sons of the enemy, by contrast, are taken to exemplify the malignant masculinity, the swaggering brutality, that feminists in other contexts have seen as a consequence of war's masculine ideology.

There is, to be sure, a literary and historical record of maternal identification with "other" mothers and their children—including those of the "enemy". Despite the pull of parochial loyalty, fear, and distorting fantasy, at least some mothers can see in "other" and "enemy" mothers a real, particular, variant of the passionate attachments and connections that determine the shape of their own lives. In Argentina and Chile, mothers (*madres*) who suffered quite particular and brutal assault against their children came in the course of protest to identify with children who suffered the violence of tyranny and poverty. In Israel and its occupied territories, Palestinian and Israeli women work together to create conditions of peace for their peoples. These and many other movements of women in resistance express the active responsibility and cross-cultural compassion on which public maternal nonviolence will depend.[1]

It is clear that *some* mothers can extend, tentatively and imperfectly, the difficult disciplines of the nonviolence they have practiced. Even if peacemaking mothers cannot themselves translate their daily principles into public action, maternal practice and thinking might offer to people who are already anti-militarist a useful example of ordinary peacemaking. Yet even a committed and mother-respecting anti-militarist will not find it easy to extend the principles of domestic maternal nonviolence to public conflict.

---

[1] I wrote about the Madres in *Maternal Thinking, op. cit.,* Chapter 8. Of the Israeli movements, I am most familiar with "Women in Black," although during the recent war I learned from Israeli and Palestinian women of other women's peace groups. Movements of women in resistance may not be explicitly maternalist but, given the association of women and mothering, these groups usually draw upon and also redefine cultural meanings of maternal responsibility.

Paradoxically, one difficulty in taking mothering easily is the ease of imagining, on the model of mothering, more successful strategies of disarmament and far less violent ways of settling disputes. (It is embarrassingly easy to do this in the recent Gulf war even if one suppresses any memory of events before August 2, 1990.) Yet if imagining peace 'maternally' is all-too-easy, it is also, in the absence of mothering power, all-too-difficult.

Maternal nonviolence depends upon *mothers*—people with real power committed to self-restraint. Most state governments and their leaders are not bad mothers—they are not mothers at all: they are not even initially committed to relationships whose success is measured by their *inability* to dominate or their ability to sustain relationships with citizens and neighbor states alive with their own histories and desires. Indeed, if governments were compared to mothers, then many of them would be figures of a child's nightmare. These "mothers" use their powers in mystifying ways, prey upon their "children's" greed and fear, arm and train them to hurt and be hurt, command their obedience, punish conscientiousness, and then declare themselves ready to terrorize and injure if they can assert their "will" in no other way.

Nor is war only the creation of governments. Peacemakers cannot, as mothers must, depend upon loving enough "children"— citizens who, despite intense jealousy and rage, can be cajoled into making peace. The current obsession with media presentations of war suggests that, if only the workings of diplomacy and battle were spelled out, citizen-subjects would also prove "loving enough" to reject militarism. But even when all the pictures and reports are in, it may be that too many people want war—or at least they want, more than peace, the territory, resources, control, national glory, community solidarity and moral self-righteousness that war promises and sometimes delivers. Even those who reject war may not value or retain a capacity for conscientiousness, when, without the protection of maternal conscience or power, they are subject to governments that reward obedience and punish "objection".

Anti-militarists who want to politicize maternal nonviolence will have to create *new* ways of thinking and of relating to subjects and neighbors that do not depend on anything like maternal will or child-like compliance. They will then have to devise strategies for inserting politicized maternal conceptions into a public discourse which has simultaneously taken mothers' thinking for granted and disdained it. Both conceptual creation and political strategy will depend upon many more mothers presenting themselves—and thereby representing mothering—as resistant, insistent instruments of peace.

I cannot, as I would like, write optimistically of mothers becoming peaceful or of maternal peacefulness achieving political change. I will nonetheless end, as mothers often learn to do, on a note of hope. Nonviolent mothering offers one construction of power which refuses domination, respects bodily, willful life, yet does not let evil stand. Hence, often enough, mothering expresses, and perhaps can come to symbolize, the new forms of "wish and responsibility" which a "fierce and human peace" will require. This particular model of nonviolence originates in everyday life where, also, fantasies and experiences of violence originate. Many women and men, to a greater or lesser degree, are mothers. Most people have at least one mother whose practice—in its degrees of nonviolence and violence—was enacted upon their bodily spirit at its most vulnerable. Anyone who is willing to listen attentively and realistically to maternal nonviolence at work can learn its lessons Mothering is surely only one of many ordinary practices that offers hints of peace and of the price of its violation. Given the pervasiveness of warism and the multiple costs of war, peacemakers can ill afford competition amongst themselves for best peacemaker. It is enough if mothering is a practice whose ubiquity and emotional potency makes it one distinctly valuable resource for peace.

Eugene Lang College, The New School for Social Research

⑨ The Morality
of Nonviolence

Robert L. Holmes

The past century has witnessed a gradual awakening to the power of nonviolence. Models of nonviolent commitment have emerged in disparate parts of the world. These include Tolstoy in Russia, Gandhi in India, Martin Luther King, Jr. in the United States and, more recently, Mubarak Awad in the Middle East and the Dalai Lama in the Far East. But this awakening has not been confined to a few remarkable individuals. Thousands of ordinary persons have turned to nonviolent action as well: in Scandinavia during World War II, the U.S. during the civil rights era, the Philippines during its revolution, and in Poland, China, Czechoslovakia, the West Bank, the Baltic republics, and the Ukraine in the dramatic events of the 1980s and early 1990s.

Some of this nonviolence has been spontaneous. Some of it has been expedient. And some of it has been tainted with violence. But all of it is part of the historical unfolding of an empowering way of dealing with conflict, and beyond that, of living and being in the modern world.

Viewed in one light, nonviolent action—particularly concerted action by large numbers of people—is simply the exercise of power. It is power that employs different means than are involved in the use of force. Rather than trying to prevail by marshalling greater force than than one's opponent, it seeks to undermine the bases of an opponent's power. Governments, armies, occupying forces and institutions of any sort that control and regulate people's lives require the cooperation, or at least the acquiescence, of large numbers of people. Withdraw that cooperation and the foundations

*Earlier versions of this paper were presented at a conference, "The Ethics of Nonviolence," in Moscow, USSR, November 27-29, 1989; the national meeting of Concerned Philosophers for Peace, University of Notre Dame, September 21-23, 1990; and the University of Missouri, October 29, 1990.

of such power crumble. Nonviolence studies techniques by which to do that. These techniques require studying with as much care as traditionally has gone into the study of violence and warfare. As important as it is to understand the practical side of nonviolence, however, it is important to understand the theoretical dimensions as well. This is needed in the interests of clarity. It is also needed to understand whether nonviolence can be justified, and if so, in what ways. It is enough for some that nonviolence often works as a tactic. It is enough for others that it can be used when weapons are unavailable. It is enough for still others that it makes a useful supplement to the standard methods of violence. But for some, nonviolence represents a deeper commitment. It represents a commitment to remainnonviolent even when this or that tactic fails, and even when weapons of violence are available. It is nonviolence in this sense that I propose to examine. My aim will be primarily clarificatory. I shall map out the different ways of understanding nonviolence. But I shall also try to show how I believe nonviolence can most plausibly be defended as a moral position.

Let me begin by locating the moral concern within the broader perspective of a philosophy of nonviolence.

The Philosophy of Nonviolence

A philosophy of nonviolence may simply describe and elucidate nonviolence. Or it may instead, or in addition, propose and defend its adoption. That is, it may be normative or non-normative. I shall examine nonviolence understood to be normative in this sense.

Now sometimes nonviolentists (as I shall call advocates of nonviolence) say that while *they* ought to be nonviolent, others must choose for themselves. Thus they refrain from prescribing nonviolence for others. This represents a common and important position. But it is not the one I want to examine. I want to examine nonviolence understood to be a moral position with an interpersonal character to it—that is, as a position meant for others as well as oneself.[1]

---

[1] It is important at the outset to distinguish nonviolence from pacifism. Pacifism is opposition to war, nonviolence opposition to violence. While one cannot be a nonviolentist without being a

Moreover, nonviolence as an interpersonal position may be held on either moral or nonmoral grounds. I shall call the former, *Principled nonviolence*, the latter, *Pragmatic nonviolence*. Moreover, principled nonviolence may tell us either to *be* certain sorts of persons, or to *act* certain sorts of ways, or both. It may tell us, in short, to be nonviolent and/or to act nonviolently. In the first case, it belongs to the ethics of virtue; in the second, to the ethics of conduct. These distinctions can be represented as follows:

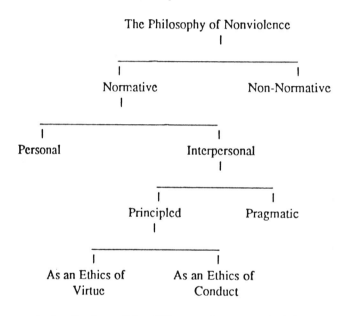

The Philosophy of Nonviolence

Normative — Non-Normative

Personal — Interpersonal

Principled — Pragmatic

As an Ethics of Virtue — As an Ethics of Conduct

What are the implications of the differences between principled and pragmatic nonviolence?

It is tempting to say that pragmatic nonviolence stresses consequences, whereas principled nonviolence does not. But this is not necessarily so. Just as morality may emphasize consequences (as in utilitarianism), so may principled nonviolence. Whether it does so depends upon the overall moral position of which it is a part. If

pacifist, one can be a pacifist without being a nonviolentist. One can, that is, oppose warfare without necessarily opposing other modes of violence (such as in personal self-defense, or by the police, or in the form of capital punishment).

that position is consequentialist, it will assign as much weight to consequences as does pragmatic nonviolence; if it is nonconsequentialist, it will not.

It is also tempting to say that pragmatic nonviolence values effectiveness in achieving social and political ends, whereas principled nonviolence does not. But this, too, need not be so. To be concerned with effectiveness is to be concerned with achieving ends, goals, and purposes. And this concern typically characterizes principled nonviolence as well as pragmatic nonviolence. Any of the ends of pragmatic nonviolence can become ends of principled nonviolence, provided they have a moral justification. This was the case with some of the better-known uses of principled nonviolence by Gandhi and King.

Finally, it is tempting to say that principled nonviolence renounces violence in all conceivable circumstances, whereas pragmatic nonviolence does not. But once again, this is not necessarily so. *Absolute* nonviolence renounces violence in all conceivable circumstances.[1] But conditional nonviolence does not. It allows there are conceivable circumstances—whether ever realized in the world or not—in which it would be permissible to use violence. Pragmatic nonviolence is conditional in this sense. It advocates nonviolence to the extent that it "works." It may consider violence permissible or even necessary when nonviolence fails. On the other hand, principled nonviolence, held conditionally, concedes there may be hypothetical circumstances in which violence would be justified. But it contends these are rarely, if ever, actually realized.[2] This reflects a difference in the ends or goals of the two approaches. Pragmatic nonviolence typically has social, political or national goals. Principled nonviolence may have, either in addition to or instead of these, broader moral ends, like promoting a certain way of life, maximizing value, or showing reverence for life. Its concern, we might say, is with moral effectiveness rather than merely practical effectiveness.

---

[1]The ancient Jains came as close as anyone to holding nonviolence in this absolutistic way.

[2]Gandhi clearly was a conditional nonviolentist of this sort. He maintained that if the choice were between violence and cowardice, one might better choose violence.

There is, clearly, a sharp distinction between absolute and conditional nonviolence. Hence there will be a sharp distinction between principled and pragmatic nonviolence when the former is held absolutistically. But when principled nonviolence is held conditionally, the difference between it and pragmatic nonviolence will be one of degree (just as the difference between a conditional nonviolentist and someone who rejects nonviolence but thinks violence is justified in only a narrow range of cases will also be one of degree).[1] In practice, principled nonviolence opposes violence in a broader range of (actual and hypothetical) cases than does pragmatic nonviolence. And it opposes them on moral and not simply social or political grounds.

Both will maintain that nonviolence has a justification. But for principled nonviolence that justification will be moral, whereas for pragmatic nonviolence it will be social, political, economic, nationalistic, etc. For principled nonviolence, it is necessary and sufficient for the final justification of nonviolence that it be justified from the moral point of view. For pragmatic nonviolence it is not. An important consequence follows from this. It is that whereas principled nonviolence cannot (knowingly, at least) be used for immoral ends,[2] pragmatic nonviolence can. It is an instrument which is neutral in and of itself. It can be used by the wicked as well as by the good.

This latter consideration brings us, however, to the question of what exactly nonviolence says. The first task here is to locate it in the broader context of types of normative theory.

Interactive and Reactive Conduct

Two areas of conduct are of concern to ethical theory. The first is the normal interactions among people in everyday life. The second is people's response to wrongdoing, either against

---

[1] I am drawing these distinctions along roughly the same lines as in my "Violence and Nonviolence," in Jerome A. Shaffer ed., *Violence* (New York: David McKay, 1971), pp. 103-135.

[2] As Gandhi said of his nonviolent method, Satyagraha, "There can be no Satyagraha in an unjust cause." M.K. Gandhi, *Non-Violent Resistance* (New York: Schocken Books, 1951), p. 56.

themselves or against others. The first we may call interactive conduct, the second reactive.

Nonviolence in its interpersonal dimension tends to be concerned with reactive conduct. It proposes an alternative to violence when one confronts those who threaten violence, or who engage in wrongdoing of a more general nature. It may also say something about how we should act in the normal course of our lives—when, that is, we are engaged in interactive conduct. But this will be only when it takes the form of principled nonviolence. Pragmatic nonviolence, as I am understanding that term, does not presume to tell people what constitutes good or proper conduct in their everyday lives. It presumes only to show them a practical alternative to violence when confronted by violence, injustice, or oppression. Nonviolence held only as a purely personal commitment, which makes no claim that others should be nonviolent as well, may govern either interactive or reactive conduct, or both.

I shall in what follows confine my attention to nonviolence as a moral position with an interpersonal character, that is, to principled nonviolence. Specifically, I want to ask whether it is possible to formulate a morality of nonviolence that is clear, coherent and plausible.

The Scope of Nonviolence in Governing Conduct

Notice at the outset that virtually any moral theory, if it describes normal conduct in an ideal world, would describe it as nonviolent. With the exception of those few who extol violence for its own sake, everyone believes the world would be better off if individuals and nations renounced violence.

This suggests that nonviolence is problematic only in a world in which some people are violent and others are not. Does nonviolence remain plausible for such a world (which, of course, fits the description of the actual world)? There are several possible objections to supposing that it does. The first is largely theoretical, the others substantive.

The theoretical objection holds that because nonviolence is negative in character, it cannot provide a positive guide to conduct in general. And if it fails to do that, it cannot provide an adequate moral position.

The point here is that nonviolence is defined negatively by reference to what it rejects rather than by reference to anything it is for. So, even if we should accept nonviolence, it would at most provide us with only limited guidance. It would tell us only to refrain from violence in circumstances in which we might otherwise be tempted to resort to it. But most of our interactions with others occur in circumstances in which violence would be pointless and counterproductive. Therefore no decision need be made about whether to use it. Nonviolence provides us with no guidance in these circumstances, which make up by far the largest part of ordinary lives.

It may be, of course, that nonviolence is held as a rule or principle. If it is held as one principle among others, or as a rule which presupposes a more basic principle, it would not presume to cover the whole of morality. It would apply only to the area of conduct involving conflict or dispute. Hence this objection would merely point out what is conceded in advance.

But the objection has some force against certain ways of understanding nonviolence. Even if nonviolence is presumed to govern the whole of conduct, if it is understood simply as the principled renunciation of physical violence, it would indeed leave unspecified how we should act throughout most of our lives. It would not preclude the possibility that we could be nonviolent and still treat people badly. This is because physical violence is only one mode of violence. There is psychological violence as well. We can insult, humiliate, degrade, demean, and oppress people; treat them unkindly, unfairly and unjustly; and cause them untold physical and psychological harm—without resorting to physical violence against them. A theory which prohibits only physical violence could claim at best to represent only a part, not the whole, of a plausible moral position.

A fuller conception of nonviolence, however, extends to these other sorts of conduct as well. Even if we understand nonviolence negatively as opposition to violence, we still need to distinguish psychological violence from physical violence. To commit oneself to nonviolence in this fuller sense is to commit oneself to renouncing all of the subtle as well as the overt ways of causing mental harm. Racism and sexism often cause their greatest harms not through physical violence, but through the systematic destruction of self-esteem through subtle psychological devices that are not fully understood or even consciously adopted by those who use them. The sort of fuller commitment to nonviolence of which I am speaking requires cultivating a sensitivity to the countless ways in which language, practices, and social institutions can *do violence* to people even while not using physical violence against them.

More than that, nonviolence may, as I mentioned earlier, ask that we strive to *be* certain sorts of persons as well as that we *act* certain ways. The Jains maintain that we should be nonviolent not only in action and speech, but in thought as well. One can fail to do this if one is committed only to nonviolence in the narrow sense, which renounces physical violence alone. For without ever using physical violence one can still be judgmental, manipulative, unfair and unkind. And one can harbor ill-will toward others, and think unkindly of them, even if one does not outwardly treat them in these ways. In this way nonviolence may be understood to be, at least in part, an *ethics of virtue* as well as an ethics of conduct.

It will be useful, in light of this, to distinguish two different forms of principled nonviolence: *Minimal Nonviolence,* which renounces only physical violence; and *Maximal Nonviolence,* which renounces all violence, physical and psychological. Although either form could advocate the development of the appropriate traits of character as well as the performance of the appropriate actions, Maximal Nonviolence lends itself most readily to becoming an ethics of virtue. It will be either an ethics of conduct or an ethics of virtue depending upon whether it requires only that we be nonviolent in our conduct, or requires also that we be nonviolent persons.

Now, the objection that nonviolence is inadequate as a comprehensive moral position because it does not provide guidance for the whole of life is valid against Minimal Nonviolence. But it is not, I suggest, valid against Maximal Nonviolence. For the nonviolentist can maintain that if we remain nonviolent in *all* that we do (i.e. in situations pertaining to psychological as well as to physical violence), and particularly if we strive to be nonviolent in thought and speech as well as conduct, then whatever we otherwise do in our interactions with others will be permissible. Nonviolence in this maximalist sense does govern all of our life. Once we satisfy its requirements, we may in other respects act as we choose towards others. Even though I have stated it negatively, it has, for all practical purposes, a positive content. It tells us to *be nonviolent.*

This, I suggest, answers the theoretical objection. But another objection needs considering, even against nonviolence understood in this fuller sense. It grows out of the ambivalence some people feel toward nonviolence and pacifism.

Nonviolence and the Defense of the Innocent

On the one hand, many people regard nonviolence as admirable. That some people should never resort to violence strikes them as extraordinary. Such people are often regarded as saintly. It also strikes many people as admirable, if a little strange, that some people should not only refrain from using violence to get their way with others, but should also refuse to use it even in self-defense; that they should be willing to suffer ill-treatment, harm and even death rather than do unto others what others do unto them.

On the other hand, many people consider it contemptible that anyone would stand by while innocent persons are attacked, beaten and perhaps killed, refusing to assist them merely because that would be to resort to violence. And on a larger scale, it is considered contemptible to refuse to sanction the use of violence by oppressed peoples to resist or overthrow oppressive colonial or totalitarian regimes, even if one does not engage in the violence oneself. It is one thing, they say, to refuse to defend yourself if attacked; it is another to refuse to defend others, particularly the innocent, or to approve the use of violence in national defense or for national liberation.

I consider this a serious objection. Before responding to it, however, I want to examine a closely related objection.

Keeping One's Hands Clean

Sometimes this objection is put in the following way: The nonviolentist (and the pacifist, for as I say, this objection is frequently brought against pacifists as well), it contends, does not want to dirty his hands. He is more concerned with his own moral purity than with the lives and well-being of others. So long as *he* refuses to kill or use violence, he is satisfied, even if this means letting others suffer and die. He keeps his hands clean at their expense.

This objection may be understood in either of two ways. It may mean that to refuse to use violence to help others is wrong, and to do this simply out of revulsion at killing or using violence is cowardly. If this is how the objection is understood, then it is just another way of making the first objection, and it will be covered by what I say later. But the objection can be taken in another way. It may mean that the nonviolentist keeps his hands clean in the sense of refusing to do anything wrong. On this understanding, the objection *concedes* it is wrong to kill and use violence even in defense of others. But at the same time it implicitly maintains that sometimes one must do what is wrong; in some situations it is necessary. To keep one's hands morally clean by refusing to do wrong even to help others betrays a self-righteous preoccupation with one's own moral purity.

Understood in this way, the objection, I suggest, is either incoherent or it advocates immorality. If the point is that sometimes it is morally right to do what, by hypothesis, is morally wrong, then the objection is incoherent. If it is wrong ever to resort to violence, and one does so in defense of others, it cannot at the same time be right to do so. If, however, the point is that it is wrong to kill even in defense of the innocent but sometimes one should do so anyway, then the position expressly advocates wrongdoing, hence arguably is immoral.   Theoretically, of course, one might contend that violence in these cases is necessitated by other considerations (the justifiers of violence, at least since the time of Augustine, appeal to an unexplicated conception of "necessity" allegedly operating here). These considerations might be those of self-interest or national interest. But they might also be such considerations as those of sympathy, compassion, caring and love. The claim would then be that, when considerations of these sorts conflict with what morality prescribes, they override morality. This represents a problematic metaethical claim. Whether it can be rendered plausible there is not space to examine here. The objection still reduces to the judgment that in these situations we should act immorally. And so it does not constitute an objection to nonviolence understood as claiming that the morally correct thing to do is to refrain from violence.

Consistency and the Defense of the Innocent

So let us return to the first objection. It does not concede that it is wrong to use violence on behalf of the innocent. To the contrary, it says it is wrong *not* to do so. Nonviolentists do not keep their hands morally clean by refusing to use violence; they keep their hands clean only by aiding the innocent, even if that means dirtying their hands with the blood of the guilty and sometimes that of the innocent as well. This objection lies at the heart of the assessment of nonviolence as a moral position. To respond to it fully would require a more comprehensive explication and defense of nonviolence than I am able to undertake here. But we may take note of several points relevant to assessing the objection.

Sometimes it is said in support of the view expressed in the objection that the very concerns which prohibit violence sometimes mandate it, such as when it is necessary protect the innocent.

This is maintained by Jan Narveson and Paul Ramsey, and is at least implied, in somewhat different form, more recently by Nel Noddings.[1] Ramsey argues from a Christian perspective. He contends that the very love which prohibits killing requires that in some circumstances one be prepared to kill lest many more innocent persons die. Narveson argues that the pacifist's very opposition to violence (he characterizes the nonviolentist as a pacifist) should compel him to resort to violence when it is the only way to prevent the violation of rights. Noddings contends that caring for persons may require killing in defense of self or others so long as caring itself is not endangered. Narveson's argument in particular is complex, and there is not space to do justice to it here. I merely want to note that all three positions have one thing in common: they maintain (Ramsey and Noddings implicitly, Narveson

---

[1] See Jan Narveson, "Pacifism: A Philosophical Analysis," *Ethics* Vol. 75, 1965, pp. 259-271; and "Violence and War," in Tom Regan (ed.), *Matters of Life and Death: New Introductory Essays in Moral Philosophy* (New York: Random House, 1980), pp. 117-128; Nel Noddings, *Caring: A Feminine Approach to Ethics and Moral Education* (Berkeley: University of California Press, 1984), pp. 100-101; Paul Ramsey, The Just War: Force and Political Responsibility (Lanham, MD: University Press of America, 1983), pp. 150-151.

explicitly) that the strength of one's commitment to something (love, caring, or nonviolence) should lead one to do the very thing normally prohibited by that commitment in circumstances in which that is the only way to prevent those things from being done by others. Ramsey and Noddings accept this as part of the understanding of love and caring respectively. Narveson contends it shows why pacifism (nonviolence) is incoherent, since it reveals the manner in which pacifists' opposition to violence commits them to using it in certain circumstances.

But this is implausible. If I am a teetotaler, it is not a test of the strength of my commitment to abstain from alcohol that I be prepared to drink some in order to prevent others from drinking. And if I am a vegetarian, my commitment to refrain from eating meat does not require that I be prepared to eat some if that is the only way to prevent others from doing so. The measure of my commitment not to do something (whether it is to refrain from drinking alcohol, eating meat, killing, or using violence) is whether *I* consistently refrain from doing it. If, in addition, I believe others should do likewise—that is, if I hold this as interpersonally binding and not merely as a personal commitment—then my initial commitment (to refrain *personally* from doing these things) limits what I may do to oppose the doing of those things by others. Although it is true that if my commitment to renounce violence compelled me to engage in it in certain circumstances, my position would be inconsistent, it is false that such a commitment in fact compels me to engage in such conduct.

This, however, even if correct, does not altogether meet the original objection. It does not show that there is not something reprehensible about refraining from saving the innocent when one does so because saving them would require using violence. What it shows is that the preceding attempts to explain why it is wrong fail.

It should be noted before proceeding that nonviolentists need not stand passively by while innocent people are assaulted or the nation attacked. It is always open to them to resist nonviolently. Gandhi's followers at times insinuated themselves between assailant and victim in the bloodshed between Muslims and Hindus, absorbing the blows themselves. And on a national scale, there is a growing movement in various countries today to promote the idea of nonviolent national defense (or Civilian-Based Defense, as it is sometimes called). It is not my aim here to detail the various techniques one might use at the personal, social, or international levels to try to defuse the threat of violence or to minimize harm once it has commenced; this has been admirably done by Gene Sharp and others. My aim is only to point out that nonviolence as understood by most of its recent practitioners is not passive but active. It cannot simply be assumed that in the many kinds of circumstances in which one might be positioned to intervene to try to prevent violence against the innocent, nonviolent methods would not be as effective as, or sometimes more effective than, violent methods. That is a factual question which can only be answered empirically.

Suppose, however, we confine ourselves to cases in which, by hypothesis, violence would save the innocent and nonviolence would not. It is easy to conceive of such cases. And critics of nonviolence can focus directly upon them. (One could also consider cases in the past where violence succeeded in saving the innocent and then speculate about whether nonviolence could have done so as well; and while these deserve as much attention as purely hypothetical cases, I shall not try to go into them here.)

The problem with hypothetical cases of this sort is that they distill out certain salient features of a situation and selectively exclude others. Unless one is able to assess all of the relevant features, it is difficult to say with justifiable confidence what the morally correct course would be.

Take the case of an assailant and an innocent child. To stipulate that the child is innocent is to say only that it is free of wrongdoing. It is not to say that it would remain so forever. It does not preclude the possibility that it might grow up to be a mass murderer, a serial rapist, or another Hitler. From a consequentialist or utilitarian perspective, these are relevant considerations. By the same token, those who advance cases like this presume that the assailant is guilty. But need that be so? What if the assailant has been confronted with the choice of either killing this one innocent child or allowing 10 or 100 or 1,000 innocent children to die? Perhaps as a good utilitarian he has concluded with great regret that he must kill the child. To rule this out we would need to specify that he is not a utilitarian, or that utilitarianism does not have this consequence, or that the agent is not confronted with a choice of that sort. Or, to introduce some deontological considerations, perhaps there is a God, and the assailant believes that whatever God commands is right. And perhaps further, as with Abraham, the child is the potential assailant's son, and the assailant has been commanded by God to sacrifice his son.

To extract the conclusion the critic wants would require tailoring the example so that virtually all considerations that would support anything other than violent intervention have been expressly excluded. The potential assailant might have to be described as not only guilty, but guilty beyond redemption; the child as not only innocent, but destined to remain so. Countervailing consequentialist and deontological considerations would have to be selectively eliminated.

Now, one can do this. One can stipulate anything one wants in hypothetical examples. But to do this risks designing question-begging assumptions into the example which virtually entail the conclusion one wants. If one characterizes the example in such a way as to leave no *conceivable* circumstances in which it would be right to refrain from violence to save the innocent, one refutes at most only those nonviolentists who hold their position in absolutistic form (I say "at most," because even this will not refute absolutists who doggedly insist that killing is wrong in all conceivable circumstances, for they will simply disregard all the additional considerations the critic brings to bear, no matter what they are).

If, on the other hand, one leaves some conceptual space in which it would be right to use violence, and constructs an example to conform to the assumptions defining that space, conditional nonviolentists will concede the example. They will simply contend that there are no such cases in the actual world, or so few as not to undermine a general commitment to nonviolence. And they will insist that they subscribe to nonviolence as a guide to conduct in the world as we know it, not as it might be in philosophers' imaginations. The question then will be whether cases of that sort are ever in fact encountered, or are at all likely to be encountered, in ordinary life.

This is not to say that hypothetical counter-examples cannot sometimes be effective. They can. If they remain faithful to the assumptions framing the nonviolentist's commitment to nonviolence, and at the same time highlight a dimension of that commitment he has overlooked—whether in the way of possible consequences, or in the way of what he is prepared to concede are relevant deontological considerations—they may lead him to reconsider or even abandon his position. They can, in other words, be effective against a position that is inconsistent or ill-thought-out. But otherwise they cannot.

The Commitment to Conditional Nonviolence

It is a conditional nonviolence that I want to propose as the most plausible candidate for a moral position. Expressed as a principle, it says: One ought always to act nonviolently. This will be understood to preclude both physical and psychological violence. But it may also be understood to require that we strive to be nonviolent persons, meaning that we strive to incorporate nonviolence into thought and speech as well as action, to make it a part of our very character. Aristotle says that virtue requires not only performing the right acts, but choosing them in knowledge for themselves, and in such a way that the choice proceeds from a firm and unchanging character. So, we may say, *being nonviolent* requires not just performing nonviolent actions, but doing so because they are nonviolent (and not just out of expediency) and in a way that naturally flows from a nonviolent character. In other words, nonviolence as a principle belonging to the ethics of conduct may prescribe the cultivation of the kind of character belonging to an ethics of virtue.

The distinguishing feature of nonviolence understood in this way lies in its recognition of the limitations of our knowledge in situations of conflict. This is a point stressed by Gandhi, in his method of Satyagraha. The resort to violence presumes that one knows one is dealing with willful wrongdoers and that one's own position is righteous. We rarely know this in complex social, political and international situations involving large numbers of people. We can only make estimates of varying degrees of probability regarding where the truth lies. Given the limited nature of our knowledge of right and wrong in such situations, we have two choices. On the one hand, we can assume that because we cannot be certain where the truth lies, we should act on the presumption that the best course lies in following conventional morality. We should then abide by the laws of the state or by the customs and practices of peoples. This, in effect, is the course taken by St. Augustine. He recognizes that since sin is a corruption of the soul, and we can never be certain from a person's actions alone whether he or she sins (only God can know that), we do best to abide by the rules that preserve the social and political order. This is a conservative position which favors the status quo. Gandhi, on the other hand, and in certain respects Tolstoy before him and Martin Luther King, Jr., after him, see this epistemological condition as requiring a a new *methodology*. We need a manner of dealing with others which enables us to stand by our own convictions regarding what is best in the situation, while at the same time acknowledging that we may be mistaken; which enables us to stand by our belief in the injustice of our adversary, while allowing that we may be mistaken about that as well. The aim, then, becomes to find the truth. Prevailing over the other is not the objective. Nothing morally worthwhile is gained if you prevail but were wrong to do so. One strives to engage the other in a way that maximizes the possibility that the truth will eventually emerge, whatever it may be, and whomever it may favor.

It is this which, on the view I am proposing, dictates the commitment to nonviolence. For you cannot justifiably kill other people at the same time you acknowledge that they may be acting with a significant measure of the truth whose realization it is your aim to foster. Killing closes off the possibilities for such realization. You must engage opponents only in ways sanctioned by the search for truth. This represents a different way for the nonviolentist from the one chosen by Augustine and most Christians since his time. It means that one must often go, not only against custom and practice, but against law itself. This inevitably brings the nonviolentist into conflict with the state. It is not surprising that Tolstoy, as thoroughgoing a nonviolentist as one finds in Western thought, is led to anarchism, and that Gandhi moves decidedly in that direction. For the state by its nature regulates conduct by force and violence. It holds the threat of punishment over its citizens for failing to do what it decrees or for doing what it prohibits. And when its conflicts with other states are severe enough, it resorts to war. Typically it coerces its citizenry to do the killing and dying which that entails. The *consistent and thoroughgoing* nonviolentist, as Tolstoy saw, will be an anarchist.

Finally, one further aspect of nonviolence needs emphasizing. It requires asking what the harm is we seek to avoid when acting nonviolently. What harm does violence cause that leads the nonviolentist to oppose it by others (including its manifestations in social, political and economic systems) and to renounce it in one's own conduct?

There are, of course, the harms of physical and psychological violence already mentioned. But perhaps equally important is the moral harm suffered by wrongdoers in oppressing others, killing them, or destroying their possessions. Nonviolence seeks to engage wrongdoers in a way which shows a regard for their moral, physical and psychological well-being as well as for that of their victims. When Gandhi's followers stepped between assailants and victims in the Muslim/Hindu clashes mentioned earlier, they did so as much to prevent the assailants from becoming murderers as they did to protect the victims. There is a long philosophical tradition, from Socrates and the Stoics through Augustine and Kant, which holds that the only real harm (or in Kant's case, the worst harm) that can befall one is corruption of the will. Others can deprive you of possessions and even life. But only you can make yourself morally corrupt. And that is a worse harm than anything others can inflict upon you.

Thus, when we rightly condemn the injustice of Apartheid in South Africa, perhaps we should do so as much because of its effects upon the oppressing white minority as because of its more conspicuous effects upon the oppressed black majority. Or when we express concern about Israeli treatment of Palestinians in the occupied territories, perhaps we should do so as much because of its brutalizing effect upon young Israeli soldiers as upon the Palestinians injured or killed in the process. When we deplore the tragedies of Vietnam and Afghanistan, perhaps we should do so because of the effects upon the surviving American and Soviet soldiers as well as because of the suffering of the Vietnamese and Afghan people. Violence can sometimes put a stop to wrongdoing. It can kill or disable the wrongdoer. Or drive him off in fear. But it rarely produces the conditions under which he confronts the true nature of his acts and freely chooses to turn away from them (and when it does so, it usually does so incidentally, and not as part of one's intention in dealing with him). Principled nonviolence can do that. It does not always succeed. But in seeking the best solution in each situation of conflict, it weighs into the scales the physical, psychological, and moral well-being of all of the persons involved.

Understood in this way, principled nonviolence differs from most of the standard ethical theories in one important respect. Most of them (Kantianism, Utilitarianism, Egoism, etc.) leave largely unchallenged the basic structures of society: the police, courts, prisons, economies, armies and war systems of modern states. Nonviolence asks us to reconsider all of these. It asks us to reflect upon whether they hinder rather than help us to move to a higher plane of moral conduct than humankind has previously achieved. It asks us to seek new and creative ways to relate to others; to consider that the capacities for good and moral growth that we share with all peoples are ultimately of more importance than the divisions of race, sex, class, religion and nationality that separate us. In short, it projects a vision of a new world and asks us to join together in trying to create it.

University of Rochester

Part II

Nuclear Deterrence
and Deterrence Discourse

Introduction to Part II:
Nuclear Deterrence and Deterrence Discourse

Richard Werner

The first three articles in Part II attempt to reveal the consequences of particular deterrence policies and, thereby, to determine the morality and rationality of these policies. Such thinking represents a consequentialist approach to morality and rationality, for it is solely the value of the foreseeable consequences of an action which determines the rightness or correctness of that action. Hence, if deterrence policy produces more good than harm, the ends justify the means, and deterrence is justified. If it produces more harm than good, then the ends do not justify the means, and deterrence is not justified.

Many opponents of nuclear deterrence subscribe to a version of the following argument.

1. If the threat to use nuclear weapons fails to prevent the other from launching nuclear weapons, then nuclear deterrence policy fails and produces catastrophe.
2. Since deterrent threats are bound to fail at some future time, nuclear deterrence policy will eventually fail and produce catastrophe.
3. Therefore, nuclear deterrence policy ought to be abandoned for it threatens inevitable failure and catastrophe.

While many who defend deterrence policy question the second premise, Jonathan Schonsheck challenges the first premise of this argument. Even if deterrent threats eventually fail and nuclear war ensues, it is possible that no alternative nuclear weapons policy—including the policy of unilateral disarmament—would have proven superior to nuclear deterrence policy. If catastrophe occurs regardless of the policy we pursue, then nuclear deterrence policy cannot be singled out as a failure simply because it leads to catastrophe. Accordingly, those who assert the aforementioned · argument against nuclear deterrence policy are left in the unenviable

and difficult position of establishing that nuclear catastrophe could •
have been avoided, if we had not pursued a policy of nuclear
deterrence.

Such a position is unenviable because it rests on the
counterfactual claim that "Nuclear war would have been avoided, if
we had not pursued a policy of nuclear deterrence" which sounds
suspiciously like: "Hitler would have been victorious in World War
II, if Nazi Germany had invaded England" or "I would have been a
great rock star, if I had spent as much time playing guitar as I spent
studying philosophy." Defending such claims is difficult just
because they seem to rest primarily on opinion rather than fact. If
Schonsheck has successfully shifted the burden of proof in this
manner, then the defender of the aforementioned argument cannot
legitimately claim that nuclear deterrence policy fails because the
deterrent threat fails, even when nuclear war erupts .

Philosophers who find nuclear deterrence acceptable and those
who do not both tend to concentrate their attention on counterforce
deterrence (i.e., the targeting of the other's nuclear weapons and
military centers). Steven Lee directs his attention to countervalue
or finite deterrence (i.e., the targeting of the other's population
centers).

Lee, following others, indicates that there are two types of
stability in deterrence theory. If a nuclear power possesses the
ability to destroy the other's nuclear arsenal in a first-strike, it might
under crisis conditions be willing to initiate war, while the other,
fearing under crisis conditions that it might be attacked, would be
tempted to initiate its own preemptive attack. Crisis stability is the
consequentialist advantage that finite deterrence possesses in
comparison with counterforce deterrence. To have multilevel or
strategic stability a nation must be prepared to fight successfully a
limited nuclear war, which requires extensive counterforce
deployment, which in turn generates crisis instability for the
aforementioned reasons. To have strategic stability a nation must
forsake some crisis stability, and to have crisis stability, it must
forsake some strategic stability. A nation cannot have both
strategic and crisis stability to a high degree, which is the
stability/instability paradox.

Consequentialist defenders of deterrence usually argue that while
the *effects* of a nuclear war would be catastrophic, the *risk* of the war
occurring is so low as to make deterrence preferable to unilateral

disarmament. Unilateral disarmament, they argue, may decrease the destructive effects of a nuclear war but it also increases significantly the risk of its occurrence. Moreover, other nuclear powers could use their dominance to compel concessions from the disarmer. Such coerced concessions are known as "nuclear blackmail." In tandem, these considerations are presumed to show that deterrence rather than disarmament is optimific.

The stability/instability paradox makes clear that whichever strategy of nuclear deterrence is chosen, there are respects in which nuclear deterrence will increase the risk of war as well as respects in which it will lower the risk. The paradox suggests that nuclear deterrence may not lower the risk of major nuclear war sufficiently to make it a better option than unilateral nuclear disarmament. Thus, the importance of the stability/instability paradox is that it allows the consequentialist critic of nuclear deterrence to explore the dangers of nuclear deterrence in a manner which applies not just to counterforce deterrence but to countervalue deterrence as well.

David Lewis argues that each nuclear power should deploy a small arsenal of very sophisticated nuclear weapons, targeted on the nuclear weapons of opponents. By so doing, Lewis reasons, such a finite counterforce policy wii be at least as effective as any other in preventing nuclear attack and superior in limiting damage to oneself after nuclear war has begun.

While Douglas Lackey concedes that Lewis's finite counterforce is morally superior to current countervailing strategy, it still fails in comparison with other possibilities. First, countervalue strategy deters better than finite counterforce, since the punishment that one can expect to suffer from a countervalue attack is greater than the punishment one can expect to suffer from a counterforce attack. The loss of one's major population centers is a greater loss than the loss of one's missiles. Second, the chance of nuclear attack is greater under finite counterforce than under nuclear pacifism (i.e., unilateral nuclear disarmament). The existence of counterforce weapons provides a reason for the other to attack. Third, a nation is more likely to launch a first-strike with counterforce weapons than with countervalue weapons, since the former have many more acceptable military uses.

Lackey indicates that the main problem with finite counterforce is what occurs when it destabilizes in the second stage of a nuclear war. After an initial counterforce attack by one superpower, the size of both arsenals is reduced, and each side is tempted to launch in order to preempt launch by the other. Neither will find it rational to quit since the adage "use them or lose them" will come into play, and the war will continue until both arsenals or populations are exhausted. The destabilization produced by counterforce is morally less attractive than that caused by nuclear pacifism since, from the consequentialist perspective, a nuclear response will cause more expected harm than good in comparison with disarmament and, from the deontological or nonconsequentialist perspective, the president violates principles of distributive justice in *killing* Soviets rather than *allowing* Americans *to die* in a nuclear attack.

The middle three articles in Part II employ the just war tradition in an attempt to determine the morality of nuclear deterrence. The just war tradition represents a nonconsequentialist approach to morality, for it holds that the value of the foreseeable consequences of an action do not *solely* determine the rightness or wrongness of that action. The intentions of the agent must be balanced against the value of the consequences of the action. The ends do not justify the means, *simply*; one must also have right intention. Consequently the distinction between the intended consequences of an action and the unintended but foreseeable consequences looms large in the just war tradition (the Principle of Double Effect).

In *Nuclear Deterrence* (1987), Joseph Boyle, along with the book's other authors, argued that the practice of nuclear deterrence by the U.S. and its allies is immoral and ought to be abandoned. Central to the argument is the claim that it is immoral to conditionally intend to kill innocents in the manner evidenced by present deterrence policy (i.e., "We will kill your innocent civilians, if you launch an attack against us"). Boyle believes that while some of the arguments of their book have been rendered obsolete by the demise of the Soviet Union and the resulting new world situation, other arguments of theirs stand fast. In particular, he presents a new, abstract version of the moral argument offered against deterrence policy in his earlier book.

Boyle is interested in a certain kind of action: an act of deterring in which one threatens intentionally to kill innocents, and in which one is neither bluffing nor keeping open the decision about killing if the threat fails, but in which one is resolved intentionally to kill innocents, if the conditions calling for the threatened act are fulfilled. Consequently, this is the kind of act which includes the conditional intention to kill innocents found in present deterrence policy.

Following Gregory Kavka's usage, the Wrongful Intentions Principle holds that it is wrong to intend to do what it is wrong to do. Unlike Kavka, Boyle embraces the principle. The question now becomes, "Does the Wrongful Intentions Principle apply to the conditional intentions involved in deterrent acts?" The answer is "Yes," given:

1. We do not employ strict consequentialist considerations to block the application of the principle to deterrent situations;
2. There is resolve to do the threatened action, and not merely a prediction that one will do it;
3. When the resolve exists even with the recognition of the possibility of changing one's mind in the future, and even in the presence of the improbability of the need to carry out the threat, and even when the threat is made so that the need for carrying it out becomes less likely.

Thus present nuclear deterrence policy, which is a token of the type of deterrence under discussion, is immoral.

Finally, Boyle responds to a criticism of Steven Lee, namely, that present nuclear deterrence policy is the action and intention of a group, while the moral analysis of actions and intentions provided in *Nuclear Deterrence* is of an individual.

John Kultgen agrees with Boyle that nuclear deterrence is wrong, but he disagrees with the arguments offered in *Nuclear Deterrence*. Briefly put, the central argument of *Nuclear Deterrence* is as follows:

1. It is wrong to use nuclear weapons, because their use involves the wrongful killing of innocents in violation of the Just War Principles of Discrimination and Proportionality.
2. It is wrong to intend to do what it is wrong to do (The Wrongful Intentions Principle).
3. Nuclear deterrence (i.e., the possession of nuclear weapons) involves the intent to use nuclear weapons.
4. Therefore, nuclear deterrence (i.e., the possession of nuclear weapons) is wrong.

The Principle of Discrimination tells us that noncombatants must not be directly (i.e., intentionally) attacked. The Principle of Proportionality tells us that noncombatant casualties that occur as indirect (i.e., unintended) consequences of military actions must not be disproportionate to the evil fought against or the good sought. The arguments of *Nuclear Deterrence* entail that any number of civilian causalities are countenanced as long as these are inflicted impartially and in accord with the Principles of Discrimination and Proportionality. But if we grant that nuclear weapons eliminate the distinction between combatants and noncombatants while destroying or blighting untold numbers of lives, this fact renders the argument of *Nuclear Deterrence* untenable, Kultgen argues. Indeed, Kultgen continues, these considerations show that nuclear war is immoral as well as demonstrate the failure of Just War Theory.

In place of Just War Theory, a thoroughgoing consequentialism is recommended. All of the foreseeable consequences of an action are considered and not merely those which are directly intended or disproportionate. The rationale is that better consequences will accrue if people are held responsible for pursuing the best total results of their actions rather than if they are held accountable only for their intentions.

Boyle and Kultgen both believe that the Wrongful Intentions Principle expresses a fundamental truth about deterrence, but Kultgen's justification is consequentialist. The intention to use nuclear weapons is morally corrosive given the damage which the deterrent system wreacks on democratic political processes (e.g., the security state) and the moral character of both leaders and citizens (e.g., political cynicism and passivity, slackening private morals). The morally corrosive effect of nuclear deterrence policy again reveals the immorality of deterrence

Unlike Kultgen, **Ronald Santoni** argues that Just War Theory entails the conclusion that the proper implication of the principle of restraint in the nuclear age is renunciation of the use of nuclear weapons. There is no instance of military necessity which would compel that justice be served through the disproportionate and indiscriminatory death and destruction which nuclear hostilities threaten, particularly since the wartime use of nuclear weapons threatens nuclear omnicide. Here Santoni is in agreement with both Boyle and Kultgen. In agreement with Kultgen, he holds that the morality of nuclear weapons policy cannot be restricted to the intentions of their users but, instead, spills over into the unintended but foreseeable consequences of their use.

Next, Santoni argues that commonly accepted notions of self-defense are violated by almost any use of nuclear weapons. Ordinary notions of self-defense entail that only necessary force be used in war, and the principle of necessary force is violated by the uncontrollable, disproportionate destruction caused by nuclear weapons. The condition that the agent harmed in an act of self-defense must be the same agent threatening harm is frustrated by the fact that any use of nuclear weapons will harm some who did not threaten harm. The proviso that the agent harmed in self-defense must be culpable is violated by the the fact that it is virtually impossible to confine any nuclear retaliation to the culpable party. Each of the limiting conditions of self-defense is violated by the indiscriminate, uncontrollable, and excessive destruction of nuclear weapons.

Finally, Santoni argues that his position is reinforced by international law. To cite but a few of his examples, the 1945 *Charter of the International Military Tribunal* for the adjudication of Nuremberg Trials, the 1945 *Charter of the United Nations*, the *Genocide Convention* of 1948, and the 1949 Geneva conventions reinforce and extend the protection of noncombatants and the requirement of proportionality in armed hostilities. U.N. General Assembly resolutions condemn any use of nuclear weapons as committing a crime against humanity and call for the permanent prohibition of the use of nuclear weapons. In addition, Article 1 of the *U.S. Constitution* gives Congress authority to "define and punish offenses against the Law of Nations."

The Charter of the United Nations, the *Nuremberg Charter*, and the *Genocide Convention* condemn even the deterrent threat to employ nuclear weapons, argues the author. Nor are appeals to national self-defense relevant, as Santoni has already argued that such appeals fail when applied to the use of nuclear weapons.The last three articles in Part II consider the language of nuclear deterrence. They attempt to reveal how we are deceived by the language which political analysts, politicians, and the mass media employ. By revealing these concealings, they hope to clarify our understanding of nuclear deterrence policy and help us avoid some of the ways we are mislead by such rhetoric.

Following in the tradition of such disparate philosophers as
Nietzsche and Heidegger, Kuhn and Hesse, Davidson and Rorty,
Ron Hirschbein holds that master metaphors guide thought and
conduct in most communities. Just as Newtonians liken the
universe to a great machine and Marxists liken the social world to
an organism, mainstream political analysts and decision-makers
have their master metaphors as well.

A problem is created by two main aspects of metaphors. First,
metaphors are literally false. While "love is blind" may be a decent
rule of thumb, it is literally false. Second, the fictive nature of
metaphors usually goes unnoticed. We use such phrases as "the
arms race," "the peacekeeper missile," and "political realism"
without attending to the presuppositions these metaphors contain.
Each exaggerates similarities with their literal extensions, while
concealing important differences. The arms race is no race, for there
is no way to win. Peacekeeper missiles are missiles (i.e., weapons
designed for mass destruction), but whether they keep or violate the
peace is an open-question. Political realism is surely political, but
whether it is as judicious, objective, or farsighted as the highly
positive word "realism" connotes is debatable. The bottom line is
that the two aforementioned aspects of metaphors often cause us to
be duped by their use.

Hirschbein argues that while equilibrium is an intelligible
concept in algebra or in a laboratory, it is not an intelligible concept
in international relations. Its use dupes us into likening the arms
race to an antique laboratory balance where all will be well if we
balance the scale. Notice the misleading image of the scales of
justice. But, in fact, there is no way to balance the scale, let alone
justly, for different perspectives yield different senses of what
nuclear equilibrium might be. Accordingly, the metaphor fuels the
arm race by allowing both sides to argue continually and
persuasively that they are outweighed by the other.

In place of the image of a scale in equilibrium, Hirschbein asks
us to consider the metaphor offered by the skeptic Sextus
Empiricus, who taught that every weighty argument can be balanced
by an equally substantial counterargument. Hirschbein's metaphor
reveals what is concealed by the political realists' metaphor of
equilibrium: all positions on arms escalation, maintenance, or
reduction are equally arguable. It is mere sophistry to think that the
weight of reason rests on the side of escalation alone.

Whereas Hirschbein concentrates on the metaphor of equilibrium, William C. Gay looks at the myth of protection. Since the early days of civil defense, the U.S. has used language which suggests that the population can be protected from a Soviet nuclear attack by adopting the appropriate technology. While the appropriate technology was once fallout shelters, now it is a Star Wars defense system.

It is fairly obvious, as Gay indicates, that the intent behind Star Wars carries an offensive component. If the U.S. can use a Star Wars missile defense system to protect its nuclear weapons from Soviet attack and the U.S. has a credible first-strike capability with new, extremely accurate warheads, then the U.S. could either use its first-strike with impunity, since it could disarm a Soviet counterattack with the Star Wars system, or it could repel any Soviet offensive strike. The U.S. mentions only the latter, making Star Wars seem solely defensive. Consequently, we are duped by the myth of protection: we ignore the offensive capabilities of the weapons system while focusing solely on its defensive capabilities.

In fact, as with most weapons, Star Wars has both an offensive and a defensive capability. We tend to think that a weapons system is either offensive or defensive, but not both. We are trapped by bi-polar thinking. Obviously it serves the interests of the U.S. to sell Star Wars to the populace as a defensive system while suppressing its offensive capabilities. Gay goes on to argue that our bi-polar thinking traps us with other dichotomies such as active vs. passive defenses and U.S. vs. Soviet intentions.

Gay indicates that there is evidence that our nation's design for Star Wars is, in fact, offensive. Obviously, a nation need not *use* its weapons to gain advantage. If a nation can credibly threaten their use at times of heightened international tension, it can gain an advantage without using the weapons. One of the purposes of Star Wars, Gay argues, is the demise of a mutual deterrence policy (MAD) and its replacement by a nuclear use policy (NUTS).

Lyle V. Anderson turns our attention from the strategic policy of nuclear deterrence *policy*, to the domestic use of deterrence *discourse.* Elaborating on a point hinted at by Hirschbein and Gay, the author argues that one of the primary functions of deterrence discourse is to affect the consciousness of U.S. citizens. Deterrence, like the U.S. itself, is presupposed as infallible in the pursuit of U.S. interests, i.e., "justice." This major presupposition of deterrence discourse goes unmentioned. To mention it is to make it subject to analysis and criticism.

Prior to the end of the Cold War, deterrence discourse served us well. It allowed the U.S. to spend trillions of dollars on defense which created a rich and powerful military-industrial complex for the wealthy—and a crushing national debt for the rest of us. Given the recent demise of the Soviet Union as a credible advisory, deterrence is credited with the victory. No internal or independent explanation of recent events in the breakup of Soviet power are even considered relevant, not even that communism simply fell under its own weight. *Nuclear* deterrence is presupposed by the state as the cause of the Soviet demise, so *conventional* deterrence must still perform its role of making the rest of the world serve our interests, i.e., act "justly." The Persian Gulf War becomes an extension of U.S. deterrence discourse and its presupposition of infallibility in the pursuit of U.S. interests, i.e., "justice."

Following such thinkers as George Orwell, Noam Chomsky, and Edward Schiappa, Anderson is concerned with the use of language by the government to create a *picture* of the world which is misleading. That picture, Anderson indicates, serves the interest of the military-industrial complex at the expense of the vast majority of U.S. citizens. The production and consumption of that picture of the world presupposes that deterrence is the very condition for discourse about U.S. interests and intentions. That picture of the world is behind the justification offered for the U.S. attack on Iraq during the recent war (the Nuclear Non-Proliferation Treaty) and for our *blitzkrieg* attack during the war (win before popular support dwindles). Deterrence discourse as justification for U. S. foreign policy has come full circle, just as U.S. hegemony, disguised as "the new world order," is completed.

Hamilton College

10 On the Success and Failure of "Nuclear Deterrent Threats" and "Nuclear Deterrence"

Jonathan Schonsheck

Introduction to the Issues

In a series of papers, I have come to the defense of nuclear deterrence. I have argued that the "moral debits" of deterrence are not so great as it might seem,[1] and that it is a methodological mistake to reject nuclear deterrence on moral grounds without a moral assessment of alternative nuclear weapons policies.[2] It is unlikely that nuclear deterrence will be superseded by the "Strategic Defense Initiative."[3] Furthermore, mutual suspicion and hostility among competing groups is to be expected.[4] Finally, the United States

---

[1] "The End of Innocents: An Array of Arguments for the Moral Permissibility of a Retaliatory Nuclear Strike," *Journal of Social Philosophy*, Volume XVIII, No. 2 (Summer 1987); "Hostages or Shields? An Alternative Conception of Noncombatants & Its Implications as Regards the Morality of Nuclear Deterrence," *Public Affairs Quarterly: Philosophical Studies of Public Policy Issues*, Volume 1, No. 2 (April 1987).

[2] "Wrongful Threats, Wrongful Intentions, and Moral Judgements about Nuclear Weapons Policies," *The Monist*, Vol. 70, No. 3 (July 1987).

[3] "Philosophical Scrutiny of the Strategic 'Defence' Initiatives," *Journal of Applied Philosophy*, Vol. 3, No. 2 (1986) (excerpted in *Ethics and Strategic Defense: American Philosophers Debate Star Wars and the Future of Nuclear Deterrence*, ed. Douglas P. Lackey (Belmont, California: Wadsworth Publishing Co., 1989); "Confusion and False Advertising of the Strategic 'Defense' Initiatives, *International Journal on World Peace*, Vol. V., No. 3 (July-September 1988).

[4] "On the Implications of Sociobiology for Nuclear Weapons Policy," *Issues in War and Peace — Philosophical Inquiries*, eds . Joseph Kunkel and Kenneth H. Klein (Wolfeboro, New Hampshire: Longwood Academic, 1989).

ought not absolutely minimize its deterrent weaponry and threats, but rather make the threats and maintain the weaponry to achieve the stability of "nuclear stalemate" with the Soviet Union.[1] In this paper, I once again come to the defense of nuclear deterrence—in this instance, against the charge that it doesn't work (or at least that we are not justified in having confidence that it works). Steven Lee, in an article recently published in *QQ: Report from the Institute for Philosophy & Public Policy*,[2] answers the title's question—"Does Nuclear Deterrence Work?"—in the negative. He concludes that "Having nuclear deterrence [is] worse than having no system of military deterrent threats at all."[3]

I believe that the arguments leading to this conclusion are defective, and that taken together, they do not secure this conclusion. Let us have a look at the arguments, and then assess them.

The Incentive to Conform

Lee begins with an investigation of deterrence in the context of the criminal law—an institution with which we are quite familiar. Lee claims,

> Now, if the belief that the threatener is able and willing to carry out its threat is to lead the threatened parties to conform their behavior to the required standard, they must be assured that if they do so conform, the harm threatened for nonconformity will not be inflicted upon them; otherwise they would have no incentive to conform in order to avoid this harm.[4] [emphasis added]

---

[1] "Nuclear Stalemate: A Superior Escape from the Dilemmas of Deterrence," forthcoming in *Philosophy & Public Affairs*.
[2] Steven Lee, "Does Nuclear Deterrence Work?" *QQ: Report from the Institute for Philosophy & Public Policy*, Vol. 8, No. 1 (Winter 1988).
[3] *Ibid.*, p. 12.
[4] *Ibid.*, p. 10.

This is false. Granted, we speak casually of complying with criminal statutes to avoid prosecution, and of threatening nuclear retaliation in order to prevent nuclear war. And the simplest sort of deterrent relationship is this: if one does not conform to the threatener's wishes, one will be visited with the threatened evil; if one does conform to the threatener's wishes, one will not. But deterrent relationships need not be this straightforward (and most, I suspect, are not). A person can be subjected to criminal prosecution *despite* obeying the law; a nation could become the victim of a nuclear strike despite its following the wishes of the threatening nation. Conforming one's behavior to the wishes of the threatener does not *guarantee* escaping the threatened evil—but so what? It just doesn't follow that one has "*no* incentive to conform." The conforming behavior may well reduce precipitously the prospects of becoming the victim of the threatened evil, even though it does not absolutely preclude it. Consider a case such that, if the threatened party does not conform, the probability of receiving the evil approaches 1.0; by conforming, the threatened party reduces the probability to .01. While the harm *might* be inflicted *despite* conforming, it would be quite mistaken to hold that the threatened party has "no incentive to conform." Unless the threatened harm is exceedingly mild, or the conforming behavior particularly arduous, one would have great incentive to conform—*viz.* to reduce the probability of being subjected to the threatened evil from nearly 1.0 to .01. Consider another case: if one fails to conform, the probability of the evil is .7; if one conforms, the probability is .2. In such a case one *still* has *some* incentive to conform—though not as much as in the prior case, and perhaps not sufficient to warrant conformity. (But still more than "no incentive.") Indeed, one could construct nonfantastic cases—the threatened party wants to act in some way, but not very much; the threatened evil is substantial—such that the threatened party would have *great* incentive to conform, even if its conforming behavior reduced only *slightly* the probability of becoming a victim of the threatened evil.

Generalizing: the incentive that one has to conform to the wishes of a threatener depends upon a number of factors, including the ability and inclination of the threatener to carry out the threat, the difficulty of conforming one's behavior to the threatener's wishes (including the motivation for *not* conforming), and the prospect of being subjected to the threatened harm despite one's conforming behavior. And generally, the more likely one is to avoid evil by exhibiting the conforming behavior, the stronger the deterrent. But the claim that one has "no incentive to conform" unless *guaranteed* that one will thereby evade the threatened evil is not correct. In the nuclear context: the fact that a nation may become the victim of a nuclear strike despite its conforming behavior does not mean that that nation has "no incentive" to take seriously its adversary's threats, and thus to appropriately constrain its geopolitical behavior. Lowering the probability of one's becoming a nuclear victim may well be sufficient motivation for conforming one's behavior to the demands of the threatening party.

Does Deterrence Require Its Own Failure?

I believe that Lee is correct in claiming that "deterrence is a pervasive relation among persons and institutions at all levels of social groupings, from the family to the nation to the world order."[1] I also agree that, usually, it

> . . . the basis for the belief that the state is willing to carry out legal threats is to be found in the state's past behavior of legal threat executions. To create the belief that it is willing to carry out legal threats, the state must have a history of having done so.[2]

Deterrent relationships *do* pervade human social life, and one can come to understand the nature of deterrent relationships only through knowledge of instances of noncompliance followed by the infliction of the threatened harm. Lee continues,

> To put the point paradoxically, the general success of legal deterrence is dependent on its occasional failure. Legal deterrence does not merely tolerate failures, maintaining its overall success despite

---

[1]*Ibid.*, p. 9.
[2]*Ibid.*, p. 10.

them, but actually makes use of them, and even
requires them for its overall success.[1]

Great care must be exercised here. I agree, it is not credible that
people could come to an understanding of deterrent relationships
unless some people, some times, were undeterred and were punished.
More narrowly, criminal statutes have deterrent effect (to the extent
that they do), and citizens attain an understanding of the legal
deterrent, by witnessing the infliction of evil on those who are not
deterred. But it does *not* follow from this that some *particular*
statute cannot deter unless that statute itself is sometimes violated.
Once people have a firm grasp of the institution of legal deterrence,
it is perfectly plausible (i.e., nonfantastic) to imagine a society
enacting a criminal statute against some action *a,* and that statute's
never being violated. Imagine that the citizens have some
inclination to go about *a*-ing (and remark to one another that, were
it not illegal, they would in fact engage in it), but it is virtually
impossible to *a* without being detected at it, and the state is
determined to prosecute *a*-ing vigorously (and the state has proved
itself competent in its enforcement of other criminal statutes), and
the penalty for *a*-ing is quite severe. I don't know what *a*-ing is.
But that doesn't matter.

The point is this: even if "deterrence" *qua* social practice
"requires" its own (occasional) failure, even if people come to
understand the institution by its failures, it does not follow that a
particular deterrent threat does not in fact deter unless it sometimes
fails to deter. While the *practice* "requires failures, a particular threat
can deter, even if *it* never fails, is never violated. Returning again
to the context of nuclear deterrence: it is perfectly intelligible to
maintain that the U.S. threat of nuclear retaliation deters the Soviet
Union, *even though* it has never failed, *even if* it never fails, even if
the Soviet Union is never undeterred. (I do not commit Lee to the
position that a deterrent threat cannot deter unless it sometimes
doesn't; he doesn't say that. My point is that that claim cannot be
validly inferred from what he *does* say—though it would be quite
easy to think that what he does say implies it.)

---

[1]*Ibid.,* p. 10.

A Key Distinction: "Failure of a Deterrent Threat" versus "Failure of the Policy of Deterrence"

Consider now the following inference:

> The point is often made that nuclear deterrence can tolerate no failures, that is, no instances of nonconforming behavior (assuming that such an instance would be or would lead to nuclear war). If there was an instance of nonconforming behavior, the likely result of destruction of society would mean that the system of deterrence as a whole had failed.[1]

To see that this is not so, first reflect on the following two scenarios:

Scenario One: The United States repudiates its policy of nuclear deterrence (but maintains a conventional military). Over a period of ten years there are several military conflicts between the U.S. and the U.S.S.R., as their respective geopolitical interests (continue to) conflict. Tiring of this competition, and strapped by its expenses, the Soviet Union launches a massive nuclear strike against the U. S., devastating the population.

Scenario Two: The U.S. maintains its nuclear deterrent, and the policy of deterrence. Tensions wax and wane, as superpower interests collide in more and less serious ways. After a century, as the globe's fossil fuels near exhaustion, the conflict escalates. The Soviet Union becomes undeterred, and launches a nuclear attack on the United States, devastating the population.

I have been careful here to distinguish "the deterrent" from "deterrence." The former is the deterrent *threat*; the latter is the *policy* of *issuing* deterrent threats. This distinction is crucial when considering the matter(s) of success and failure. A particular deterrent *threat* has failed when nuclear weapons are launched despite the threat of retaliation. (There are, of course, various *degrees* of

---

[1]*Ibid.*, p. 12.

failure. The deterrent could fail in that there ensued a limited nuclear exchange; it could fail in that there ensued a massive, central-systems exchange.) In Scenario Two, the deterr*ent* threat fails. Does this mean that the policy of deterr*ence* has failed—as claimed by Lee? Not necessarily; that does not follow from the failure of a particular deterrent threat. As a *policy*, "nuclear deterrence" is a failure just in case some other nuclear weapons policy option would have proved superior. That the adopting of some policy was a mistake is not proved by pointing to its bad consequences *in isolation*—for it remains possible that the adopting of *any other* policy would have had *worse* consequences. Now arguing in this sort of way is difficult—as is always the case when arguing for counterfactuals, and consensus may be unattainable. Nonetheless, *this* is the burden of proof, *this* is what must be argued, if one is to make good on the claim that some *policy* has failed. Put another way: it would be at least disingenuous, and probably just bad faith, to claim "nuclear deterrence had failed" while believing that no alternative nuclear weapons policy would have proved superior.[1]

This point is illustrated in comparing Scenario One and Scenario Two. When considering just these two alternatives, the correct assessment is that a deterrent threat had failed, but that the policy of nuclear deterrence succeeded—it forestalled the nuclear devastation of the U.S. population for ninety years. It "made the best of a bad lot"—a matter of great significance to several generations.

Now it may be thought that Scenario One is not very likely. But that's not relevant; all that is needed to prove that the failure of the deterrent threat does not entail that "the system of deterrence as a whole had failed" is a pairwise comparison of two scenarios such that the one in which a particular deterrent threat fails at some point is nonetheless superior to an alternative policy option.

Reluctance to acknowledge this stems (I suspect) from the presumption that there *must be* some policy option that could be selected whose consequences are superior to those of the failure of the deterrent threat. But that must be argued, and not merely

---

[1] I owe this formulation to Steven Lee, it was made during the discussion of an earlier draft of this paper at the Third Annual Conference of Concerned Philosophers for Peace, University of Notre Dame, September 21-23, 1990.

assumed. Nuclear disarmament followed by Soviet domination may be superior—perhaps it's better to be Red than dead—but that's got to be argued. And of course the issue is complicated by the necessity of estimating probabilities: of Soviet domination in case of nuclear disarmament, of the failure of the deterrent threat. The failure of the deterrent at some time *t* need not be the worst thing that could happen. Minimally, it's better than the same failure at some time *prior to* time *t*. Again: there is no guarantee that the U.S. has some cheerful policy option available to it. Sometimes the "bad lot" that one has to make the best of includes *no* option that would "allow the social order to continue."[1]

The "Amulet" and its Contrapositive

Consider now the final chunk of argument offered by Lee:

> For nuclear deterrence to have absolute deterrent
> value, we may say, the probability of its failing
> (say, per year) must be so low that it is very
> unlikely that a failure would occur over decades or
> even centuries. If nuclear deterrence cannot
> guarantee that it is very unlikely to fail over an
> extended number of years, it must be regarded as
> ineffective in an absolute sense. Unless nuclear
> deterrence can do a substantially better job at
> deterring aggression than history has shown
> general military deterrence has been able to do,
> then nuclear deterrence is absolutely ineffective,
> because general military deterrence can tolerate a
> much higher rate of failure without social
> breakdown (or destruction) than nuclear deterrence
> can.[2]

I confess to some perplexity about this passage. I don't know what it means to say that nuclear deterrence might be "ineffective in an absolute sense." Nor do I understand how it is that deterrence can avoid this charge by "guaranteeing" that "it is very unlikely to fail

---

[1]Lee, *op. cit.*, p. 12.
[2]*Ibid.*, p. 12.

over an extended number of years." (Indeed, I do not understand what it *could* mean for a policy *per se* to "guarantee" *anything*.) Furthermore, the conditional claim that "nuclear deterrence is absolutely ineffective" is ambiguous between (i) "ineffective in the absolute sense" (which I have already confessed I don't understand) and (ii) *very* ineffective—which I deny.

Let us agree that general military deterrence can tolerate a higher failure rate than can nuclear deterrence. This is simply the claim that societies can tolerate conventional conflicts (as many have), but societies are less likely to be able to tolerate nuclear conflict. But this does *not* show that nuclear deterrence is "absolutely ineffective." It shows merely that there are limits to the relevance of drawing an analogy between general military deterrence and nuclear deterrence— *viz.*, that societies can tolerate failures of the former, but not of the latter. It does *not* show that Soviet behavior would not be different if the United States were to abandon its nuclear deterrent, or both its nuclear deterrent and its general military deterrent.

Consider a third scenario:

Scenario Three: The U.S. maintains its nuclear deterrent, and the policy of nuclear deterrence. There is *never* a nuclear exchange between the superpowers. (Pick any reason you like: AIDS kills off the species, or the Death Star Nemesis destroys virtually all life on Earth. Or a new sort of weapon is developed, as destructive as nuclear weapons, but "cleaner," nuclear weapons genuinely become obsolete).

Would it be true that the United States' policy of deterrence had in fact deterred the Soviet Union, preventing a nuclear war? Well, that would have to be argued. But it would be quite mistaken to claim, without argument, that the policy of nuclear deterrence, that the making of deterrent threats, had *not*.

At the outset of the article, Lee retells the famous amulet story: a person is certain that wearing an amulet is keeping elephants away, because no elephants have been seen since the wearing began.[1] But to deny the effectiveness of nuclear deterrence in a case such as Scenario Three, without argument, is to urge the contrapositive of the story of the amulet: if there has been no

---

[1] *Ibid.*, p. 9.

nuclear exchange, it cannot have been due to the maintaining of the nuclear deterrent. And that inference is no more justified than the original inference.

Concluding Summary

If my arguments are sound, I have shown the following. First, it is possible for the nuclear deterrent to in fact deter—i.e., secure conforming behavior—even though it is not certain that that conforming behavior precludes the threatened evil, the nuclear attack. Second, although the social practice of deterrence requires some failures, a particular deterrent threat can prove effective without itself failing. Third, the failure of a particular deterrent threat (i.e., the threat of retaliation does not, in some instance, deter an adversary) does not entail the failure of deterrence, i.e., the policy of seeking safety through making deterrent threats. It is possible that nuclear deterrence is the optimal policy—that there is no policy whose consequences are better—even if some particular deterrent threat, at some point in the future, fails.

Le Moyne College

11 Nuclear Deterrence and the Stability/Instability Paradox

Steven Lee

In this paper, I hope to fill what I believe is a lacuna in the discussion of the ethics of nuclear deterrence, in particular, in that ethical discussion that adopts a consequentialist or utilitarian perspective. Some consequentialists favor nuclear deterrence and some oppose it. To put it roughly, some find nuclear deterrence less dangerous and some find it more dangerous than unilateral nuclear disarmament. But the degree of danger may depend on the form of nuclear deterrence policy in question, that is, on the strategic nature of the policy, on the strategy that informs decisions about weapons development and deployment as well as plans for their use should deterrence fail. Nuclear deterrence may be more dangerous under some strategies than under others. More to the point, it may be that some strategies make nuclear deterrence more dangerous than unilateral nuclear disarmament, while others make it less dangerous. Unilateral nuclear disarmament may have better consequences than nuclear deterrence under some strategies, while having worse consequences than nuclear deterrence under other strategies. An adequate consequentialist account must initially consider not nuclear deterrence *simpliciter*, but policies of nuclear deterrence under different strategies.

The two general kinds of nuclear strategy which I will consider, and which I will assume, when understood broadly, to be exhaustive of possible nuclear strategies, are counterforce deterrence and finite deterrence. Counterforce deterrence involves an extensive deployment of nuclear warheads with counterforce targets. Counterforce targets are military targets, or targets of military importance, including, most importantly, the strategic nuclear forces of the opponent, but also including conventional military targets. Different versions of counterforce deterrence go under the names of flexible response, graduated deterrence, countervailing strategy, prevailing strategy, and nuclear war-fighting. Doug Lackey refers to this kind of strategy as victory strategy. Finite deterrence, sometimes called minimum deterrence, involves a relatively small number of nuclear warheads aimed primarily (though not necessarily exclusively) at so-called countervalue targets, that is, economic and civilian targets, mainly large cities. Lackey refers to this as detente strategy. Sometimes finite deterrence is referred to as existential deterrence, though these are not quite the same thing.

Consider, first, those consequentialists who favor nuclear deterrence. Most of them, such as Greg Kavka, support finite deterrence over counterforce deterrence, believing the latter to be far more dangerous than the former. Whether they would regard counterforce deterrence as more dangerous than unilateral nuclear disarmament may not be clear, but their position is that finite deterrence is less dangerous than unilateral nuclear disarmament. On the other hand, those who argue against nuclear deterrence from a consequentialist perspective usually focus almost exclusively on the dangers of counterforce deterrence, tending to identify the dangers of counterforce deterrence with those of nuclear deterrence in general. (Lackey is an exception in this regard.) The reason for this may be that many of those who argue against nuclear deterrence in consequentialist terms give greater weight to the deontological or just-war arguments against the policy, so that their consequentialist examination of the policy tends to be cursory. In any case, the result is that finite deterrence does not always get the careful critical attention in consequentialist terms, since those favoring nuclear deterrence support finite deterrence and so give their critical attention largely to counterforce deterrence, while those opposing nuclear deterrence also set their sights largely on counterforce deterrence rather than finite deterrence.

The lacuna I seek to fill concerns a particular line of consequentialist criticism of finite deterrence which, for the reasons discussed above, has largely been ignored in philosophical discussions of nuclear deterrence. A version of this line of criticism is sometimes offered by strategic thinkers who favor counterforce deterrence over finite deterrence, as a way of trying to show that finite deterrence is less effective than counterforce deterrence. This version of the criticism is that finite deterrence lacks credibility. But the criticism cuts much deeper than counterforce advocates generally realize, and it is this deeper form of the criticism, which has been labeled the stability/instability paradox, that I want to consider. As it will turn out, the stability/instability paradox counts against counterforce deterrence as well as against finite deterrence. Neither the credibility problem nor the stability/instability paradox are much discussed by those who consider the ethics of nuclear deterrence. In what follows, I will first present the criticism that finite deterrence lacks credibility, then examine the consequentialist advantages of finite deterrence, and finally discuss the nature and implications of the stability/instability paradox itself.

Proponents of counterforce deterrence criticize finite deterrence on the grounds that the threats involved in this policy lack credibility. The argument is that threats cannot be effective unless they are credible and the threats involved in a nation's policy of finite deterrence, threats to destroy the society of the opponent, are not credible, because carrying them out would bring on the destruction of the nation's society in retaliation. Finite deterrence results in self-deterrence, because its threats are, in effect, threats to commit suicide. Note that, according to this criticism, credibility is lacking only in regard to threats to respond with nuclear retaliation to the opponent's military aggression short of an all-out nuclear attack. Thus, the criticism is that finite deterrence cannot effectively deter aggression at what are called "lower levels of violence." Counterforce deterrence, on the other hand, avoids the credibility problem, because an extensive counterforce arsenal provides the opportunity to retaliate with nuclear weapons in a way that avoids destroying the opponent's society, so that the nation's nuclear retaliation would not inevitably lead to the destruction of its own society (assuming, of course, that nuclear war can be kept limited).

Whatever the force of this criticism, however, proponents of finite deterrence have a strong consequentialist argument in favor of their policy, and it is an argument that consequentialist defenders of finite deterrence usually appeal to. A fair characterization of the consequentialist advantage of finite deterrence comes from a critic of the policy, Colin Gray.

> . . . the development of nuclear weapons has imposed a technological peace [which has] solved the problem of premeditated war between nuclear-armed states, because the initiator will know that it cannot deny the enemy the capability of

destroying its society in retaliation. . . . The
balance of terror is thus massively indelicate.[1]

To say that deterrence is massively indelicate is to say that it is
very unlikely to lead to war. Because each side believes with near
certainty that it could gain nothing by initiating nuclear war,
moreover that it would suffer grievously as a result, the likelihood
that either side would initiate a nuclear war is extremely small.
Finite deterrence is, as a result, highly stable, in the sense that it is
very unlikely to collapse into war.

This stability is a consequentialist advantage of finite deterrence
in comparison with counterforce deterrence. Counterforce deterrence
lacks a high degree of stability because an extensive deployment of
weapons with counterforce targets may threaten, or be perceived to
threaten, the ability of the other side to retaliate after a surprise first-
strike. If either side possessed such a "full first-strike capability," it
might, under certain crisis conditions be willing to initiate a war
and, more importantly, the other side, fearing under those conditions
that it might be the object of an attack, would be strongly tempted
to initiate its own preemptive attack. Because this form of stability
exhibits itself in crisis situations, it is referred to as crisis stability.
Crisis stability is the consequentialist advantage that finite
deterrence possesses in comparison with counterforce deterrence.

So much is standard fare in the strategic debates. But perhaps
this consequentialist stand-off between finite and counterforce forms
of nuclear deterrence, represented by the opposing tendencies of
considerations of credibility and crisis stability, can be pressed
further. Colin Gray does this by casting the objection to finite
deterrence on the grounds of its lacking credibility into the language
of stability.[2] Gray takes issue with the claim that finite deterrence
has the advantage of greater stability by contesting the notion of
stability itself. Gray argues, in effect, that the stability of a policy
of nuclear deterrence should be judged in terms of its credibility. A
policy of nuclear deterrence is not stable if it is liable to break
down, and when its threats are not credible, it is liable to break
down. Finite deterrence, which is not credible at the lower levels of

---

[1]Colin Gray, *Nuclear Strategy and National Style* (Lanham, MD:
Hamilton Press, 1986), p. 140.
[2]*Ibid.*, Chapter Five.

violence, is thus liable to break down at those levels, and so is, in that sense, unstable.

A policy of nuclear deterrence should have, according to Gray, "multilevel stability," and this "requires that there be a measure of *instability* at the central war level—translated as a potential for U.S. advantage."[1] This is a revealing quotation, for it shows that Gray is not so much redefining stability as claiming that there is another kind of stability than the crisis stability championed by proponents of finite deterrence, and that this other kind of stability (call it strategic stability) is more important than crisis stability in evaluating deterrence policy. Further, this quotation suggests that one kind of stability can be bought only at the price of the other. To have multilevel or strategic stability, a nation must be prepared successfully to fight a limited nuclear war ("a potential for U.S. advantage"), which requires an extensive counterforce deployment, which generates crisis instability for the reasons discussed above. Gray's discussion does two things. It casts the consequentialist discussion over which form of deterrence is preferable in terms of the notion of stability, and it suggests that the two forms of stability are exclusive, in the sense that a nation's nuclear deterrence policy cannot at the same time have both to a high degree. To have strategic stability, a nation must forsake some crisis stability, and to have crisis stability, it must forsake some strategic stability.

This last point is the stability/instability paradox. It is the claim that a form of nuclear deterrence that is stable in one sense is at the same time unstable in the other. The claim, as presented by Glenn Snyder, is that

> the greater the stability of the "strategic" balance of terror [that is, what we call crisis stability], the lower the stability of the overall balance at its lower levels of violence. The reasoning is that if neither side has a "full first-strike capability," and both know it, they will be less inhibited about initiating conventional war, and about the limited use of nuclear weapons, than if the strategic balance were unstable. Thus firm stability in the strategic nuclear balance tends to destabilize the

---

[1]*Ibid.* , p. 146 (emphasis added).

conventional balance and to activate the lesser
nuclear "links" between the latter and the former.[1]

As Robert Jervis puts it: "To the extent that the military
balance is stable at the level of all-out nuclear war, it will become
less stable at lower levels of violence."[2] As these characterizations
make clear, the claim is not, strictly speaking, a paradox, since there
are two different kinds of stability involved. There is no one kind of
stability that a policy of deterrence both has and lacks; rather, there
is one kind it has and one kind it lacks, and, more importantly, it
lacks the one because it has the other, and vice-versa.

Jervis is a critic of counterforce deterrence. He recognizes the
stability/instability paradox, hence that there are two different kinds
of stability involved;, but he argues, in effect, that crisis stability is
more important than strategic stability. Thus, he is at the opposite
end of the issue from Gray, who argues, in effect, that strategic
stability is more important than crisis stability. What is Jervis's
argument? He acknowledges that the presence of one form of
stability is in inverse proportion to the presence of the other when
he says that "there remains a trade-off between the perceived risk of
total conflict and the possibilities for adventurism." But he claims
that though crisis stability may make it "relatively safe" to risk
conflict at lower levels of violence, "'relatively safe' may not be safe
enough and even a slightly credible threat of all-out war may be
credible enough to deter the other side."[3]

As this quotation suggests, Jervis's basic response to the
problem is to appeal to what Thomas Schelling has called "the
threat that leaves something to chance," that is, the risk that conflict
at lower levels of violence will escalate to all-out nuclear war is
sufficient to deter the opponent's aggression at those lower levels.
The risk of escalation, in other words, solves the credibility
problem. In amplification of this point, Jervis argues that the
situation of mutual assured destruction involves a threat of

---

[1]Glenn Snyder, "The Balance of Power and the Balance of Terror," in
Balance of Power, ed. Paul Seabury (San Francisco: Chandler, 1965),
pp. 198-99.
[2]Robert Jervis, *The Illogic of American Nuclear Strategy* (Ithaca:
Cornell University Press, 1984), p. 31.
[3]*Ibid.*, p. 31.

destruction in two senses—in the sense of an explicit threat of such destruction, which may lack credibility for the reasons discussed above, and in the sense of a general danger that any conflict could, whatever the parties intend, escalate to mutual destruction.[1] It is the latter threat that succeeds in deterring conflict at the lower levels of violence.

In recognizing the stability/instability paradox, both Jervis and Gray admit that there are consequentialist considerations favoring each form of deterrence, such that choosing one strategy or the other, finite deterrence or counterforce deterrence, involves a trade-off. Each argues that that trade-off favors the form of strategy he champions. Thus, each argues, in effect, that the balance of consequentialist considerations favors his preferred strategy over the other. Unfortunately, however, this is not the conclusion either needs to prove. The consequentialist question is not just which form of nuclear deterrence is better than the other, but whether either form is better than unilateral nuclear disarmament. The stability/instability paradox provides some reason to think that neither is. The choice of continuing a policy of nuclear deterrence over unilateral nuclear disarmament has always been seen as involving an important consequentialist trade-off, different from the one involved in choosing a strategy of nuclear deterrence in the face of the stability/instability paradox. This more basic trade-off is between lowering the likelihood of major war and increasing the potential destructiveness of such a war should it occur. Nuclear weapons are said to do both. But the defenders of nuclear deterrence have always argued that, despite the weapons' destructiveness, this is a trade worth making because nuclear deterrence makes the risk of war almost negligible.

What the stability/instability paradox does is to raise serious problems with this argument. The trade-off between risk of war and destructiveness of war may not be worth making. For the argument shows that, though nuclear deterrence may lower the risk of major war below what it would be in the absence of nuclear weapons, it does not lower it as much as defenders of nuclear deterrence have argued. This is because the stability/instability paradox makes clear that, whichever strategy of nuclear deterrence is chosen, there are respects in which nuclear deterrence will increase the risk of war as

---

[1]*Ibid.*, p. 150.

well as respects in which it will lower this risk. This suggests, though it does not prove, that nuclear deterrence does not lower the risk of major war sufficiently for the trade-off to be worth making. Thus, the importance of the stability/instability paradox is that it allows the consequentialist critics of nuclear deterrence to talk about the dangerousness of nuclear deterrence in a way that applies not just to counterforce deterrence, but to finite deterrence as well, that is, to nuclear deterrence however it is practiced. In other words the stability/instability paradox provides what many have sought to present, a consequentialist critique of nuclear deterrence *simpliciter*.

Hobart and William Smith Colleges

12 Kill Like a MADman; Destabilize Like a NUT: A Critique of David Lewis's "Finite Counterforce"

Douglas Lackey

For many years philosophers have presented a moral critique of nuclear deterrence which goes something like this:

If you practice nuclear deterrence, you must practice either the countervalue version or the counterforce version. The countervalue version is immoral because it involves a direct threat to innocent life. The counterforce version is immoral because it is unstable and recklessly raises the risk of nuclear war. Thus we must practice nuclear pacifism.

Obviously this argument presumes that only two versions of nuclear deterrence are available, and defenders of deterrence like Bruce Russett, James Sterba, and Anthony Kenny have devised versions of deterrence which do not fit easily into the "counterforce" or "countervalue" mold.[1] The latest and perhaps most elaborate maneuver along these lines is the 63 page essay by David Lewis entitled "Finite Counterforce," published in 1989 in a volume edited by Henry Shue and issued by Cambridge University Press.[2]

Lewis's essay, I believe, is a failure, but it is an impressive failure. What Lewis suggests is that each nuclear power should deploy a very small arsenal of very sophisticated nuclear weapons, targeted on the nuclear weapons of opponents; we should, he writes,

---

[1] See Bruce Russett, "Assured Destruction of What? A Countercombatant Alterative to MADness" (Abbots Langley, England: Catholic Information Services. 1981); Anthony Kenny, *The Logic of Deterrence* (Chicago, Chicago University Press, 1985); James Sterba, "Between MAD and Counterforce," *Social Theory and Practice* (Summer, 1986).'

[2] David Lewis, "Finite Counterforce," in *Nuclear Deterrence and Moral Restraint*, ed. Henry Shue (New York: Cambridge University Press, 1989). According to Lewis, this essay was written in 1986.

"Buy like a MADman; use like a NUT."[1] The prudential case for such a policy is strong. Assume that one's national priorities are that one sets highest value on preventing nuclear attack on oneself and second highest value on limiting the damage of nuclear war to oneself should it occur. According to Lewis, the suggested Finite Counterforce policy is at least as effective as any other in preventing nuclear attack. Among those policies that are equally effective in preventing nuclear attack, Finite Counterforce is superior in limiting damage to oneself after nuclear war has begun.

Notice, furthermore, that the standard moral critique of nuclear deterrence does not touch Finite Counterforce. Since the policy is a finite *counterforce* policy, it does not involve direct threats to innocent life. By providing scrupulous and prudent nuclear responses, it does not require the moral immorality or rational irrationality of countervalue strategies. Since it is a *finite* counterforce policy, it does not tempt leaders towards preemptive strikes, because it is manifestly impossible with small nuclear forces to eliminate the second-strike forces of the opponent. Since one's opponents know that their second-strike capacity is secure, they too experience no temptation to preempt. Thus Finite Counterforce is as stable as any countervalue policy.

Compared with the current Countervailing Strategy, Lewis's Finite Counterforce is positively virtuous. Unlike the Countervailing Strategy, it involves no search for nuclear superiority, and generates no Prisoner's Dilemmas or arms race treadmills. Unlike the Countervailing Strategy, it does not extend itself to defense of allies; unlike the Countervailing Strategy, it is consistent with the abolition of tactical nuclear weapons and the disentanglement of conventional military planning from nuclear options. In all these respects it is morally superior to present arrangements.

---

[1]Here 'MAD" stands for 'Mutual Assured Destruction," a policy of responding to a nuclear attack by destroying the opponents cities and society, and NUTS stands for "Nuclear Utilization Target Selection," the policy of targeting one's weapons against the military (especially nuclear) capacities of the opponent. See Spurgen M. Keeny and Wolfgang Panofsky, "MAD vs. Nuts," *Foreign Affairs* (Winter 1981-82).

Though Lewis doesn't mention this, Finite Counterforce has another virtue not often found in philosophers' proposals regarding nuclear weapons: it is politically feasible. It cannot be charged with disarming the United States. It will keep the military-industrial complex happy with demands for more precise and more sophisticated weapons. It will keep Congress happy by not requiring massive weapons purchases. Indeed, though Lewis says that his policy will require substantial changes from current deployments, my feeling is that his scheme corresponds quite closely to present procurement patterns. The Defense Department gets its MX, its D-5, its B-1, its Stealth bomber, but the Congress will buy only a few of each. Thus by accident we have Finite Counterforce. If Lewis is correct, Main Street is almost all right. Nothing could be more distressing to philosophers or more agreeable to politicians.

But I come not to praise Finite Counterforce, but to bury it. Let me begin by questioning whether it is true that Finite Counterforce reduces the risk of nuclear attack as well as all alternative policies. Lewis argues that there is no difference between the deterrence effectiveness of Finite Countervalue and the deterrence effectiveness of Finite Counterforce, since it is the mere existence of nuclear weapons that deters attack, not the numbers or types of nuclear weapons.[1] (This point has often been made to support Finite Countervalue strategies, but Lewis ingeniously notes that it supports Finite Counterforce as well.)

Now it seems to me that Lewis is wrong here about the relative risk of nuclear war. Obviously the policy generates less risk of nuclear war then Countervailing Strategy. What interests me is the claim that a finite counterforce policy is less likely to produce a nuclear war than a finite countervalue policy or nuclear pacifism. It

---

[1]Thus Lewis accepts "existential deterrence," an unfortunate policy label that seems to have been introduced by McGeorge Bundy in "Existential Deterrence and its Uses," in *The Security Gamble*, ed. Douglas MacLean (Totowa, NJ: Rowman and Allanheld, 1984). For the most elaborate presentation of the idea that it matters much whether a nation has nuclear weapons but that it matters little which nuclear weapons a nation has, see William A. Schwartz, *et. al.*, *The Nuclear Seduction: Why the Arms Race Doesn't Matter — and What Does* (Berkeley, CA: University of California Press, 1990). All of the defenders of existential deterrence except Lewis dislike counterforce weapons.

seems to me simple logic that if I am contemplating an action that will lead to my suffering punishment, the greater the punishment, the less likely it is that I will perform the act. It may be true that I dread any punishment, and that as a result it is very unlikely that I will perform the act even if the punishment is small. Nevertheless, it is just wrong to say that I am just as likely to perform the act if I am confronted with a small punishment as I am if I am confronted with a big punishment. So even if Finite Countervalue and Finite Counterforce are both likely to deter attack, Finite Countervalue still fares better than Finite Counterforce.

Furthermore, I do not agree that the chance of nuclear attack is less with Finite Counterforce than with Nuclear Pacifism. The main wartime use of nuclear weapons is to deter or preempt nuclear attack by others. If this is so, nations that do not possess nuclear weapons need not greatly fear nuclear attack. Yes, I've heard about Hiroshima, but that was before the effects of nuclear weapons were understood and before there was a taboo on the use of nuclear weapons. Of course, the chance of nuclear attack with Nuclear Pacifism is not zero, but it is not zero under any policy.

So far we have compared the policies as regards the chance of nuclear attack on the United States. But obviously in a moral analysis we must consider not just nuclear attacks on the United States but nuclear first-strikes by the United States. Here Finite Counterforce is inferior to Finite Countervalue and both of these are inferior to Nuclear Pacifism. One can agree with Lewis that it is very unlikely that the United States will launch a nuclear first-strike from either a Finite Countervalue or Finite Counterforce posture. Nevertheless, counterforce weapons by definition have more uses and, from the standpoint of standard military training, more acceptable uses, than countervalue weapons. Consequently, the United States is more likely to launch a first-strike with counterforce weapons than with countervalue weapons.

When Lewis says that Finite Counterforce is as safe as Finite Countervalue, he appeals to the fact that Finite Counterforce is nearly as safe as Finite Countervalue, and that the difference between the risks of nuclear war posed by these policies is small compared to the overall risk of nuclear war posed by either. But when the outcomes are very bad, small chances do matter. When I get on to a bus, I think it very unlikely that the bus will have a serious accident. (If I did, I would not get on.) Nevertheless, if there is an accident, I am much more likely to be killed if I sit in front, and much more likely to be killed if I sit on the left hand side of the bus. If I have a choice of seats, then, it is rational to ride in the middle on the right hand side, even though the increase in my life expectancy brought about by this choice is small relative to the expected length of my life.

Perhaps Lewis would concede these points, but dismiss them as trivial. He might agree that Finite Counterforce generates a slightly greater risk of nuclear war, but that this greater risk is compensated for by the great superiority of Finite Counterforce after nuclear war begins. So let us assume that a nuclear war has started and let us assume with Lewis that it starts with a Soviet nuclear attack on the United States. What we should do, then, according to Lewis, is to direct a nuclear second-strike against nuclear weapons forces in the Soviet Union. Lewis, however, does not tell us whether this second-strike is directed against ascertained reserve forces of the opponent, or whether it is directed against targets which have been designated as objectives before nuclear war begins. We must consider both possibilities, though frankly I think that it is far more likely that the second-strike will go out against pre-assigned targets.

Suppose that we are firing against pre-assigned targets. Given pre-assignment, we might be firing against weapons that have already been fired off. On the other hand, we might be firing against weapons that are still there but which will not be fired off no matter what we do. If so, we cause destruction with no compensating gain. Now suppose that we are firing against ascertained targets. It still might be the case that we are firing against weapons that will not be fired no matter what we do. Furthermore, it might be the case that we are firing against weapons that would not be fired were it not for the fear that American counterforce weapons might take them out.

This last difficulty is a serious one, and perhaps the most serious that afflicts the Finite Counterforce system. Once the United States has experienced a nuclear attack, Finite Counterforce is no longer finite. Arsenals on both sides have been sharply reduced, on the one side by launch, on the other side by attrition. When these two reduced arsenals confront each other, the usual instabilities of counterforce emerge. Each side is tempted to launch in order to preempt launch by the other side. Neither side will find it rational to quit, and the war will grind on from stage to stage until the arsenals are exhausted. For both sides this is worse than if the United States suffered a first-strike and did nothing at all. In short, Finite Counterforce destabilizes in the second stage of nuclear war. Note that Lewis cannot solve this problem by arguing that we do not know if nuclear wars will consist of a succession of stages. His entire argument for damage limitation depends on the assumption that some Soviet weapons will be held in reserve for later stages of a nuclear war.

It seems that the only scenario in which Finite Counterforce could provide genuine damage limitation would be one in which the Soviet Union reserves some weapons for later use in a nuclear war, and would actually launch those weapons even if the United States had no capacity to preempt. I consider that this scenario is possible. It follows that if we do not launch a second-strike, this result may be the deaths of millions of Americans. But if we do launch the second-strike we will surely kill millions of Soviet citizens. You do not have to think that there is a moral difference between killing and letting die as such to find that actually killing people is morally more repugnant than possibly saving people.

Now suppose that you do not find the difference between "possible" and "actual" here helpful to the moral analysis. You might say that "actual" is just the same as "100% possible" and that all we should do in this analysis is deal with different consequences multiplied by differing probabilities. How should we rate the expected consequences? My solution is the standard one of favoring the policy that has the best expected consequences—the greatest balance of possible good over possible harm. But Lewis is no utilitarian and he does not accept this solution. He thinks that it is legitimate to launch a second-strike even if it causes more expected harm than good—provided that the harm falls on the Soviets. Lewis argues this point with a candor that plainly incapacitates him for higher elective office:

> It would be right for a commander-in-chief to proceed as if he values the lives of his enemy's subjects somewhat, but less than the lives of those on whose behalf he is fighting. That judgement has two parts: first, the judgment that it is permissible to undertake a responsibility to serve the interests of some people more than others and

second, the judgment that one who has done so is
permitted, indeed required, to be partial towards
those he has undertaken to serve. Whoever the
commander-in-chief may be, he will have accepted
either a high position in government or a
commission in the armed forces. Either way, he
has undertaken a special responsibility towards his
countrymen. (And to those they have taken on as
allies.) He betrays his obligation if he chooses to
no longer serve his countrymen but rather to
become an impartial servant of mankind at large.
When he deliberates between alternative courses of
action, such as waging counterforce warfare or not,
he is entitled and required to weigh the
consequences — but with a finger on the scale.[1]

Now I do not think that Lewis would have bothered to introduce
this "finger on the scale" argument if he felt that counterforce
attacks really did produce the best consequences overall. If they did,
he would cite that fact as his argument. So he must believe, as I do,
that a counterforce second-strike would take more expected lives
than it saves. Nevertheless, no one but the President is entitled to
engage in this inefficient exercise of risk shifting. His argument is
based not on an appeal to rights or to self-defense or to the
permissibility of deflection or to a shift in the locus of
responsibility for the outcome. It is a simple appeal to the
responsibilities of office.

I suppose that we all feel the intuitive force of this appeal. The
question is whether our intuitions are any good. I am myself
suspicious of deontological intuitions in general and intuitions
about role responsibilities in particular. But suppose that we buy
into this style of ethics. Then, I say, we must buy not isolated
judgments but an entire moral package. We will start by affirming
the existence of rights, and then we must proceed to make a moral
distinction between acting and allowing things to happen, and then
to distinguish causing harms from failing to provide goods. But if
we distinguish morally between harms and goods, that is, between
driving a person down three utility units from level X and failing to

---

[1]Lewis, *op. cit.*, p. 92.

supply him with the three units he needs to reach level X, then we will differentiate between rules of distributive justice as regards the distribution of goods and rules of justice as regards the distribution of harms.

With this in mind, when we turn to the part of the package where we have installed role responsibilities we will still distinguish between killing and failing to save, between distributing harms and distributing good. We will say that the President has a responsibility, when it comes to saving four Americans or ten Russians, to save the Americans—a responsibility, when it comes to killing four Americans or killing ten Russians, to kill the Russians. But none of this justifies launching the second-strike , in which the President kills Russians to save Americans. We will say that, when it comes to distributing goods, the President can favor Americans over Russians, but that, when it comes to distributing harms, he must distribute them impartially. Thus the.very ethics that sets up the prerogatives of roles forbids the President to launch the second-strike.

I have a final, quite different criticism, of Finite Counterforce. Even if we consider it strategically stable, at least in pre-war conditions, it is not bureaucratically stable. To overcome improved weapons defenses of opponents, Finite Counterforce requires an endless stream of new weapons programs, and weapons programs develop a momentum of their own. What starts out as Finite Counterforce may not remain Finite—MIRV and the cruise missile programs are a case in point. Furthermore, once we embrace the attitude that we must have the latest weapons, it will be difficult to forestall the lust to have the best weapons, and that will throw us back into the arms race. Long ago, McNamara discovered that the move to counterforce — in those days it was called Flexible Response—amounted to handing a blank check over to the Air Force. In a year or two he left off talk of sparing cities and invented the rhetoric of assured destruction. Even if Finite Counterforce were a morally superior policy — which it is not—it would not survive the jungles of Arlington. And when the Pentagons warps this policy into something more suited to its needs, the result will be far worse than if we had never started down the counterforce path.

Baruch College and the Graduate Center, CUNY

13 An Immoral Kind
of Deterrence

Joseph Boyle

Moral Arguments About Deterrence
and Recent Changes in International Relations

In *Nuclear Deterrence, Morality and Realism* (1987), John Finnis, Germain Grisez and I argued that the social act by which the United States and its Western allies deter the Soviet Union is immoral. To establish this conclusion we argued, in effect, that

(1) there is a kind of deterrence which is morally impermissible, namely, one which includes a conditional intention to kill innocents, and
(2) the American deterrent (which I will call "the deterrent") is an act of that kind.

Thus, we were not talking about anything as general as nuclear deterrence or deterrence or nuclear weapons, but about a complex yet logically singular action, the social act which we think has been done continuously by the United States since at least the 1960's and is probably still being done. The only *kind* of action with which we were concerned was the kind which, we argued, the deterrent instantiates: threatening to kill innocents with the conditional intent to carry out the threat.

Since, as we argued, the deterrent is an act of an impermissible kind, and the reasoning for this judgment included a consideration of the circumstances which might make it acceptable to continue with the deterrent even for a time, we drew the obvious conclusion that the United States should abandon the deterrent. In the context within which he wrote, that seemed a very drastic step indeed. For the deterrent was the cornerstone of Western defense against Soviet power, and abandoning it in the face of that power seemed tantamount to handing world hegemony over to the Soviets.[1]

Unilateral abandonment of the deterrent, together with such other steps required for being responsible about abandoning the deterrent requires, would, we thought, amount to something very much like surrender to Soviet power. For alternatives to the deterrent—such things as purely conventional forces, defensive strategies like Star Wars, and genuinely counterforce deployment of nuclear forces—do not seem capable of deterring or effectively defending against the power of a hostile force capable of final retaliation against population centers.[2] Without the deterrent, efforts to deter, contain or defend against the Soviets looked like an irresponsible invitation to disaster. In spite of these bleak prospects, we thought that the moral course was clear: unilateral abandonment of the deterrent, and the implementation of the steps needed to avoid disaster in the absence of deterrence.

Of course, the world situation has changed enormously since we wrote *Nuclear Deterrence, Morality and Realism* in the mid-1980's. The Soviet Union no longer seems capable of or interested in world domination. So, unilateral abandonment of the deterrent does not seem likely to have the bad consequences we expected. Furthermore, the developing international situation leaves room for elaborating alternatives for defense and deterrence which are not of the same moral kind as the deterrent.

Still moral qualms about the deterrent do not seem to have affected American policy makers, and the deterrent, pretty much as we described it, appears to remain in place, surely, it has not been renounced. However, given the likely changes in power arrangements during the upcoming years, strategic doctrine will probably develop considerably and deterrence policy along with it. Surely there will be some change in the words by which deterrent threats are issued and in the military and strategic deeds which back them up and make them credible.

These new words and deeds might constitute and express a different moral reality than the deterrent. But they might not. In

---

[1]Finnis, J., Boyle, J. & Grisez, G., *Nuclear Deterrence, Morality and Realism* (Oxford: Oxford University Press, 1987), pp. 70-77, 324-337.

[2]Ibid., pp. 147-154.

either case they might serve to disguise and obscure the moral reality of our strategic posture, and thus continue a tradition of strategic pronouncements and actions in which the moral issues are systematically, if not deliberately, fudged. This tradition is well established in the Western democracies and goes back at least to the public statements of strategic bombing policy during World War II.[1]

In any case it seems unlikely that there will be a clear repudiation of the deterrent, and so, given the changes that are sure to occur, it is likely to become much more difficult in the years ahead to morally identify the descendants of the deterrent. In addition to the fact that new doctrine will enhance, not curtail, the possibilities for rationalizing and dissembling on the part of policy makers, strategists and moralists, its development and implementation will complicate the factors which, in the recent past, made it possible to identify the moral character of the deterrent.

For example, talk about counterforce strategies, whether sheer rationalization, wishful thinking or honest analysis, could a few years ago be shown to be irrelevant to the basic moral issue raised by threats of final retaliation, because such strategies were plainly needed to fill gaps within the ladder of deterrence, the foundation of which had to remain the threat of final retaliation. "Had to" because we faced an enemy itself capable of final retaliation even if our counterforce power was fully and effectively used. That kind of argument is not available if we face enemies with lesser capacities.[2] More generally, many of the "necessities" to which one could appeal in arguing that the deterrent was in fact an act of a murderous kind have themselves been dependent upon the situation of mutual deterrence between powers capable of final retaliation, and incapable of safely taking steps towards genuine alternatives to threats of final retaliation.

In a word, the new world situation raises the question whether the argument of *Nuclear Deterrence*, and perhaps of any moral analysis developed within the context of the cold war, is now obsolete. Surely, some moral arguments about the deterrent will become or have become obsolete. Michael Walzer's argument that something like a condition of supreme emergency justifies the

---

[1]*Ibid.*, pp. 18-26, 38-44.
[2]*Ibid.*, pp. 143-154.

Western deterrent,[1] or perhaps consequentialist arguments which depend on a precise estimate of the outcomes of keeping or abandoning the deterrent.

As already noted, *Nuclear Deterrence* included projections about the consequences of abandoning the deterrent, and an extensive effort to morally identify the deterrent. Both of these parts of our argument will require substantial revision and explication if the kind of argument we made is to lead to concrete evaluations of likely future developments in deterrence policy. In particular, the effort to identify the moral kind of the actions by which the United States deters potential enemies is likely to be very difficult. However, one component upon the context of the cold war, namely, the argument that there is an impermissible kind of deterrence. In what follows I will lay out a version of this argument.

I think this is worth doing, because abstract arguments against certain kinds of actions have an enduring role in moral discussion and reflection. This is true even if it is difficult or impossible to identify instances of the action. For the kind of social criticism which is one of the tasks of moral philosophy, and which requires the effort to identify instances of morally evaluated kinds of action, can proceed even in the face of substantial empirical ambiguities, and this kind of social criticism is not the only or the primary purpose of moral analysis.

Policy makers and citizens can be guided in their planning and public-decision making by moral considerations, and attending to the moral kinds of actions they might consider doing is surely part of such prospective moral evaluation. This sort of moral reflection does not require the difficult and detailed argumentation to morally identify an act which is needed to convict someone of wrongdoing. The requirements of a quasi-legal argument which seeks to establish from a third-person perspective that someone is doing an act of an impermissible kind are obviously quite different from the considerations which an agent needs to guide her or his decisions. So there is some value in determining whether there is a sound moral argument against a kind of deterrence.

---

[1]Michael Walzer, *Just and Unjust Wars* (New York: Basic Books, 1978).

To keep the focus clear and make the subject manageable, I will set aside two components of the normative view which underlies the argument:

(1) I will not discuss the arguments against consequentialist approaches to the deterrent or into the arguments about consequentialism more generally.[1] This is an essential part of the dialectic by which we defend our overall deontological approach to deterrence issues, but here I will simply assume that approach.
(2) I will not try to derive what I think is the basic moral norm governing these matters—the prohibition against intentionally killing the innocent—from more basic normative principles.[2] Again, I will assume the truth of this norm, and assume that it is an absolute norm.

Of course, these assumptions are controversial, as indeed are the attempts to defend them in *Nuclear Deterrence*. Still, these assumptions form part of the moral outlook of many people, including many who do not reject the deterrent as immoral. Thus, these assumptions do not themselves determine whether there is an immoral kind of deterring. For deterrence is not killing but threatening to kill, and so reasoning is needed to determine whether the threat involved in at least one kind of deterrence renders acts of that kind immoral. Therefore, my effort in what follows is to exhibit that reasoning. While not sufficient to justify the moral evaluation of a kind of act of deterrence, such an effort is necessary, and so important for the ongoing discussion of the deterrent.

A Kind of Deterrence

I begin the argument by delineating a kind of human action from what seems to me the proper moral perspective: that of the intentions, practical reasoning and choices of the agents involved. Let us consider, then, a certain kind of act: an act in which one intentionally deters another.
What does one undertake when choosing to deter? I take it that one deters when one wants to control the behavior of another in

---

[1]Finnis, *op. cit.*, pp. 238-267.
[2]*Ibid.*, pp. 297-319.

some way; namely, by giving the other a certain kind of reason not to do something one does not want the other to do. The kind of reason one gives the other is the credible threat to do something the other does not want one to do. So, intentionally deterring presupposes the belief on the part of the one who deters that there is an outcome that the other fears and which one can bring about, and the belief that threatening to bring about that outcome will give the other reason not to do certain things. The action of deterring is making the threat so that the other, believing that one will cause the feared outcome if he or she does certain things, will refrain from doing them.

So, here is a possible action someone might take: one commits oneself to achieving the benefit involved in another's refraining from doing something one regards as harmful. That benefit is what one intends in choosing to deter. That benefit is achieved by causing the other to fear certain things one could do, and so causing that fear is the precise means one chooses to achieve the intended benefit of deterrence.

But it is equally clear that the feared action one threatens need not be something one intends, even conditionally, to do. Perhaps one knows that one cannot do the act, but can cause the other to believe that one can. In that circumstance, one's threat is a bluff in a fairly obvious sense (as when Dirty Harry says `Make my day' knowing his revolver is empty). It also is possible that the person issuing the deterrent threat is just resolved not to do the act if the conditions calling for it are fulfilled, but thinks she can achieve the benefits of deterrence by causing the other to believe falsely that she will, if necessary, do what is threatened. Here again we have a bluff. And whatever the morality of these kinds of bluffing, they are not acts involving the choice to do the threatened act.

If one is not bluffing in making a deterrent threat, there seem to be two possibilities: either one chooses precisely to do the threatened action if the conditions calling for it are fulfilled, or one leaves open for a later choice the question of whether or not one will do the act should the conditions calling for it be fulfilled.

In the first of these possibilities the resolve to do the threatened act is clearly part of what one intends in the act of deterrence: one's choice includes the resolve to do the act if the conditions calling for it are fulfilled. Causing the other to fear something the other believes one could do is, as noted above, essential to an act of deterrence, and resolving to do the threatened act if the conditions calling for it are fulfilled is surely one sensible way of contributing to the causing of that fear. This resolve alone will not cause fear, but it surely can help. For the reality of this resolve, if effectively communicated, will help remove the possibility that the other will think the threat a bluff. One way to get one's threats to be taken seriously is to be ready to carry them out, and so the will to do the feared act is a natural way of realizing the essential deterrent means of causing fear.

In the second of these possibilities, the act of deterrence does not include the firm resolve to do the threatened act if called for. In this case what contributes to causing the other's fear is one's openness to choose in the future to do the act, however that may be expressed or disguised. So one's will is not firmly fixed on doing the threatened act if called for.

However, the moral significance of this difference in intentional structure is not great—not at least in the context of the argument I am developing. For, as will become clear, what is pivotal in this argument is one's will towards doing the action one threatens, since it is impermissible to do the threatened act. Although there is a difference between choosing to do such an act if the conditions calling for it are fulfilled and keeping an open mind about whether one will do it, that difference does not mark the line between permissible and impermissible choices. For it is wrong to maintain an open mind about doing immoral things; such possibilities should be firmly rejected.[1]

There is a difference between maintaining an open mind about future wrongdoing and doing something which has as a side-effect the creation of future temptations. In the first case one's choice is precisely to leave open the possibility of choosing evil, whereas in the second case one's choice is not to be open to doing evil but to do the act which brings about the temptation. The latter can be compatible with an upright will, but not the former.

Still, to make the main moral argument perspicuous, let us set aside this possibility of leaving one's options open, and consider the case in which one deters precisely by choosing to do the threatened action should it be called for. Now it is clear that among the things one might threaten to do in deterring another are some that it is

---

[1]*Ibid.*, pp. 110-112.

impermissible to do. The kind of act of deterring I will evaluate is one in which the threatened act is the act of intentionally killing the innocent. I use "innocent" in the standard way to refer to those who are neither convicted capital criminals nor engaged in which unlawful, violent action.[1] I call the threatened killing "intentional" not to indicate that the causing of deaths is itself a benefit, but according to the common usage in which what one does purposefully as part of one's plan is "intentional" in contrast to what one brings about as a side-effect of carrying out that plan.

The interlocking intentions of deterrent acts and of the acts threatened in deterrent acts, as well as the relationships between one's intentions towards what one threatens as one threatens it in deterring and those involved in actually doing the threatened act should deterrence fail, make for considerable difficulty in identifying a threatened act as one of intentionally killing the innocent. I am concerned with the clear case in which one does threaten to kill innocents, however one would describe that to oneself or others.

It is perhaps worth noting that, although there are some genuinely difficult cases here, there are also some transparent rationalizations in which the threat to kill innocents is plainly present, though not acknowledged. Thus, for example, the long list of strategic statements in which American officials disavow any interest in targeting or destroying cities or attacking civilians. The disavowals are almost always followed by a reminder that, of course, cities and civilians cannot escape destruction. It is clear, therefore, that the fear on the part of the Soviet leaders that these innocents will be killed is part of what American leaders take steps to bring about and apparently want to bring about. Consequently, even if the deaths of these innocents were genuine side-effects of the military actions which would carry out the threat if deterrence should fail, these deaths would not fall outside one's deterrent intentions. For in deterring one chooses precisely to cause fear, and what one chooses to cause the other fear is part of one's plan and intention.[2]

The difficult cases arise when (1) the action one threatens is predicted to have effects the prospect of which will contribute to the other's fear of the threatened act, but (2) one refuses to take steps designed specifically to cause the other to fear just those effects. In

---

[1]*Ibid.*, pp. 86-90.
[2]*Ibid.*, pp. 91-93.

this case, one cannot but welcome the fact that the prospect of these effects is fearful to the other, since they contribute to one's deterrent purposes. And it seems true even if there are other reasons why one may not welcome such effects, such as one's judgment that it is not permissible to act with a view towards causing that fear. This case is difficult, because welcoming what contributes to one's purpose is often a sign that one intends it, but the refusal to take steps to bring something about is a sign that one does not intend it. Although I am inclined to believe that it is possible not to intend such effects, it seems to me that the only thing to which one can appeal in many cases is one's conviction that one does not in fact intend them, that one is not interested in them even as a bonus, and that one brings them about only as a side-effect of threatening something else. Happily, my argument does not require that the difficulties raised by this possibility be settled.

To return to the main argument: I have delineated a certain kind of action: an act of deterring in which one threatens to intentionally kill innocents, and in which one is neither bluffing nor keeping open the decision about killing if the threat fails to work, but in which one is resolved to intentionally kill innocents if the conditions calling for the threatened act are fulfilled. This is a kind of act which *does* include the conditional intention to kill innocents—either because that is precisely what is threatened or because what one wants to cause the other to fear includes the deaths of innocents.

The Moral Evaluation of this Kind of Deterrence

This, at last, is a kind of act which it is profitable to morally evaluate. The argument to show that acts of just this kind are immoral seems to me relatively straightforward. The basic premise in the argument for this conclusion is what Gregory Kavka has called the "wrongful intentions principle:" the idea that it is wrong to intend what it is wrong to do. So, it is wrong to intend the deaths of innocents, just as it is wrong to intentionally kill them. This step in the argument seems uncontroversial.

The further application of the wrongful intentions principle to conditional intentions is generally uncontroversial. One who intends to rob a bank only if the guard is absent surely has a wrongful intention and it is seen as such by an uncontroversial application of the wrongful intentions principle.

It is the application of the wrongful intentions principle to the case of deterrent intentions which seems abstract and mistaken. Kavka has provided one of the chief reasons for this appearance: in acts of deterring, the conditional intention has what he calls "autonomous" consequences—consequences which arise from forming and expressing the conditional intention independently of whether the threatened action is carried out.

Kavka uses this observation to ground a consequentialist argument for blocking the application of the wrongful intentions principle to a class of deterrent intentions. This argument assumes that what justifies the wrongful intentions principle is that intending to do something bad (usually) increases the likelihood that one will do it. It proceeds to claim that in deterrent situations in which the bad outcomes one wishes to prevent are worse or roughly as bad as the evil conditionally intended, one may act with the deterrent intention.[1]

But the assumption of this argument is unavailable to those who wish to proceed with moral analysis on nonconsequentialist lines. For nonconsequentialists, the wrongful intentions principle is not the result of applying the consequentialist method to the causal connections between willed acts and outcomes, but a reminder about what moral evaluation deals with. Moral standards, according to this nonconsequentialist conception, direct people in their use of freedom. Consequently, free choices and their underlying intentions are the *main* subject of moral evaluation; behavior is not independently significant but morally relevant as the execution and expression of choices. So the wrongful intentions principle does not provide a bridge for connecting a subject of derivative or secondary moral evaluation to the primary subject, but is a reminder that moral norms direct our lives just insofar as our lives are the exercise of our freedom, and so apply just as much to choices which are not carried out in overt behavior as to those which are.[2]

For all of us have difficulty in keeping in focus the precise kind of action which Kavka and I are discussing: one which *does* involve

---

[1]*Ibid.*, pp. 180-181; Gregory Kavka, "Some Paradoxes of Deterrence," *The Journal of Philosophy*, Vol. 75 (1978), pp. 285-302.

[2]Finnis, *et. al.*, *op. cit.*, pp. 78-81.

the conditional intention to kill innocents. If the factors which blur this focus are explicitly considered, it becomes plausible to think that the wrongful intentions principle applies.

This focus is hard to maintain, because some deterrent acts involving this conditional intention are similar to acts having a different intentional structure, and because some of them have features which make the presence of this intention less than perspicuous.

Some deterrent acts involving a conditional intention to kill innocents are easily confused with actions in which a person does something with the expectation that doing this will give him or her reason at some future time to wrongfully kill, for example, in a bluff in which one recognizes that one might be sorely tempted to carry out the threat. This kind of act is intentionally different than the one Kavka and I discuss. For we are considering an act in which there is not simply an expectation that one might make an imoral choice in the future. One's choice is already made: one is resolved to do the threatened act if the conditions calling for it are fulfilled.

Deterrent acts involving the conditional intent to do what one threatens are also easily confused with acts in which one the condition includes some further choice which one has not made. This is the situation in the old example of the monk who decides that if he ever chooses to go to a bordello he will not go in his habit. Since the monk has not chosen to go to the bordello, that his will in not fixed on abandoning his habit in the way the will of one deterring with the conditional intention to carry out the threat is fixed on carrying out the threat. What is conditional in this deterrent case is not conditioned on one's future choices, but on factors which operate independently of it.

A deterrent case which is perhaps more like that of the monk is one in which one's choice is to keep one's options open, but that, as I said above, is not the case under consideration. Even this kind of deterrence differs from the monk's case in that in the latter there is no will to abandon the habit, since there in no will to fulfill the condition on which that action depends, whereas in the former, the fulfillment of the conditions calling for the threatened action are outside one's control, and one does have a will to at least remain open to doing what one threatens.

I turn now to a consideration of some of the factors which may obscure the presence of the conditional intention to do what one threatens in acts of deterrence in which that intention is *ex hypothesi* present. One such factor arises when the threat involving the conditional intent is made in circumstances such that the conditions calling for carrying out the threat are not likely to be fulfilled immediately, thus allowing for time to change one's mind. In such a case it might seem that one cannot be choosing anything more than to keep one's options open. But a conditional intent to do what one threatens is compatible with having time within which one might change one's mind. The fact that one foresees that one will be able to change one's mind has no tendency to show that one had not made up one's mind in the first place; quite the contrary.

Likewise, the fact that one judges it most unlikely that the conditions calling for the performance of the threatened act will be fulfilled might obscure the presence of a conditional intention, but it is compatible with there being such an intention. One can surely resolve to do something if necessary while believing that one probably will not have to do it. And even if the threat containing the conditional intention is made precisely to render the need for carrying it out unlikely, one can make the threat with that intention.

Finally, the fact that one does not want to carry out the threatened act can obscure the intentional structure of an act of deterrence, but is compatible with threatening with the conditional intention to carry it out. Here the language of intention is perhaps problematic, because carrying out the threat when one does not want to carry out presupposes that doing the threatened action is not regarded as a benefit, and not, in that sense, intended. But people plainly are capable of choosing to do things which they do only reluctantly and with great loathing. Thus, it seems possible to conditionally intend to do something one does not want to do. Indeed, that is what would be going on in the relevant class of deterrent acts, supposing that those who issue the threats do not want to carry them out.[1]

It is perhaps worth noting that there is a form of reluctance which is incompatible with deterrence, but the incompatibility has nothing specifically to do with the conditional intentions involved in some deterrent threats. If one had overriding reasons not to carry out a deterrent threat, and no good reason to carry it out when the conditions calling for it were fulfilled, then not only could one not

---

[1] *Ibid.*, pp. 81-86.

conditionally intend to carry out the threat, but one could not plausibly threaten it to deter, even as a bluff. To guarantee that a threat is credible as a threat, one must do what one can to exclude the appearances that one is bluffing; and that requires that one foresee and communicate that one will have reason to carry out the threat if the conditions calling for it are fulfilled. So, the kind of reluctance incompatible with the conditional intent to do the threatened act is incompatible with deterrence as such. MAD can't be literally mad and still work as a deterrent; moreover, there clearly is a motive which one could expect people to act on, even in final retaliation: vengeance. This is not perhaps a good reason, but it is a sufficient motive.

In short, many of the reasons for resisting the application of the wrongful intentions principle to deterrent intentions are factors which lead people to suppose that the relevant conditional intentions do not exist. But the case at hand is one in which the conditional intention to do wrong is assumed to be be present. There appears to be every reason to apply the wrongful intentions principle here for the resolve to kill innocents involved in this kind of deterrence is a real willingness and readiness to do it. The will of one doing the act is set. The will to kill is conditional, but the condition is not a further determination of one's will, but rather the fulfillment of conditions which do not depend on one's will. Since the wrongful intention principle applies to deterrent intentions, the kind of action I have delineated is immoral. Any act a person contemplates doing which is seen to be of this kind should be rejected as a temptation.

Social Acts and Bluffing

Now, deterrence by a nation is not the act of an individual, but of a group. This surely complicates the moral analysis, in particular, an analysis which puts so much emphasis on intention and choice. Who is making the choice and forming the deterrent intentions? Steven Lee argues that difficulties in answering this sort of question are the Achilles heel of the argument of *Nuclear Deterrence* (and indeed of any attempt to apply just war analyses to policies of deterrence rather than to actual warfare). He thinks these difficulties emerge in our rejection of the possibility that the deterrent is a bluff. He says:

The authors adopt a deontological perspective concerned with assessing the intentions of individuals, but then to show that nuclear deterrence cannot be a bluff, they apply this perspective, through the notion of a social act, in such a way that the intentions of individuals become no longer morally determinative.[1]

Plainly, an argument against a kind of deterrence would be fantastic if its conclusion could be applied to actions of that kind done by a group only by accepting group intentions and choices which are wholly unrelated to the choices and intentions of group members.

But the claim which Lee reports by saying that "the intentions of individuals become no longer morally determinative" is *not* that there are no individual choices which are necessary or sufficient for social actions. We say otherwise:

> The deterrent, too, is a social act. The US deterrent, for instance, came into being and is kept in being by official acts of presidents, members of Congress, and others, in accord with their constitutional, statutory, or other public responsibilities.[2]

As this suggests, our claim is that members of a group can make choices and have intentions which are different from and inconsistent with those they make as participants in a group action.[3]

However group actions are to be understood, there surely are such things: teams play games, countries declare war, families go on vacation, universities adopt admission standards, and so on. I take it that the decisions of some within the group under some circumstances are necessary and sufficient to create an act of the group. There is no general way to say whose decisions, made under

---

[1]Steven Lee, "Morality and Nuclear Weapons Policy," *Philosophy and Public Affairs*, Vol. 19, pp. 95.
[2]Finnis, *et. al.*, *op. cit.*, pp. 122.
[3]*Ibid.*, pp. 121-123.

what conditions, count as the decisions of the group, since the authority structure of groups is variable and more or less formally established, But this indeterminacy does not leave group decisions hanging in the air, independent of anybody's choices and intentions. Consequently, adding to the act of deterrence evaluated in the previous section the circumstance that its agent is a group does not put it into moral limbo, nor, as far as I can see, provide a circumstance that substantially changes its moral character.

This general response to Lee's criticism can be amplified by putting it into the context of *Nuclear Deterrence*'s argument that the deterrent cannot be a bluff. This argument does not include the claim that social acts cannot be bluffs. They plainly can be. A small group who could and did communicate among themselves that a threat they corporately issued was not to be carried out would be bluffing.[1]

Variations on this simple possibility suggest the complexities in the relationships between group and individual decisions and point to some of the reasons for thinking that the deterrent cannot be a bluff. Suppose the leader of the group proposes to the others that they engage in a bluff, and the others agree, but the leader is lying and plans to go through with it: is the act of the group a bluff or not? Suppose that it is not the leader who is lying about bluffing but one or another of the members who would have to refrain from carrying out the threat if that were called for: is the group action then a bluff or not?

A natural way to resolve these puzzles is to regard as the act of the group the act which is proposed to group members, for endorsement if necessary and for cooperation and compliance. Thus, if a group is asked or told by its authorities to bluff, then those who cooperate are engaged in a common action of bluffing. But if they are asked or told to be ready to carry out a threat, the common action in which they are wittingly cooperating cannot be a bluff. A person might pretend to cooperate in the common action of deterrence while resolving never to do his or her part in carrying out the threat; perhaps we might say that the person is bluffing, but surely that has no tendency to show that the joint enterprise is a bluff.

These conceptual points are applied to the deterrent in the following way: what has been proposed by its leaders to the

---

[1]*Ibid.*, pp. 114.

American people for their support and acceptance, and to many
Americans for much more active cooperation than that, is not that
the US deters by bluffing, or for that matter by keeping our close
options open, but that we should be ready and willing to carry out
murderous threats. This is what is on the table: what Congress is
asked to appropriate money to support, what the military is asked to
implement, and what citizens are asked to support. All might wish
it were a bluff, and many of those in a position to contribute to
carrying out the threat if called for, including perhaps the President,
or the President on some days but not others, might resolve not to
carry it out. But the social act is not changed by such private
resolves.

Thus, given the way in which American policy is established
and the large and complex nature of the cooperation needed for
deterrence, it seems impossible that the public proposal be a bluff—
that would be tantamount to announcing to the other side that our
threat was just a bluff.

To sum up: what provides some room between individual
intentions and the intentions which constitute social actions are the
protocols for authoritative decision making in any group and the
need for communication of proposals for cooperative action to those
who will wittingly cooperate. These facts do not altogether break
the link between personal choice and social action, and they do not
by themselves rule out the possibility of social acts of bluffing.
What rules out the possibility of bluffing in American deterrence
policy is the is the conjunction of these factors with the demands of
public decision making in a democratic society (public in our world
even to one's enemies).

Our argument that the deterrent cannot be a bluff was
undertaken as part of the effort to block the rationalizations which
prevent the correct moral identification of the deterrent. But the
necessities to which we appealed in this argument are not a function
of the Cold War relationship between the Superpowers. The
necessities depend on factors which are much less likely to change.
So, the discussion of the possibilities of bluffing are of continuing
importance if only for the light they throw on the social character of
deterrence by a modern democracy.

* * *

Where does my analysis leave us? With an argument against a kind of deterrence which is certainly a continuing possibility in a world formed by strategic bombing and thirty or more years of deterrence which surely seems to be of that kind. Are all future forms of nuclear deterrence likely to be of that kind? Hardly, or at least not clearly. But the argument suggests some questions to ask ourselves when it is not clear whether we are threatening murderously, and points to some of the ways in which we might deceive ourselves. But maybe there will be acts of altogether new moral kinds. For them we will need new moral analyses. So, I doubt there can be anything like a single, final argument against all possible forms of nuclear deterrence.

St. Michael's College, University of Toronto

14 The Natural Law Argument
Against Deterrence

John Kultgen

Finnis, Boyle and Grisez (herein, FBG) have recently published a powerful argument for the thesis that nuclear deterrence is immoral *per se*.[1] They appeal to Natural Law and argue that cost/benefit analyses of security schemes are both inconclusive (there is no way to compute the values and probabilities) and insidious (the pretence of doing so rationalizes violations of Natural Law). I shall criticize FBG's premises, but not with the aim of refuting their conclusion. I shall try rather to prepare the way for basing the same conclusion on consequentialist foundations.

There is no space here to explore the issues thoroughly. I can only provide an argument sketch and indicate the direction in which our reflections on this vital issue should go. In Section I, I will summarize FBG's position; in Section II, criticize it; and in Section III, briefly state my own reasons for condemning nuclear deterrence.

The Natural Law Case Against Nuclear Deterrence

The Moral Argument:

---

[1] John Finnis, Joseph Boyle, and Germain Grisez, *Nuclear Deterrence, Morality and Realism* (Oxford: Clarendon Press, 1987). Other works which present substantially the same argument are Anthony Kenny, *The Logic of Deterrence* (Chicago: Chicago University Press, 1985) and *The Ivory Tower* (Oxford: Basil Blackwell, 1985); and Roger Ruston, *Nuclear Deterrence—Right or Wrong?* (Abbots Langley, England: Catholic Information Services, 1981), "Nuclear Deterrence and the Use of the Just War Doctrine" in *Objections to Nuclear Defense*, ed. by Nigel Blake and Kay Pole (London: Routledge and Kegan Paul, 1984) and *A Say in the End of the World (Oxford: Clarendon Press, 1989)*.
I will discuss only Finnis, Boyle, and Grisez's version and refer to it as the Moral Argument. It is presented in more formal terms in the Appendix to this paper.

It would be wrong to use nuclear weapons in war because it would inevitably deliberately or disproportionately kill innocent people. It is wrong to intend to do what it is wrong to do. It is impossible to successfully threaten to use nuclear weapons without intending, at least conditionally, to use them (bluffing is impossible). The very possession of nuclear weapons constitutes a threat. Hence, any form of deterrence that requires possession of nuclear weapons is morally wrong.

The basis which FBG provide for the Moral Argument is the following: They define Natural Law as ordinances of reason ("moral laws") to which the individual must adhere if he is to achieve fulfillment as a human being and to which the group must adhere if it is to realize genuine community.

The ordinances include *positive imperatives* (to be implemented according to circumstances and not at all in the absence of requisite ones) and *absolute prohibitions* (to be followed without exception). To live a fulfilling life one must, positively, make commitments, assume responsibilities, and carry them out; at the same time, negatively, one must never carry them out in such a way as to violate absolute moral prohibitions, even if this makes particular obligations impossible to carry out at all.

Thus, the proper authorities of a nation—those who legitimately act for the whole—are strongly obligated to take measures to assure its security, i.e. protect its independence, the integrity of its institutions, and the lives of its citizens. But they are limited to means which are not forbidden by the moral law. Thus, positively, they are authorized to engage in wars and wage them vigorously; but, negatively, the wars they may enter and the ways they may wage them are limited by principles of justice.

The crucial Just-War principles for our purpose here are Discrimination (noncombatants must not be deliberately attacked) and Proportionality (casualties which are foreseeable byproducts of military actions must be proportionate to the good to be achieved). There can be no doubt that the use of nuclear weapons in combat between two heavily armed opponents would violate both of these principles, as the principles are construed by FBG. Hence, if the principles are valid, the critical first premise of the Moral Argument is justified. It would be wrong to use nuclear weapons in combat, either as a first use or in retaliation for their use by the enemy.

The principles of Discrimination and Proportionality are derived from Natural Law by

(a) applying to war the Law of Murder,[1] which states that the innocent must not be deliberately killed;
(b) identifying "the innocent" in war with noncombatants; (c) and maintaining (via the Principle of Double Effect) that byproduct homicide is not deliberate killing.

FBG derive the Law of Murder from the Evil Means Principle, that evil may not be done that good shall come, which they maintain is absolute. They define evil as the deliberate destruction or obstruction of a basic human good.

A basic good is a good that provides an ultimate reason for acting, so each basic good provides a reason that would justify the pursuit of it in the absence of other goods. Some examples are knowledge, friendship, justice, and (crucial for the present discussion) life. They are aspects or elements of the "full-being" or fulfillment of persons: to be a person in the full sense is to instantiate basic goods fully and harmoniously.

Individual fulfillment is possible only in community with other fulfilled persons and a degree of fulfillment among the members of a group is necessary for true community. The notion of joint fulfillment of the individual and the community is incorporated in FBG's First Principle of Morality, choose only those possibilities whose willing is compatible with integral human fulfillment.

Instantiations of basic goods are logically independent and compossible, but the finitude of the human condition precludes the material instantiation of all together and the circumstances in which individuals find themselves prevent the instantiation of particular combinations of them. In carrying out positive obligations, therefore, the individual is forced to choose among instantiations of different goods for herself and between herself and others.

Now, FBG believe that basic goods are incommensurate—when a choice between instantiations must be made, there is no objective measure to determine whether one is better than another. (They specifically deny that the pleasure or satisfaction which goods bring

---

[1]"Law of Murder" and "Evil Means Principle" are my terms. Otherwise the labels are FBG's.

is such a measure.) Consider the simplest case, where a person must choose between two basic goods for herself, for example, cultivating a particular friendship or sequestering herself in order to pursue a course of study. Consider also the case where a person must choose between two persons in instantiating a specific good, e.g., awarding a fellowship to one of two equally qualified candidates. According to FBG's account, these decisions require a totally undetermined choice between the two goods, since nothing in either instantiation provides a better reason for action than the other. The choice itself is what constitutes the good, in itself only *a* reason, as *her* reason for acting.

In the foregoing cases, FBG do not think that the agent is doing evil by failing to instantiate basic goods, since she is not destroying or obstructing them; she is simply leaving them unrealized. Other choices do involve destruction or obstruction. One paradigm is the decision of the public official to sacrifice the life of an innocent scapegoat to protect a group from a race riot or pogrom. A second is the decision of the commander to prevent an assault on his troops by holding hostages. These acts are forbidden by the Law of Murder (it is never right to deliberately take or risk the life of a person to save the lives of others), which is derived from the Evil Means Principle (the instantiation of basic goods for some persons must not be deliberately sacrificed to promote instantiations for others), which in turn is derived from the First Principle of Morality (choose only possibilities compatible with integral human fulfillment).

Counterexamples in which it seems that one ought to violate the Evil Means Principle come quickly to mind. Common morality sanctions killing in self-defense and to protect the lives of innocent people. The homeowner is permitted to shoot an intruder, if he cannot otherwise prevent the intruder from killing him or his family. The commander is permitted to commit troops to battle though he knows that many of the troops as well as the enemy and civilians will be killed or maimed, if this is required to defend his country against aggression. FBG, like other Natural Law theorists, handle these cases by the Principle of Double Effect. The acts are justified when the agent does not *intend* the deaths of the intruder or the troops and civilians, but only *accepts* them as an unavoidable byproduct of what he does intend, to ward off the murderous attack or win a crucial battle.

FBG believe that intentional homicide is evil because human life is not only a necessary condition for the instantiation of other basic goods, but a basic good in itself. Yet, as we have noted, they condone homicide in personal self-defense, and in just wars. Their justification of these lethal acts depends upon their analysis of free choice. According to them, choice is the adoption of a proposal composed of a good to be achieved (the end) and an action described in terms of its efficacy to produce that good (the means). The agent forms an intention to perform the act to achieve the end. The means-end complex exhausts the content of the intention. Side-effects of the means are not intended, even though the agent knows that they will occur. (I would add, the remote effects of the end state or the effects of external agencies which the agent's action or inaction allows to occur are also not part of the intention thus narrowly construed.)

Thus, FBG argue, one can *commit* lethal acts and *know* they are lethal without *intending* to kill anyone. This is critical for their versions of the Evil Means Principle and the Law of Murder, which are stronger in FBG's ethical theory than in common morality.

> . . . if common morality absolutely forbids intentional killing of the innocent, it does not absolutely exclude intentional killing of those not innocent. However, the argument we have offered as a rational defence of common morality's norm justifies a more general norm: any choice to kill any human being is wrong.

Nevertheless,

> Our theory . . . does not condemn all killing. The rights of innocent persons ought to be defended, even by deadly force. And the wrongs of guilty persons ought to be punished. Our thesis is that it is always wrong to choose to kill a human being. But some killing does not involve a choice to kill, and such killing may sometimes be justified, though certainly not always. Killing can carry out a choice to do a deed which in fact is deadly without being a choice to kill. Such a choice can

be to do something else, to which death will be a
foreseen side-effect. The causal consequences of
executing a choice, even if they are known to be
inevitable, are not necessarily part of what one
chooses.[1]

Objections to the Moral Argument

The entry point for my criticisms is FBG's account of deliberate
choice. Their account sanctions homicide as a byproduct of military
action as long as the deaths are not the end sought or a direct means
to the end and are not disproportionate (in FBG's special sense of the
term, discussed below). I believe to the contrary that all major
foreseeable effects of an agent's action are his responsibility,
whether or not he is seeking them. And I believe that
proportionality should be judged in the obvious way of weighing
the good and bad consequences of an action for human values.

Moreover, I reject the notion that positive duties may or must
be left undischarged whenever they violate certain moral
prohibitions. This notion requires one to refrain from intervening to
prevent others from doing evil when it would require one to "do
evil" oneself.[2] But if omissions can be as wrong as commissions,
no moral prohibition is absolute.   There are imaginable
circumstances in which one ought to do what it forbids to prevent a
great harm or promote a great good. FBG correctly point out that
discharging positive obligations can require the destruction or
obstruction of basic goods for some people in order to instantiate or
protect instantiation for other people. I draw the opposite
conclusion than they: since this is sometimes justified, even the
most basic prohibitions must sometimes give way to positive
obligations.

As far as the morality of intentions, it is true that people often
do choose actions in terms only of their ends and perceived means

---

[1]FBG, *op. cit.*, pp. 309-311.

[2]I maintain that to "do evil" in the sense of violating a moral law is
not necessarily to do evil in the more basic sense, since there are
always justified exceptions to any "law" requiring or prohibiting
specific behavior. In such cases one may violate the law without
truly doing evil.

and disregard their byproducts, their remote consequences, and the effects of outside agencies which they shape or prevent. And people often *are* excused for acting in a way that has foreseeable bad consequences which they do not aim at. However, it is my belief that they *ought* to take all of the consequences into consideration, they *ought* to choose between total packages of (major, foreseeable, controllable) ends/means/side-effects/external consequences, including the total package associated with failing to act, and they *ought* to be held responsible for all the results they can reasonably be expected to foresee.

The reason is that better consequences measured by any plausible standard—whether integral human fulfillment, irreducible goods, happiness, or pleasure—will be realized by holding people accountable for seeking the best total results in their actions rather than by holding them accountable only for their intentions in the narrow sense of selection of ends and means.

Some Just-War theorists invoke consequentialist considerations in their construal of the Principle of Proportionality. They reason that it is wrong to inflict noncombatant casualties as a byproduct of legitimate military objectives if the positive value of the objectives, measured in terms of nonmoral goods, does not outweigh the negative value of the deaths. Thus, the principal issue in their evaluation of Hiroshima is the number of lives saved counted against the number of lives sacrificed. FBG, however, are consistent in their anticonsequentialism when they construe proportionality in terms of the deontological concept of fairness. To their mind a commander observes the principle of proportionality when he is willing to allow byproduct casualties to his own citizens and allies on the same basis as the casualties to enemy citizens which he accepts, a principle violated by the Allied Command in World War II when it was more scrupulous in precision bombing of German targets in France than in Germany.[1]

---

[1]FBG maintain that "... "proportionate" and related terms do have meaning because they express assessments made by *moral standards*. The standard most usually available, and used, for these assessments is the standard of fairness (the Golden Rule, or principle of universalizability). This differentiates the impartial from the biased acceptance of harmful side-effects of military actions. ... Assuming the norms of just-war theory, the Allies unfairly accepted the harm

214   Just War, Nonviolence and Deterrence

This is one of the theses that convince me that FBG's position is faulty in its foundations. If I have not misread their analysis, they countenance any number of civilian casualties as long as these are inflicted impartially as a byproduct of otherwise legitimate military actions. One of the unique horrors of nuclear weapons is precisely that they swamp the differences between combatant and noncombatant, as well as between enemy, ally, and bystander. There is a monstrous impartiality about them. They exterminate everyone with even-handed indifference. It is the number of lives they destroy or blight, not whose lives, that makes them so wicked.

Proportionality in the straightforward sense of a balance of goods over harms (primarily of nonmoral goods over nonmoral harms[1]) is the key principle for evaluating belligerent acts. If we accept the principle in this form, we have to face up to the fact that the moral belligerent chronically must decide whether to sacrifice some instantiations of basic goods in order to preserve or produce others. Choose among basic goods he does and choose he must. It does not help to tell him that basic goods are incommensurable. Rather a way must be found to enable him make choices on something like an objective basis. Fortunately (!) the choice

---

their bombing caused to German civilians. It is unfair, not as "too much" in some other way, that the incidental harm thus accepted is reasonably said to have violated the requirement of proportionality." *Op. cit.*, pp. 263-264.

[1] Once principles of morality which define actions in terms of their non-moral consequences exist, there come into existence specific moral goods and evils. They consist in doing what is right or according to the principles and avoiding what is wrong or contrary to the principles. This intrinsic good that resides in the very effort to do what is right is added to the consequences of making that effort and, in some instances, of succeeding in it. Moreover, the moral good of trying to do what is right may be sufficient to counterbalance the non-moral evils which come from mistakes about what is right. However, the evil consequences that would be caused by nuclear warfare and that are avoided by refraining from it are so massive as to make the moral goodness of acting with good intentions insignificant whenever those intentions significantly increase the risk of nuclear war. Hence, I do not take the specifically moral good of following principles such as that of fairness into consideration in my analysis of proportionality.

relating to nuclear weapons is clearcut. The nonmoral evils that would result from using them are so immense that fine comparisons are not needed. We are not forced to decide, for example, whether, having assigned a value of 100 to the life of Bush, we should rate Gorbachev's life at 90 or 120 or how low to rate Saddam Hussein's or how high to rate our own. All lives would be in jeopardy in a nuclear exchange and the few goods that might be achieved are negligible in comparison.

The distinction between combatant and noncombatant ultimately carries no weight in evaluating casualties. A soldier's death is just as great an intrinsic evil as a civilian's, though it may be more justified instrumentally (it usually contributes more to just victory to kill enemy soldiers than enemy or friendly civilians). This renders problematic the applicability of the Law of Murder to war.[1] But that law is not needed to evaluate the use of nuclear weapons. Those who enter war or wage it must judge whether their objectives are important enough to outweigh the prospective casualties among combatants and noncombatants alike, on both their own and the enemy's side, as a result of both their own actions and the enemy's responses to their actions. The gains have almost never been worth the costs in the most just of wars. They almost certainly would not be in any modern full-scale conventional war. A fortiori it is inconceivable that they would be in a nuclear war.

What Is Wrong with Nuclear Deterrence

I take it as obvious, then, that use of nuclear weapons in combat would cause much greater harm than any good that it might achieve. The military casualties prior to escalation would be disproportionate to any military advantage. Escalation would bring an immense number of additional casualties not only to combatants but to noncombatants on both sides and neutral populations. The damage to the environment and cultural assets would be incalculable.

---

[1] There seems a fundamental confusion in identifying combatant/non-combatant with guilt/innocence and calling non-combatant homicides murder and combatant homicides not murder, despite vigorous efforts of many Just War theorists to justify these conceptions.

But deterrence, if it works, is not open to this criticism. Its purpose is to prevent nuclear exchanges. What must be judged, therefore, is whether nuclear threats are justified when their objective is good. The most defensible reasons for maintaining a nuclear arsenal are prevention of nuclear war and preservation of national independence. More debatable is the aim of spreading freedom and justice in the world. Most problematic is the aim of propagating Christian values or the American Way of Life or US economic interests.

The attempt to advance even the legitimate objectives in the above list by nuclear threats is wrong because:

(a) All existing and proposed systems of deterrence are inherently unstable, given the inevitable shifts in political relationships among and within nations and the dynamics of technology.[1] Hence, deterrence is unacceptable as a system of security even on its own narrow conception of security. The fact that a single failure of the system would be catastrophic and probably irreparable forbids permanent reliance on it.

(b) The goal of preventing aggression against the United States or its allies and interests is too narrow for a policy of national security. The only adequate basis for genuine national security is a world order based on cooperation, the fair sharing of resources and restraints on their consumption, and respect for the autonomy of integral (political, national, cultural) groups. Nations and the individuals who compose nations will never reach complete fulfillment in their histories and lives, or enjoy real security in the level of fulfillment that they do achieve, until such an order exists.

---

[1]Proponents of nuclear armaments argue that forty-five years of research and planning, trial-and-error implementation, technological advances and political experience have produced a stable system of mutual deterrence despite a number of touchy moments. They have in mind, however, a stability predicted on a standoff in power between the NATO and Warsay Pact blocs, with no serious third-party rivals. Even if they are correct about the equilibrium of past decades (which is open to serious question) current events (at the time of this writing and at any other time of the reader's choosing) should remind us that assumptions of perfmanence cannot be made the basis of life-and-death policies.

(c) Implicit in the first two points is the notion that use of terror to prevent aggression does not insure true security even when it "works" in the short term. While fear inhibits the weak from attacking the strong for the present, it incites them to become strong or else prostitute themselves to strong patrons and thereby mount a threat to those who have threatened them. Worse, reliance on terror and threat for immediate narrow national objectives is a positive obstacle to the larger goal of a world order based on cooperation, justice and mutual respect. Fear feeds on fear, suspicion on suspicion, injustice on injustice—and hostility on all of these.

(d) The Security State which is required to maintain an effective nuclear deterrent (that is, as effective as the nature of the nuclear deterrent permits) corrupts the nation which adopts it. It subverts democracy and curtails civil liberties; it perverts science and academia; it distorts public communication; it condemns its citizens to live under a pall of fear. While one cannot say that nuclear weapons have created the Security State—they are as much its effects as its cause—and one cannot claim that all of the pathologies of our society are due to the Security Establishment, the State and the Establishment have surely aggravated infections that were already present and introduced new ones. More to the point, it is difficult to imagine how we might cure these infections as long as the Security State is maintained.

(e) *The Revised Moral Argument*: While some of the implications of the second premise of FBG's argument, that it is wrong to intend to do what it is wrong to do, are problematic, it does express a fundamental truth. As a result of the connection between doing and intending in the structure of human actions, people who sanction actions of their leaders which violate their personal principles suffer from cognitive dissonance. Dissonance produces either political cynicism and passivity, slackening of private morals, or both. Moreover, fear never ennobles a people. It turns them inward to indulge in private concerns or causes them to seek scapegoats for public evils and turn their hostility upon out-groups in other nations and in their own. Our nation's system of nuclear deterrence and the Security State of which it is an integral part have contributed to these irrationalisms. Nuclear deterrence, then, is both imprudent and wrong.

But perhaps we have no way out of the hole humanity has dug for itself. Relations between nations may be so Hobbesian that moral principles have no role to play. Relations may be so unstable that enlightened self-interest cannot find a firm point to exert its leverage.

I cannot resign myself to these despairing conclusions. It is true that nuclear weapons cannot be uninvented. It is probable that, however they offend our moral and prudential sensibilities, the landscape will teem with them for a long time to come. Bemoaning them will not make them go away nor prevent our society from clinging to them in the illusion of security. But we can make the best of a bad thing. We can use our weapons as a basis for negotiation. We can use them to forestall proliferation, vertical as well as horizontal, and work to reduce nuclear arsenals until conditions are ripe to eliminate them altogether and insure that they will never be reintroduced. If bargain we must, bargain we should. It is clearly time to use our obscene pile of chips.

To put it more precisely, our weapons provide us the wherewithal for unilateral "sacrifices"—initiatives that could show the way to a more secure world to other actual and potential nuclear powers and regain such moral authority as we once had in the cause of a more just world.

Fruitful negotiation and true leadership, however, presuppose valid objectives. We private citizens must hold our leaders to a higher aim than national security in the narrow sense of the ability to beat off attackers and beat down those who offend our sensibilities or compete with us for material privileges. Such an aim is a just and cooperative world order. Indeed, leaders must be brought to see that security in the narrow sense is impossible until a decent world order is achieved. They must be brought to see that the national interest is in fact identical with the interests of humanity.

University of Missouri, Columbia

Appendix

The Moral Argument Against Nuclear Deterrence

Premises

P1. It is wrong to use nuclear weapons in combat.
P2. It is wrong to intend to do what it is wrong to do.
P3. If one threatens to do something, one either intends to do it or one is bluffing.
P4. Nuclear bluffing is impossible.
P5. To possess nuclear weapons is to threaten potential adversaries.

Conclusions

C1. It is wrong to intend to use nuclear weapons in combat. (From P1 and P2)
C2. If one threatens to use nuclear weapons, one intends to use them. (From P3 and P4)
C3. If one possess nuclear weapons, one intends to use them. (From P5 and C2)
C4. It is wrong to possess nuclear weapons. (From C1 and C3)

Grounds for P1

Natural (Moral) Laws:
> First Principle: Choose only possibilities compatible with integral human fulfillment.
> Evil Means Principle: Evil may not be done that good may come.
> Law of Murder: It is wrong to kill the innocent deliberately.

Just-War Principles derived from the Law:
> Discrimination: Noncombatants must not be directly attacked.

> Proportionality: Noncombatant casualties as side-effects of military actions must not be disproportionate to the evil fought against or the good sought.

Factual Claim:
> Because of the nature of nuclear weapons, any use of them would be indiscriminate and/or disproportionate.

15 Nuclear Weapons: Neither Moral Nor Legal: An Indirect Plea for Abolition

Ronald E. Santoni

In preceding papers,[1] I have critically examined attempts on the part of contemporary just war theorists to recover just war theory for a nuclear age. I have argued strongly against the attempts of "just war" advocates to allow for the moral possibility or justifiability of any nuclear war, no matter how restrained in intent.

In the present paper, I wish, first, to summarize the conclusions of my study of some contemporary interpretations of "just war" doctrine. I then want to address, however briefly, the "right of nuclear self defense" argument offered by both "just war" proponents and advocates of nuclear deterrence. In the final portion of my paper, I propose to show that my moral indictment of any use of nuclear weaponry is strongly bolstered by commonly accepted international law or, more specifically, what has come to be called the emergent "law of armed conflict".

Conclusions of My Study of Modern "Just War" Contentions

James Turner Johnson, quite likely the best of the contemporary historians of the "just war" tradition, has maintained that "The first requisite of moral use [of weapons of war] is human

*This paper was initially presented to the Global Studies Seminar at Denison University on November 19, 1989, and to International Conference of the International Philosophers for the Prevention of Nuclear Omnicide, held in Moscow, U.S.S.R., between May 28 and June 3, 1990. I am grateful for the discussion which attended the presentation of my paper, and I again express gratitude to my colleagues in Concerned Philosophers for Peace and IPPNO for the ideas which I have developed and shared with them over the last decade.

[1] See e.g., Ronald E. Santoni, "Just War and Nuclear Reality," *Philosophy Today* (Fall, 1985).

control."[1] Yet committed to the just war tradition's emphasis on restraint, and believing that the principle of restraint can be exercised morally by the use of "more controllable" or "more manageable" weapons of war, he—like other prominent "just war" proponents of our time[2]—concludes that some nuclear weapons qualify for moral use. Although I endorse the view that human control is a necessary precondition of morality, as well as the premise that human control is essential to moral use, I arrive at the following opposing conclusions.[3]

First, the inherent indiscriminacy of nuclear weapons and their capacity for excessive destruction, violate just war's moral principle of *discrimination*; that is, they violate the prohibition against the harming or killing of innocents. The technological uncontrollability of nuclear weapons prevents the moral use of any nuclear weapons and, hence, any "just nuclear war." For, if human control is essential to moral use of nuclear weapons, and if all exploded nuclear weapons have some foreseeable uncontrollable consequences (e.g., long-term radioactive effects and disproportionate injury) on innocent non-combatants, then a case cannot be made for their moral use.

Secondly, insofar as the "technological recalcitrance" of nuclear weaponry—that is to say, the unpredictability, uncontrollability, and "accidentability" of them—works against the possibility of any justice in the methods or weapons of nuclear war (*jus in bello*), it in turn works against the possibility of justifying any *resort* to nuclear war (*jus ad bellum*). It would not make sense to argue that there is "just cause" for resorting to a nuclear "war" for which there are no means or weapons which could be employed morally. For, as Robert Holmes has pointed out, "waging war requires justifying the means of so doing": "unless one can justify

---

[1] James Turner Johnson, *Can Modern War Be Just?* (New Haven: Yale University Press, 1985), p. 85.

[2] See, e.g., W. V. O'Brien, "Just War in a Nuclear Context," *Theological Studies*, 44 (1983), pp. 212-213.

[3] These are some of the conclusions of my study, "Just War and Nuclear Reality," *op. cit.*, pp. 175-190. My study constitutes, to a large extent, a detailed response to James Turner Johnson, *op. cit.* I am grateful to Robert Lechner, former ed. of *Philosophy Today*, for encouraging me to do a close critical study of this work.

the actions [and weapons] necessary to waging war," one "cannot justify the conduct of war and the pursuit of its objectives"; and if one cannot justify the conduct and objectives of war, one "cannot justify going to war."[1] So, in respect to modern nuclear "war," the inability to provide a moral rationale for justice in war (*jus in bello*) excludes the possibility of justifying the resort to war (*jus ad bellum*)—even if the "war" is intended to be limited or restricted.

Thirdly, the "technological recalcitrance" of nuclear weaponry calls radically into question the claim that there are "necessities" which "compel that justice be served only through (nuclear) force,"[2] that is, that there are certain situations in the nuclear context in which justice may be carried out by resorting to nuclear "war." There would seem to no "necessity" — or "overwhelmingly just cause" (W. V. O'Brien) or "supreme emergency" (Walzer)—which would allow morally for the *disproportionate* destruction and indiscriminacy that resort to nuclear weapons and nuclear hostilities would bring about. For such a consequence would clearly violate the principles of discrimination and proportionality generally endorsed by both "just war" and "self-defense" moralists. Even the preservation and defense of a country's highest values, often offered as the basic rationale of the just war tradition, loses much of its force and consistency in the face of the devastation of life and values that nuclear hostilities would effect. No human value or ideological commitment would appear to justify resort to a "war" that might escalate to the ultimate indiscriminacy and disproportion—nuclear omnicide. And to argue that any does would amount, I believe, to breaking with moral tradition and civilization"[3]—a form of what I have called "nuclear insanity."[4]

---

[1] Robert Holmes, *On War and Morality* (Princeton: Princeton University Press, 1989), pp. 178, 181. For a discerning and thought-provoking account and discussion of issues related to the morality of war, I again commend this book to the attention of readers.

[2] James T. Johnson, *op. cit.*, p. 189.

[3] Ronald Aronson uses this expression in *The Dialectics of Disaster* (London: Verso Press, 1983). I have profited much from our exchange in panels and forums in this country and abroad.

[4] See, e.g., Ronald E. Santoni, "Nuclear Insanity and Multiple Genocide" in I. Charny, ed., *Toward the Understanding and Prevention of Genocide* (Boulder: Westview Press, 1984).

Fourthly, to use similar grounds, my argument against a just or moral resort to war is strengthened by the "firebreak" argument. That any use of nuclear weapons and any waging of war in a nuclear age might escalate to an all-out nuclear "exchange", and in turn to a nuclear "holocaust" or, possibly, to nuclear omnicide, is a compelling moral reason against the justifiability of waging *any* modern war. Moreover, the "lack of control" inherent in nuclear weaponry increases the possibility of "firebreak." Given the technological "slipperiness" of nuclear weapons, even the possession of them for *defensive* or *deterrent* purposes enhances the risk of an accidental launch and, hence, the likelihood of an indiscriminate and disproportionate nuclear "war".

Fifthly, the conventional just war requirement of restraint (= "economy of force" = "least force necessary") cannot be applied to the nuclear context and to nuclear weapons in the manner that it has been applied to conditions and events of the pre-atomic era. To attempt to do so is to be involved in *pre-atomic* thinking and to fail to appreciate the vast qualitative difference between pre-atomic and post-atomic reality.[1] The technological recalcitrance, the disproportionate destructiveness, of nuclear weapons or of waging nuclear war prevents, in a morally significant way, the imposition of restraints or morally adequate limitations. Nuclear weapons *cannot* be restricted to the intentions of their users. If anything, they frustrate those intentions: they are uncontrollable, unpredictable and subject to accidents. And the fact that some weaponry, e.g., neutron bombs, are *more* controllable or *more* discriminate does not make them controllable, discriminate, or open to moral use. Morality's "first requisite" (Johnson) of controllability is still lacking. Although James T. Johnson and other just war theorists do well to stress the importance of *intending* restraint even in "war", they are unrealistic, finally, in respect to the *recalcitrant* or "defiant" forces that work against the possibility of exercising "controllable restraint." They appear to delude themselves into believing that the *intention of restraint* can guarantee restraint and thus meet the criteria for moral action. But, as the American Catholic Bishops have pointed out, "modern warfare is not readily contained by good

---

[1] I develop this point in "Nuclear Insanity and Multiple Genocide," *op. cit.* Once more, I refer to this pattern as an instance of "nuclear insanity."

intentions" and the "moral issue" is "not resolved by the design of weapons or planned intention for use."[1]

In conclusion, I contend that the proper implication of the principle of restraint in a nuclear age is renunciation of any use of nuclear weaponry and any resort to war. Just war principles did not emerge from the nuclear age and must not be tailored to accommodate it. As Michael Walzer has pointed out, "Nuclear weapons explode the theory of just war. They are the first of mankind's technological innovations that are simply not encompassable within the familiar moral world. . . .Our familiar notions about *jus in bello* require us to condemn even the threat to use them."[2] The use of nuclear weapons, even "small" tactical ones, for what the strategists sometimes call a "surgical strike", is like a terrorist's attempt to apply poison gas restrictively to a selected "enemy" quarter of a major city. Control and restraint are not among the choices which nuclear weaponry can guarantee. In another context, Chernobyl alone is testimony to this. If we are to take seriously the "just war" tradition's emphasis on restraint, we must come to understand that the only way to insure restraint, discrimination and proportionality is by forsaking modern war and nuclear weaponry. The "actualities" of the "real" nuclear world call not for permission to conduct limited nuclear war, but for repudiation of "war" and any use of nuclear weaponry.

The Right of Self-Defense Argument:
A Brief Response

Both proponents of just war theory and advocates of a nuclear deterrence strategy have appealed to the right of *self-defense* as a basis for justifying morally the resort to nuclear war or the use of nuclear weaponry in certain circumstances. And certainly tradition

---

[1]American Catholic Bishops, "The Challenge of Peace: God's Promise and Our Response," *Origins* (April 14, 1983), p. 715.
[2]Michael Walzer, *Just and Unjust Wars* (New York: Basic Books, 1977), p. 282.

in philosophy, religious thought and political thinking has granted the moral right to self-defense—particularly in life-death situations. Just war theory since St. Thomas has traditionally viewed "self-defense" as a "just cause,"[1] and international law, following the lead of "just war" principles and attempting to codify them, has generally recognized self-defense as legally permissible.[2] Although the present paper is not the place for a full-scale argument regarding nuclear "self-defense" systems, I wish at least to suggest that commonly accepted conditions for the morality of self-defense are violated by virtually any use of nuclear weaponry.

Consider, for instance, the condition that "no more force must be used than necessary."[3] This is simply a version of the "proportionality" principle and, as I tried to show above, is frustrated by the uncontrollable, disproportionate destruction inflicted by self-defensive use of nuclear weaponry. In addition, the principle that "the agent harmed in self-defense must be identical to the agent threatening harm" is violated by the fact that any use of nuclear weaponry will harm—if only through radioactive fall-out—some persons who have neither harmed nor threatened harm. As I pointed out earlier, the relative unselectivity and unpredictability of nuclear weapons opposes morality's—in this case, "self-defense" morality's—prohibition against hurting innocent people, another articulation of the *principle of discrimination*.

Finally, self-defense by nuclear weaponry can hardly be justified by yet another of the closely-related conditions of self-defense. "Self-defense" moralists normally argue that harming another person in self-defense can be justified "only when the person harmed is culpable." Although the culpability of the aggressor doing or threatening harm may be known, it is virtually impossible, given my analysis, to confine any retaliation that uses nuclear weaponry—

---

[1] See, e.g., American Catholic Bishops, *op. cit.*, p. 706; O'Brien, *op. cit.*, p. 192.

[2] See, e.g., Robert Holmes, *op. cit.*, pp. 152-157.

[3] I borrow the following formulation from Tom Donaldson, *op. cit.* A shorter version of his paper was presented at meetings of the American Philosophical Association (Cincinnati, Ohio, April 1986), to which I was respondent in a paper entitled, "Donaldson, Self-Defense and Nuclear Weaponry." The reader may note that, in my response, I have contended against Donaldson that the conditions which he lists are "limiting" rather than "enabling".

even kiloton tactical weaponry—to the *culpable* party alone. And, whether we like it or not, a nuclear counter-attack might occur in response to a limited accidental launch by the other side: such a response would kill thousands, even millions, of people who cannot be considered culpable. So even this enabling condition is frustrated by the technological *recalcitrance* of nuclear weaponry.

It follows, then, that just war theorists cannot gain support for the moral justifiability of any modern, nuclear-active, war by invoking the usual conditions offered for a moral "self-defense". For each of these enabling—I prefer to say "limiting"—conditions of self-defense is violated by the indiscriminacy, uncontrollability and excessive destructibility of nuclear weaponry.

International Law in Support of Moral Prohibition

In the last part of my paper, I want to show—at least in outline form—that my position against the moral justifiability of any use of nuclear weapons is reinforced, not undermined, by an appeal to international law—to what we have come to call the "common law of nations", or, more specifically, the "law of armed conflict."[1] Although one might argue that the evolved "law of armed conflict" represents the attempt, over at least three centuries, to codify and

[1] I am grateful to political scientists Louis Rene' Beres and James Stegenga of Purdue University for suggesting that my philosophical/moral arguments against any use of nuclear weaponry would be further bolstered by an appeal to international law. Each encouraged me to do further inquiry into international law. In what follows, I owe a large debt to Professor James Stegenga, whose paper, "Nuclearism and International Law," does much explanatory work for my contentions here. His paper, to which I had access,in unpublished draft form, was presented at the Annual Conference of International Studies Association in St. Louis, Missouri, March 1988. Some of Stegenga's points are stated earlier in his "Nuclearism and Democracy," *Journal of American Culture*, Vol. II, No. 1 (1988), pp. 87-94. Since my writing of the present paper, Stegenga's "Nuclearism and International Law" has appeared in revised form in *Public Affairs Quarterly*, Vol. 4, No. 1 (January 1990), pp. 69-80. I express appreciation to Professor Stegenga for his help, and to Professor Lou Beres for his continued support of my work on this important subject.

universalize just war principles—and thus suffers some of the deficiencies endemic to modern just war thinking—I shall contend that the emergent international "common law of nations" prohibits virtually any use—offensive or defensive—of nuclear weaponry.

Without pretending to offer a complete account of the emergence of international law or consensus in respect to the bounds of international conflict, I wish to take note of common moral standards of human decency that have been built into generally accepted international conventions and treaties.[1] The progressive endorsement and practice of these conventions—which often developed *ad hoc* and prescribed rules to regulate specific conflicts between nations—emerged as the customary "law of armed conflict," the "common law of nations"—that is to say,. as dynamic international law.[2]

As early as the late 1700s, Friederick von Martens attempted to enshrine commonly accepted principles of proportionality, discrimination, chivalry and military necessity by urging governments to obey "the principles or laws of nations, as they result from. . . the laws of humanity and the dictates of public conscience." Echoes of this oft-quoted Martens clause appear, for instance, in the *Declaration of St. Petersburg* (1868)—which insists on limits to the "means of injuring the enemy" and prescribes discrimination and proportionality—the *Brussels Conference Protocol* (1874), and the *Hague Conventions on Land Reform* (1907; Annex to Convention IV, Art. 25), all of which prohibit the bombardment of undefended towns, etc. And as early as 1925, the *Geneva Protocol* proscribes the use of any "asphyxiating,

---

[1] For an invaluable collection of most of the pertinent documents, I refer the reader to Schindler, D., and Jiri Toman, eds, *The Laws of Armed Conflicts*, 3rd Edition (Dordrecht: Martinus Nijhoff, 1988).

[2] According to Builder and Graubard, "The law of armed conflict derives and continuously evolves from three sources: (1) basic principles, such as humanity and military necessity; (2) the customary practices of states in conflict; and (3) formal international agreements, such as treaties and resolutions. The law applies equally to all parties involved in conflict, whether they be aggressors or victims, and whether the conflict is declared or undeclared war. The law is binding upon all belligerents, whether they assent to it or not." (Carl Builder and Morlie Graubard: Rand Corp. 1982, No. R-2804-FF, p. vi).

poisonous. . . gases" or "analogous materials or devices." In addition, the 1945 *Charter of the International Military Tribunal for the Adjudication of Nuremberg Trials*, the 1945 *Charter of the United Nations*, the *Genocide Convention of 1948*, and the generally accepted 1949 *Geneva Conventions*—with their 1977 Protocol 1 Additional—join to reinforce and then extend the protection of noncombatants and the requirement of proportionality in hostilities. In particular, the Protocol 1 Additional prohibits the use of "weapons, projectiles, ...material and methods of warfare of such a nature to cause superfluous injury or unnecessary suffering." The *Geneva Conventions* also (Articles 33, 55) extends the commonly accepted code of armed conflict by prohibiting the use of weapons that would cause "widespread, long-term and severe damage to the natural environment."[1]

More specifically, we may take note of a few post-World War II resolutions which have direct relevance to nuclear weaponry. Resolutions of the United Nations General Assembly directly or indirectly addressed the new genocidal weaponry. *Resolution 95* (1946) unanimously reaffirmed—as binding international law—*The Principles of the Nuremberg Charter*, including Principle VI's prohibitions against listed "war crimes," "crimes against humanity," and "crimes against peace." *General Assembly Resolution 1653* (XVI) 1961, Section 1(d), characterized any use of nuclear or thermonuclear weaponry by a State as "violating the *Charter of the United Nations*, acting contrary to the laws of humanity, and committing a crime against mankind and civilization."[2] Later, in 1972, *General Assembly Resolution 2936* (XXVII) reaffirmed this 1961 denunciation by declaring that any use of nuclear weapons violates the *Charter of the United Nations*, and then solemnly committed the member states of the U.N. to "permanent prohibition of the use of nuclear weapons."[3]

Although, to be sure, commentators do not view these U.N. resolutions as establishing binding law, many scholars—as political scientist James Stegenga has pointed out—view them as "expressing emergent customary or common law" and as giving "international voice to the 'public conscience' of the Martens

---

[1]Schindler and Toman, *op. cit*, p. 645-653.
[2]*Ibid.*, p. 130
[3]*Ibid.*, p. 160

clause"[1] Certainly, these resolutions reinforce, extend and cohere with the emergent code of commonly accepted principles and rules intended to govern and bind all participants in actual or threatened armed conflict. And, in spite of obvious counterindications,[2] the U.S. government, through statements such as *Air Force Publication 110-31*, "International Law—the Conduct of Armed Conflict and Air Operation", has endorsed the binding nature of this emergent international "law of armed conflict."[3] Whether or not—to this day—this international "common law" has been ratified, part by part, by every government or nation, it stands as a set of normative principles, rules of action, and prescriptions for reinforcement, according to which nations are obligated to proceed humanely and respectfully. In fact, this Air Force document not only views the law of armed conflict as "part of 'international law'. . . governing relations between states (1.4), but acknowledges it as representing "in some measure minimum standards of civilization" (1.5). And the document goes out of its way to state that, although parts of this customary law have not been incorporated into treaties or conventions to which the U.S. has been party, "the United States, as are other nations, is bound by customary rules of international law" (1.6). Moreover, Article 1, Section 8 of the *United States*

---

[1]See James Stegenga, *op. cit.*. Stegenga credits this point to Malcolm N. Shaw in "Nuclear Weapons and International Law", (Istvan Pogany, ed., *Nuclear Weapons and International Law* (New York: St. Martin's Press, 1987), p. 13.) See, again, preceding footnote.

[2]For illustrations of clear U.S. violations of customary international law—and, in particular, of the International Court of Justice—see, e.g., Louis Rene Beres, "The United States, Nicaragua and International Law" (unpublished), and *America Outside the World: The Collapse of the U.S. Foreign Policy* (Lexington Books, 1987).

[3]One might still want to argue that this specific publication is ambiguous if not internally inconsistent. While, on the one hand, it invokes prohibitions against "uncontrollable" and "indiscriminate weapons" (e.g., "biological weapons") it, on the other hand, states in 6-5 that "The use of explosive nuclear weapons, whether by air, sea, or land forces, cannot be regarded as violative of existing international law *in the absence of any international rule of law restricting their employment*." In this regard, the document sounds like "double-talk" and in violation of its own 1-6 above.

Constitution gives Congress authority to "define and punish offenses against the Law of Nations."

On the basis of this cursory and incomplete account of evolving international law, one can readily see—as in the case of my modified interpretation of "just war" principles—that any use of nuclear weaponry would violate provisions of the so-called "common law of nations" or "law of armed conflict." Any massive "first use" of nuclear weapons, "assured destruction", massive retaliation, or other "countervalue " strike, would be a violation of virtually *all* of the provisions which I have highlighted above. Each would, for instance, violate discrimination, proportionality and "military necessity", as well as the genocide, "poisonous gases and analogous materials", and "long-term damage to environment" prohibitions of the above code. And for reasons which I have spelled out in my examination of "just war theory", so-called "limited" tactical counterforce, or even "theater," use of nuclear weapons would militate against the emergent international law regarding armed conflict. If nothing else, the *indiscriminacy* of radioactive fallout and the enduring injuries of such "poisonous" fallout represent unambiguous violations of the common law of nations.

One might add, further—though here is not the place to develop my point—that even the deterrent threat to employ nuclear weapons against another people or nations offends the developed consensus of international convention: insofar as the threat, in actuality, involves criminal, even genocidal, planning and conspiracy,[1] it violates the *Charter of the United Nations* (Article 2 (4)), the *Nuremberg Charter*, and the *Genocide Convention*—each of which has been accepted as part of the emergent, dynamic law of nations. Article 6 of of *The Principles of the Nuremberg Tribunal*, e.g., declares illegal any planning or waging of war in violation of international treaties or agreements, and condemns the same as a "punishable crime under international law."[2] The threat to commit nuclear genocide, the policy of attempting to deter nuclear attack by

---

[1] For my argument, at a moral level, that the policy of nuclear deterrence is genocidal in intent, see Ronald E. Santoni, "The Arms Race, Genocidal Intent, and Individual Responsibility," *Philosophy and Social Criticism*, 3/4 (1984).

[2] Schindler/Toman, *op. cit.*, p. 924

preparing to execute nuclear extermination under certain circumstances, is not only—as I've argued elsewhere[1]—immoral, but is also a violation of present-day laws of armed conflict.

Yet, in regard to international law, as in regard to morality, there are those who would claim license to employ nuclear weaponry by claiming an inherent right to national self-defense. They would appeal, for instance, to the self-defense provisions in Article 51 of the *UN Charter*, in the manner that self-defense moralists would invoke "self-defense" as a "just cause".

But I have already shown how nuclear weaponry violates the commonly accepted conditions of self-defense morality. Insofar as evolving international law attempts to codify "just war" morality, it is guided by the discrimination, proportionality and self-restraint principles, for instance, which this morality imposes on any type of nuclear self-defense. Traditionally—as we have seen—emergent international common law has drawn limits on the means of self-defense, and has refused to allow unnecessary suffering or destruction, or "indiscriminate" bombardment and injury of people or natural environment. So on the basis of my above summary alone, it appears that any self-defensive use of horrendous and uncontrollable nuclear weaponry could not satisfy the commonly accepted provisions of the contemporary common law of nations and of armed conflict. Even a defensive, battlefield, counterforce, use of a "teentsy-weentsy" nuclear weapon would violate the discriminacy provisions, for example, of generally accepted international law.

I conclude, then, that evolved international law and the accepted conventions for armed conflict strongly support my moral claim against any use of nuclear weaponry. Accordingly, I call upon all leaders, strategists and governments of nations in our global human community to abide by and insist on the painfully developed and utterly reasonable conventional wisdom of moral philosophy and emergent international law. I can think of no practical step which—supported by the solidarity of our international community of brothers and sisters—would contribute more significantly to the prevention of nuclear omnicide.

Denison University

---

[1]*Ibid.*

16 The Balance of Power:
A Skeptical Appraisal

Ron Hirschbein

Master metaphors guide thought and conduct in virtually every community of discourse. These metaphors define and control the way members of a particular community conceptualize and express their experience. They are so deeply ingrained that they seem perfectly natural, even inevitable. You cannot enter the Newtonian conceptual world, for example, without likening the universe to a machine. Likewise, if you would discourse with Marxists it would be appropriate to invoke the organic images of social life found in Hegel. Or, if you would associate (or rather free associate) with Freudians, you might be likened to figures in Greek drama. And, you cannot discourse with mainstream foreign policy analysts by being too literal: you must mass the tropes and liken the international world to an antique laboratory balance. Political analyst Claude Inis depicts the icon this way:

> The image is that of two scales suspended upon a fulcrum, balancing only when equal weights are placed upon the two sides.[1]

This icon legislates a particular mode of discourse that profoundly colors and shapes a decision-maker's conceptualization and behavior. Specifically, to be credible—let alone intelligible—within this community of discourse, you are expected to argue that your proposed strategy and weaponry will maintain or restore a durable equilibrium—stability is the watchword. You would no more question the aptness of the "balance of power" than a Newtonian would question the law of gravity. Indeed, if you are like most analysts, it would probably not occur to you that you are thinking metaphorically: equilibrium is a metaphorical concept

---

[1] Claude Inis, *Power and International Relations* (New York: Random House, 1962).

that has been reified and taken for an objective feature of international relations.

Such metaphors resemble Kuhnian "paradigms," but they are not merely cognitive frames that represent *what* is happening. Master metaphors also serve a largely unrecognized teleological and a normative function: they indicate *why* it is happening and *what is expected* of a decision-maker. In other words, the metaphor analyzed here is not simply the product of cognitive processing; it is an artifact of faith—an existential leap. I shall argue that the image of the international world as a simple, laboratory scale is an icon: a hallowed image that conveys a narrative—a morality play with a happy ending.

The narrative evoked reflects and reproduces the wishful thinking—the public daydreams—of the mainstream foreign policy community. Like most reified metaphors, it is self-confessional: it reveals more about how the community would like the world to be than it does about the reality of international relations. Equilibrium has become a truism that is rarely scrutinized. This paper corrects this omission by scrutinizing the ancient, persistent and irresistible metaphor that guides foreign policy discourse—the image of international relations as a precariously balanced laboratory scale.

Such scrutiny must begin with a caveat—metaphors must be evaluated in context. There are—to make a philosophic distinction—metaphors and there are metaphors. Discourse in scientific communities begins with metaphor, but it ends with algebra. (Likening the cosmos to a machine led to Newtonian formulations.) Useful, scientific metaphors prompt the construction of quantifiable, disconfirmable hypotheses. As Thomas Kuhn showed in his renowned study, when these hypotheses are continually disproved by new evidence, the hallowed, metaphorical paradigm is abandoned. (Newtonian, machine-mindedness has been abandoned among physicists, but not among certain social science types suffering from physics envy.)

But things are different outside the scientific community; metaphors are not put to the test. Master metaphors are invoked out of habit, and they exercise dominion over a community's conceptual universe as long as they satisfy a largely preconscious set of emotional and existential needs. (What conceivable demonstration, for example, would convince many of our countrymen   that America is not the "New Israel," the chosen among nations?)

In any case, this is not a paper about scientific metaphors that are ultimately put to this test. It is an analysis of the master metaphor   of mainstream strategic discourse—the icon of   a balanced laboratory scale (an image I shall refer to as "equilibrium"). This image does not generate disconfirmable hypotheses;   and it will likely persist because it offers a facile and reassuring interpretation of the threatening, ambiguous world of international politics.   In order to explore the nature and implications   of this contention, I attempt to resolve two questions:

1. How did the image of equilibrium in international affairs originate?
2. What does it mean when applied to relations between the United States and the Soviet Union?

The Roots of "Equilibrium"

Like other metaphorical constructions, the metaphors invoked in international relations often liken a complex, unfamiliar present to a simple, familiar narrative of the past. In effect, confronted with an inchoate, threatening present, strategists ask, "What's the story?" The balance of power metaphor provides the   answer. While the image of the past often refers to a tangible   reality, the relationship posited between past and present is   fictive: it is an imaginative construct, not a feature of the   world. In the words of Leibnitz, "A thing is what it is and   nothing else." Metaphors tendentiously falsify reality: they exaggerate   similarities between past and present while concealing   differences. Sometimes the fictive nature of metaphorical concepts   is recognized; often it is not.

In any case, those who liken the international world to a balance that   is—ideally—in equilibrium do so to make sense of preposterous and terrifying realities. The absurdity posed by possessing tens of thousands of apocalyptic weapons—whose use would be   irrational and unjust—is obviated by likening the situation to the salutary image of rationality and justice evoked by the simple balance found in 17th-century laboratories. The congenial notion that the arms race has, at last, established international equilibrium is celebrated in standard texts. Writing in his *The Logic of International Relations*, for example, Walter Jones reassures the reader that: "the nuclear arms race is a carefully balanced system designed not to threaten peace but to guarantee it."[1]

This is not to suggest that the arms race in conventional weapons, let alone conventional wars, readily corresponds to our usual standards of rationality and justice. Given the lethality of modern conventional weapons, and the virtually inevitable destruction of noncombatants, a certain "bad faith" is also essential in conceptualizing conventional wars: the wanton destruction of civilians (euphemistically called "collateral damage") is dismissed as a lamentable necessity for accomplishing a higher good: reestablishing (or maintaining) international equilibrium.

The story that emerges from comparing the international order to an antique balance is enticing because it sounds scientific—even just. The narrative conjures up Newtonian mechanics—for every action there is an equal and opposite reaction. When one state (or alliance) acquires inordinate power, other states increase their power, or forge alliances to rectify the balance. And, since such actions and reactions are measurable, they can be managed adroitly through careful calibration—a political science is possible.

This sanguine vision of equilibrium also evokes the archetypal image of justice—a scale in balance. From Thomas Jefferson to Henry Kissinger, advocates of the "balance of power" have taught that the restoration and preservation of equilibrium works wonders in history by ushering in an epoch of peace on earth without good will toward men. Again, to quote Inis:

> It is further assumed that the effective antidote to
> power is power. Hence, stability in
> international relations requires equilibrium;
> when the power of every state or probable
> combination of states is counterbalanced by an
> approximately equal power elsewhere in the

---

[1]Walter Jones, *The Logic of International Relations* (Glenview, CA: Scott Freeman & Co., 1988), p. 28.

system, aggressive action is unlikely to be
undertaken, or to succeed if it should be
attempted.[1]

Rousseau asserted that when the balance of power is askew
among European states, equilibrium is somehow restored through
virtually automatic mechanisms[2] — justice is blind. And
Churchill referred to the restoration and preservation of equilibrium
as "The wonderful unconscious tradition of British foreign
policy."[3]

This venerable 19th-century image of the best of all possible
international worlds (a vision closely akin to the image of the
invisible hand judiciously balancing *laissez faire* capitalist
production) has made a rather startling comeback in the 20th-
century. The concept of equilibrium is nothing less than the
master metaphor of American strategy. Indeed, the *realpolitik*
that has, allegedly, established equilibrium between the superpowers is credited with nothing less than preventing nuclear
warfare—no mean accomplishment.

As you might gather from the tenor of my remarks, I am not
entirely convinced that it is appropriate to liken strategic arsenals
on both sides of the Atlantic to a balance in equilibrium. My
reluctance to enter mainstream discourse by attributing miraculous
feats to the balance of power stems from the answer I devise to
the next question I broach: what does equilibrium mean when applied to strategic relations between the United States and the Soviet
Union?

The Meaning of Superpower Equilibrium

In strategic discourse, the ontological status of trivial,
impromptu metaphors is usually recognized. For example, the
ornithological metaphors—hawk and dove—were first invoked
during the Cuban missile crisis. When General Maxwell Taylor
was called a hawk, no one took this metaphor literally: there
were no discussions of his wingspan and visual acuity, and no one

---

[1] Inis, *op. cit.*, p. 42.
[2] See Inis, *op. cit.*, pp. 43-44.
[3] Quoted by Inis, *op. cit.*, p. 48.

objected to serving under him. "Hawks and doves" were seen for what they are in this context—figures of speech.

Unfortunately, master metaphors, such as equilibrium, are usually reified and taken literally. Decision-makers seek ways of carefully calibrating superpower relations with new weapons and clever strategies. This metaphorical notion of equilibrium is invoked uncritically and enthusiastically without definition or explanation. Could it be that the concept of "the balance of power" is so elastic that it is defined in diverse and conflicting ways? Could it be that this concept is a symbol lacking any tangible referent?

Since equilibrium is a fictive relationship between unlike things—a laboratory scale and the relations between nations—it is not surprising to discover that this metaphor means whatever a speaker wants it to mean; it is a concept without definable boundaries. As Inis notes, "equilibrium" is:

1. Used in different senses by different individuals.
2. Used in different senses by the same person at different times.
3. And, of course, there is considerable controversy about what equilibrium prevents and/or accomplishes.

"Equilibrium" is not merely an ambiguous concept; it may well be an emotive device without any publicly verifiable meaning. Several generations have passed since Richard Cobden, a political analyst, offered an observation that was insightful, iconoclastic and therefore, of course, unheeded:

> The theory of a balance of power is a mere chimera—a creation of the politician's brain—a phantasm, without definite form or tangible existence—a mere conjunction of syllables, forming words which convey sound without meaning.[1]

There are, of course, meaningful notions of equilibrium, but they are rooted in the mathematical and scientific discourse of the 17th-century. Algebraic equilibrium exists when there are equal

---

[1]Quoted by Clause, *op. cit.*, p. 13.

magnitudes on both sides of the equation. And scales are in equilibrium when the left weight balances the right. It is assumed that since equilibrium can be calculated in these disciplines, it can also be calibrated in superpower relations. Some influential analysts go so far as to assume that attaining international equilibrium is just another one of those algebraic "word problems" used by high school algebra teachers to vex hapless students. If this claim seems overstated, consider what former CIA and State Department official Ray Cline[1] teaches in his book *World Power Assessment*. We are taught that national power can be calculated by invoking the following formula:

$$Pp = (C + E + M) \times (S + W)^2$$

Applying this formula, Cline rated the U.S. 35 while the Soviet Union was rated 67.5. Predictably, Cline and others used such calculations to push for new weapons systems and bolder strategies.[3] Apparently, Cline and his colleagues have not heeded Aristotle's maxim, and they seek more precision than the discipline allows—precision is confused with accuracy. There is little consensus about what these variables mean, and even those who agree that these variables can be defined and measured seldom agree upon calculations.[4]

To be sure, most analysts who invoke the notion of equilibrium resist such facile attempts at quantification, but what—if anything—does equilibrium mean outside of formulas or laboratories? And when, if ever, does equilibrium exist between

---

[1] It was Cline who interpreted the U-2 reconnaissance and determined that Soviet missiles were to be placed in Cuba in 1962; he also advised the Ex-Comm.

[2] Pp = perceived power
C = critical mass (i.e., population + territory)
E = economic capability
M = military capability
S = strategic purpose
W = will to pursue national strategy

[3] See David Baldwin's discussion in his "Power Analysis and World Politics" in Klaus Knorr, ed., *Power, Strategy, and National Security* (Princeton: Princeton University Press, 1983), pp. 13-14.

[4] *Ibid., p. 14.*

the United States and the Soviet Union? Can the concept be
operationalized: what would have to occur for this halcyon
situation to exist? The Angel Gabriel, perhaps, may have a scale
in the next world to weigh the souls of men and nations, but no
such device exists this side of paradise. Therefore, since equilibrium
merely refers to congenial but arresting images inside the heads
of members of discourse communities, the debate about equilibrium in the strategic community is fervent and irresolvable.

Consider a hypothetical example of efforts to balance the scale
and to settle scores. Imagine that the START negotiators take a
"walk in the woods" and agree to establish a durable equilibrium by
restricting each side to ten identical weapons—M-X missiles.
(The name of this weapons system has been changed to
"Peacekeeper" to protect the guilty; each missile, apparently, is
equipped with ten 500,000 kiloton "Peaceheads"!) In any case, if
the future is anything like the past, it would not be *prima facie*
obvious that this move establishes strategic equilibrium. Imagine
the objections:

 • The Soviet leadership, if not the Soviet system, is different
from the American: the U.S. requires more weapons to
counterbalance hostile Soviet intentions.
 • Even if we grant that Mr. Gorbachev has a tractable
disposition, who might replace him? What of the "instability" in
the Soviet Union? It is better to err on the side of caution and
produce more weapons.
 • Even assuming that Mr. Gorbachev has ushered in
durable, irreversible changes for the better, don't the Soviets
suffer from technical problems in managing their strategic
weapons: what of their C^3I and their PALs?[1]
 • Since the Soviets have difficulties managing their
weapons, the U.S. requires additional counterforce weapons to
destroy Soviet weapons during times of "crisis instability."

My case need not be restricted to hypotheticals. The actual
debate about equilibrium generated by real-world strategic discourse

---

[1]This is Nukespeak for command, control, communication &
intelligence systems; and permissive action links (devises that
allegedly prevent the unauthorized use of nuclear weaponry).

would confound the Scholastics with its highly imaginative ruminations and worst-case scenarios. Within this context, I can only briefly cite a few examples:

• Before "terrorism" became a horrorific term in the popular mind, celebrated strategists and the highest officials engaged in extended debates in organs such as *Foreign Affairs* about how to attain a "balance of terror." In his article, "The Delicate Balance of Terror," for example, Albert Wohlstetter offers clinical sounding recommendations for finely titrating this balance. Suffice it to say that others who entered into the debate, such as McNamara and Kissinger did not agree upon how much was enough to terrorize the Soviet population: does the U.S. need the assured capacity to kill 1/2 or 3/4 of innocent Soviet civilians? Herbert York, former Director of the Livermore Lab and Science Advisor to several president, suggests that the debate was resolved with less than mathematical precision. According to York, it was decided that 1000 strategic missiles would provide the proper balance because 1000 was a nice, round, formidable number (100 seemed too low, while 10,000 seemed too high).

• Ralph Earle,[1] the last American Ambassador to SALT II, portrays arms control negotiations as an adversarial situation that would even vex a Philadelphia lawyer (happily, Mr. Earle is a very adroit Philadelphia lawyer!). In trying to determine what is required to restore or preserve equilibrium, the following concerns are endlessly debated:

A. Should nuclear weapons possessed by American allies be considered?
B. What of the configuration of the respective strategic triads? Does the American advantage in submarine-launched weapons counterbalance the Soviet advantage in land-based weaponry?
C. The Soviet have deployed more powerful warheads; is this balanced by alleged American advantages in accuracy and reliability?

My critique of the metaphorical concept of equilibrium is skeptical in this most literal sense. The Skeptics invoked the

---

[1]Interview with Ralph Earle, Chicago, IL, November 16, 1989.

image of a balance when Sextus Empiricus claimed that any weighty argument on behalf of a position could be counterbalanced by an equally weighty argument against it. This image of a balance devised by Sextus Empiricus—not the antique laboratory scale, let alone the scales of Justice—seems to capture the essence of strategic thought and action. In strategic discourse, doves have long argued that equilibrium exists because the virtually invulnerable U.S. submarine fleet has the capacity to incinerate thousands of Soviet targets in a second-strike. Indeed, even if the Soviets had a million reliable weapons with pinpoint accuracy, one U.S. Trident submarine could destroy Soviet civilization by destroying 240 targets with highly accurate D-5 warheads. This argument, of course, does not persuade the hawks that the scale is balanced; indeed, it appears that no conceivable argument could. The hawks offer a counter-argument that gets "curiouser and curiouser."

As psychologist Steven Kull[1] shows in his interviews, the hawks argue that while "the balance of power" may not be intelligible, both American friends and foes mistakenly believe that it is. As he explains: "They then conclude that the United States should, in effect, 'play along' with such mistaken perceptions."[2] According to Kull, this argument was first made by advocates of the Jackson Amendment. During the Senate deliberations on SALT I they allowed that, from a military point of view, it was irrelevant that the Soviets had more strategic warheads than the U.S., but the *perceived* Soviet advantage made a difference. Therefore, despite the fictive nature of the balance of power in the nuclear age, the U.S. must create the impression that the balance of power is meaningful, and that the U.S. must have numerical parity to attain perceived equilibrium. As strategist Edward Luttwak explains:

> Objective reality, whatever that may be, is simply irrelevant; only the subjective phenomena of perception and value judgment count.[3]

---

[1]Steven Kull, *Minds at War* (New York: Basic Books, 1988).
[2]*Ibid.*, p. 115.
[3]Quoted by *Ibid.*, p. 124.

In other words, equilibrium cannot be attained through algebra or weighing: it is to be attained in the increasingly semiotic world of international relations by impressions and "disinformation." But how, Lewis Carroll might wonder, can an American planner determine whether his perception of Soviet perceptions of American perceptions is accurate? Without any possibility of verification, the Newtonian principle must be psychologized: for every argument, there is an equally persuasive counterargument.

California State University, Chico

17 Star Wars and
The Language of Defense

William C. Gay

From the mid 50's to the early 60's the US experienced a fallout shelter boom. Since the mid 80's the US has been going through a Star Wars boom. As presented to the American people, the first boom and the second boom are both efforts to protect us from the Big Boom—nuclear war. While fallout shelters can be viewed almost literally as a last ditch effort, Star Wars could be presented metaphorically as an attempt to nip it in the bud—in this case to nip nuclear warheads in the ICBM bud that initially carries them.

These questions have taken on a renewed importance since the U.S. war against Iraq. The relative success of SAM Patriots against Scuds has re-kindled interest in Star Wars. Even apart from the analysis that follows, it is important to note that consideration of Star Wars involves a major shift in degree, if not also one in kind. Even SAM Patriots are not altogether successful, though the few Scuds that evaded them caused relatively little damage—at least in comparison with the destruction that even minimal 'leakage' in a Star Wars defensive system would entail. So, my first observation concerns the fundamental importance of avoiding faulty analogy between an anti-ballistic missile system that had to defend against relatively few short-range missiles with non-nuclear warheads and Star Wars as a comprehensive anti-ballistic missile system designed to respond to a full-scale strategic nuclear exchange.

Can we protect ourselves during nuclear war? The abandonment of the Fallout Shelter Program suggests that such structures offer little protection. Is it different with Star Wars? Who supports Star Wars and why?

I will approach questions about Star Wars as a philosopher. Throughout, I will be considering a particular myth about nuclear war, namely, the Myth of Protection. Within government this myth is believed by those I term nuclear fighters and is feared by

those I term as merely nuclear deterrers.[1] As such, my analysis of
Star Wars is a continuation of my on-going critique of
governmental myths.[2] In the first part of this essay, I consider the
language of defense, since government presents Star Wars as a
defensive system. Then, in the second part, I assess Star Wars
within the broader context of its actual capabilities and its relations
to other components of U.S. military technology.

Defensive Systems

Since the late 1940's there have been on-going government
efforts to develop defensive systems as means of protection against
nuclear weapons. The philosophical analysis of these efforts is
distinct from scientific analyses of their technical feasibility and
physical effectiveness. Many scientists are now questioning the
technical feasibility of Star Wars, just as they previously criticized
the physical effectiveness of fallout shelters. Philosophers are
especially well-equipped to ask slightly different questions. We can
question the *meaning* of these efforts.

1. The Myth of Protection. From the construction of fallout
shelters through research on Star Wars, many governmental planners
have ascribed to what I term the Myth of Protection in the Nuclear
Age. In fact, for years the federal govenment's main civil defense
booklet for citizens was titled *Protection in the Nuclear Age*.[3] What
is the aim of such protection? Is it to be understood primarily as a
means to save lives?

Back in 1979, Paul Warnke, a respected member of the arms
control community, exposed the real reason for the pursuit of
protection. He stated:

---

[1]William Gay and Michael Pearson, *The Nuclear Arms Race* (Chicago:
American Library Association, 1987), esp. pp. 13-15 and 204-207.
[2]William C. Gay. "Nuclear War: Public and Governmental
Misconceptions," *Nuclear War: Philosophical Perspectives*, ed. by
Michael Allen Fox and Leo Groarke (New York: Peter Lang, 1985),
pp. 11-25.
[3]U.S. Department of Defense, Defense Civil Preparedness Agency,
Protection in the Nuclear Age (Washington, D.C.: Defense Civil
Preparedness Agency, 1977).

> If it were possible for either side to protect its
> people, its facilities, and its industry—whether by
> antiballistic-missile systems and air defense or by
> sheltering its population or evacuating it, and
> hardening and dispersing its industry—then
> adequate deterrence no longer would exist.[1]

He does not say protection is the end or goal. Protection is a means. Fallout shelters and Star Wars are different means to the same end.

For the arms controller or nuclear deterrer, the mutual vulnerability of US and Soviet populations has been a guarantor of deterrence because with each side's nuclear weapons holding the other's population hostage neither side would initiate war. So, what end is facilitated by the demise of deterrence? Nuclear fighters, such as Colin Gray, recognize that deterrence of attack against oneself also entails self-deterrence, i.e., one may not be attacked, but equally one cannot dare initiate attack. With one side possessing adequate defensive systems, self-deterrence would also no longer exist. Nuclear war becomes not merely thinkable but also viable.[2] As Warnke saw, with adequate defensive systems "strategic nuclear weapons could be substantially defanged."[3] While Warnke himself considers such defensive endeavors to be both technically infeasible and strategically destabilizing, he exposes an important element in the logic of much government thinking. His statement stipulates a necessary condition for the myth of victory to become a reality.

In governmental planning, the myth of protection separates nuclear deterrers and nuclear fighters. Both see a role for nuclear weapons in the pursuit of national security and international objectives. However, whereas nuclear deterrers see only a second-use as justifiable, nuclear fighters also see a first-use as viable. Since first-use probably cannot prevent the other's retaliation, the

---

[1]U.S. Senate, Committee on Banking Housing and Urban Affairs, *Civil Defense* (Washington, D.C.: Government Printing Office, 1979), p. 4.
[2]Cf. Colin Gray, *Strategic Studies and Public Policy: The American Experience* (Lexington, KY: University Press of Kentucky), 1982.
[3]U.S. Senate, *op. cit.*, p. 5.

rejection of MAD requires belief in protection. Sidney Drell makes
the case of not only the nuclear deterrer but also of many members
of the anti-nuclear movement when he states that defensive systems,
such as civil defense, "should not be viewed as substantially
increasing the likelihood of survival or of recovery in a major
nuclear war."[1] Defensive systems do not eliminate the half-truth of
the governmental myths. Exposing this half-truth, however,
presupposes that one has not become beguiled by nuclear discourse.

2. *The Deceptive Language of Defense.* The language we use can
easily be deceptive. For example, after World War II we re-named
one important governmental department. The War Department was
re-named the Defense Department. This shift might be sincere if the
War Department had primarily been an agency for aggression which
developed offensive capabilities and if the Defense Department was
primarily to be an agency for protection which would develop
defensive systems. Since the agency and its purpose are the same,
the linguistic change is deceptive. Whether termed the War
Department or the Defense Department, that agency has always
pursued both offensive and defensive weapons and strategies.
Nevertheless, for a public leery of any plans to initiate war, the
changed designation functions semantically in a manner that creates
positive rather than negative associations with the agency.

We need to recognize that the terms "offense" and "defense" are
relative and usually occur in broader contexts which affect their
meaning. Nevertheless, it makes sense to insist that at the least any
initiative strike be designated as *offensive*, even if that countervalue
or counterforce strike is made in the name of self-defense. To call a
strike offensive does not necessarily mean that it is therefore
unjustified. Since there may well be some offensive strikes that are
justified, it would be wrongheaded to reduce that which is justifiable
to that which is defensive. Besides, even that which is defensive
may sometimes be unjustified. Moreover, not all responses to
offensive strikes are themselves defensive. A response is *defensive*
only if it seeks to *thwart* a strike by keeping it from reaching or
damaging its target. Instead of (or in addition to) trying to protect
that which someone is attacking, one can strike at something other
than the weapons being used by the attacker, thereby creating a

---

[1]*Ibid.,* p. 57.

diversion or scoring a retaliation. Diversionary or retaliatory strikes are as offensive as initiative strikes, but they are not defenses, because they neither shield the attacked nor disarm the attacker. They may be countermeasures to the current strike, but they do not lessen its damage.

The terms "offense" and "defense" are ambiguous, and given the complexities of conflict, they allow for the deceptive use of language. Systems like civil defense, ABM and Star Wars are presented as defensive. If they are defensive—if the contrast between offensive and defensive systems is real—then they defend against something which is offensive. Of course, any missiles launched by an adversary can be designated as offensive and any protection against them can be termed defensive. Yet, we do not call that agency which prepares missiles of our own for possible launch the War Department, let alone the Department for Military Offensives. Our missiles are not offensive; they are defensive. Not surprisingly, our adversary can say pretty much the same thing. To an outsider, or even to an insider with just a little critical acumen, the systems and their functions look pretty similar.

The respective governmental contrasts regarding that which is offensive and that which is defensive are not only often vacuous but also frequently instances of the fallacy of special pleading. Actually, it may be easier to see how the fallacy of special pleading occurs than how a vacuous contrast is present. Special pleading occurs when we hold ourselves to a different standard, often less rigorous or more charitable. So, saying that the ICBM's of one's own nation are defensive while saying that the ICBM's of another nation are offensive may involve special pleading.

My stronger point, however, is that the *distinction* between offensive and defensive systems is *itself* largely a vacuous one, quite apart from the added problem of special pleading. How is it that some officials claim that ICBM and SLBM systems are offensive and that civil defense, ABM, and Star Wars systems are defensive? From a functional perspective, it would make sense to say that Soviet civil defense, ABM and Star Wars systems are as defensive as US civil defense, ABM, and Star Wars systems; likewise, US civil defense, ABM, and Star Wars systems are as offensive as Soviet civil defense, ABM, and Star Wars systems.

Civil defense, ABM's, and Star Wars are operated by the military (whether it is called a War Department or a Defense

Department), and they are part of the apparatus by means of which a nation state maintains its capacity to wage war. In war all parties, whether aggressors or defenders, have always given thought to protection of their bodies and weapons. Effective offensive systems, in combination with effective defensive systems, aid war efforts. The benefit of such a combination of systems holds whether a nation is initiating an attack or seeking to respond to attack. Nevertheless, as a result of the linguistic deception facilitated by the vacuous contrast between offensive and defensive systems, the public can fail to see that civil defense, ABM's, and Star Wars can be part of an aggressive, offensive, or war fighting strategy. Such systems are not instruments of either purely offensive or purely defensive military postures and policies. Assessment of systems should not occur in abstraction from their possible use. Since they can be used to help initiate attack or to help respond to attack, and especially since they may be very effective in responding to counterattack, the designation of civil defense, ABM's, and Star Wars as defensive introduces a vacuous contrast that can be quite deceptive. Just as the Defense Department is in charge of war, even so defensive systems are instruments of war.

Making the whole problem of language even more complicated is the dilemma facing the linguistic analyst.[1] On the one hand, it does not seem appropriate to say that everything is fine with the language of defense. Our concerns about the reference and function of these words do not simply dissolve once we understand how they are used. While Wittgenstein may have given us a useful hermeneutics of language, we also need a critique of language as used. Understanding how language is used is distinct from endorsing the social prejudices that lie behind it. Just because we understand racist and sexist language does not mean we approve of it. Likewise, understanding the language of defense is not synonymous with endorsing it. On the other hand, if one is to have credibility, one is often expected to use the linguistic coin of the established political realm. So, we may find ourselves all too easily caught up in the language game of that very form of life that we seek to transform. In so doing, we run the risk of being co-opted.

---

[1]Cf. William C. Gay, "Nuclear Discourse and Linguistic Alienation." *Journal of Social Philosophy*, Vol. 18, No.2 (Summer 1987), pp. 42-49.

Yet, to be a maverick, we risk being dismissed, if not just misunderstood. We may come to feel that deSaussure is correct when he says that no individual can change even a single sign in the system of language. I believe, on the contrary, that social groups can come to change language and thereby affect both consciousness and subsequent action, but in this essay I will restrict myself to internal criticism by exposing the distortions in communication about Star Wars. Such a critique, though not sufficient, may well be necessary.

Star Wars

Ronald Reagan had a dream that nuclear weapons could be rendered impotent and obsolete. So far, it appears that George Bush shares this dream. And they are not alone in this dream. For decades many millions of people have feared nuclear weapons and wished that something could be done that would take away their threat. While this fear and wish are common, the resolve of others to produce and deploy powerful and viable nuclear weapons has been constant. Nuclear deterrers may be satisfied with nuclear weapons that are extraordinarily powerful, but nuclear fighters also want nuclear weapons that can be used successfully in pursuing a wide-range of military options. Nuclear fighters, it would seem, cannot share the dream of Reagan and Bush, because they do not want *their* nuclear weapons to be either impotent or obsolete. Yet, as is well known, nuclear fighters are among the strongest supporters of Star Wars. It is hard to imagine how, at the same time, nuclear weapons could be obsolete and viable, as well as impotent and powerful. Such inconsistencies may be possible in a dream, but not in reality. Star Wars cannot make contradictory dreams come true. So, we need to distinguish what some may wish or say regarding Star Wars from an analysis of what Star Wars would be and could do.

Star Wars is the popular term for the endeavor to develop a specific type of defensive system. Officially, this endeavor is termed the Strategic Defense Initiative or SDI. While consideration of Star Wars or SDI is often restricted to new systems being proposed for destroying ICBM's during their boost phase, there are good reasons for broadening the focus. It is hard to understand what Star Wars is when it is isolated from the other components of actual and planned defensive systems. At the least, an analysis of Star

Wars also requires discussion of ABM and ASAT systems. When viewed together, these systems more accurately suggest the specific type of defensive system envisioned by Star Wars. In order to bring out these points I will provide an analysis that will begin by treating Star Wars abstractly and will proceed to situating it in progressively broader contexts. In the initial analysis, I will reflect on Star Wars as a defensive system. In this regard, I will largely abstract from its relation to other defensive systems and will focus on defining what Star Wars would be in terms of how it functions. Then, I will proceed by assessing the capabilities Star Wars would add and their implications. To do so, I will situate Star Wars in relation to the other TRIAD defenses and will expose the manner in which such defenses undercut deterrence.

1. Star Wars as a Defensive System. The fact that Star Wars is a Strategic *Defense* Initiative gives us our initial basis for defining it as a type of defensive system. However, among defensive systems there is a distinction between civil defense and military defense. Is Star Wars to be understood in terms of one or the other of these two types of defense? Whereas civil defense programs try to protect populations and industry, military defense systems aim to protect weapons and troops. Respectively, civil and military defense parallel the distinction between countervalue and counterforce. Moreover, while civil defense is usually passive, military defense is often active. This distinction is not based on the presence or absence of motion but on the way protection is sought.

A passive defense does *not* do anything to *stop* a strike; instead, it tries to *shield* against or *dodge* the strike. Whereas fallout shelters and hardened silos are shields, evacuations of cities and evasive maneuvers by planes are dodges. Before we can decide whether Star Wars is for civil or military defense, it will be helpful to determine whether it is an active or passive defense.

The language of a "defensive shield" is sometimes used to describe Star Wars, but that use is a misnomer. Helmets, bullet-proof vests, bunkers, and fallout shelters are shields. A dome over an entire country that could deflect incoming warheads would be a shield. (Even if Star Wars were a dome, the picture is misdrawn. The dome would be over the adversary's systems and keep missiles from leaving; it would not be over one's own land and keep missiles from entering.) A system that could destroy another system before it could deliver a strike would not be a shield. Thus, the way Star Wars would operate is different from how it is often portrayed. Star Wars is not the "invisible dome" pictured in some of the advertisements for SDI; it is not a passive form of protection. An active defense *does* something to *stop* a strike; it tries to *disarm* that which delivers a strike. A sword is a better metaphor than a shield. Although a sword is primarily an offensive weapon, it can be used defensively. With a sword, you can "intercept" or deflect someone else's strike, and you can "knock out" or remove the other's sword. Such uses of a sword can be viewed as active defense, whereas "stabbing" or striking the body of an armed opponent seems offensive. (Of course, we use the expression "self-defense" to justify all sorts of attacks. Many times our contrasts eventually become quite ambiguous if not outright vacuous. Even a shield can be used offensively. You can use a shield to bash someone's head in. Moreover, even shields used to shield are sometimes moved about quite a bit, but that does not make them active defenses in the technical sense. Nevertheless, these distinctions get made and, even if vacuous, we can try to sort them out.) Star Wars is an active defense because it does something to stop a strike. Whereas ABM systems are designed to intercept incoming warheads, some Star Wars systems are supposed to be able to knock out ICBM's before they deploy their warheads.

A more interesting question is whether Star Wars is a type of civil defense or military defense. In order to address this question, we need to recognize that both civil defense and military defense can be either active or passive. Whereas a fallout shelter is an example of passive civil defense, a National Guard could function for active civil defense. Whereas a hardened missile silo is an example of passive military defense, a use of gunfire to "cover" a soldier moving from one bunker to another could function for active military defense. Sometimes, the same system can be used for either purpose. If used to protect cities, an ABM system would function as an active civil defense. If used to protect missile fields, an ABM system would function as an active military defense. The same can be said about Star Wars. Star Wars would be active civil defense if used to protect cities and active military defense if used to protect missiles. However, when a strategic missile is launched, we do not know whether its warheads are headed for countervalue or counterforce targets. The location of an ABM system can make clear whether it protects cities or missiles, but whether a Star Wars system would be preventing countervalue or counterforce strikes is indeterminate. Equally indeterminate is whether Star Wars is for offense or defense.

How a weapon can function is only part of the story. When abstracted from other considerations, Star Wars can appear to be more defensive than a sword. We know swords have a clear offensive function along with various defensive functions. Star Wars, while a form of active defense, is not as clearly offensive as a sword. However, just as we have seen that swords which appear to be offensive can be used defensively, even so we will see that Star Wars, which appears to be defensive, can be used offensively. In this regard, an analogy to a gun dual may be illuminating. While a gun can be used offensively to kill the other, it can also be used defensively to disarm the other. If one's own ICBM's are fired at the other's ICBM's and hit them before they are launched, that is like one party in a dual shooting the gun out of the other's holster. (Of course, if that holster is empty—if a missile has already been fired from the silo—the strike wastes a shot and the other may have already fired.) Nevertheless, although Star Wars sometimes gets portrayed in this manner, Star Wars does not aim for the holster. Star Wars aims for the raised gun—for an ICBM in boost-phase. (MIRV deployment during mid-phase is more like bullets being fired and leaving a gun's chambers.) With a raised gun, the target is not always clear. It may be aimed at your gun or at your heart. During boost-phase, Star Wars cannot discriminate between counterforce and countervalue attacks. (During mid-phase, such discrimination is in principle possible. During re-entry, this discriminating ability is easy but irrelevant, since ground-based ABM's are located at specific civil or military sites.)

The reason why Star Wars can appear to be more defensive than a sword is because of what it looks like, though looks can be deceiving. To see why Star Wars gets taken as defensive and a shield, we need to modify the dual analogy. Suppose one party had a holster on each hip. While the weapon in one holster is a big gun, the weapon in the other holster is a little "anti-gun." Since big guns and little anti-guns *look* different, we may forget that *both* are *guns*. We can come to think that big guns, like swords, are offensive and little anti-guns, like shields, are defensive. To see how such thinking arises, we need to continue our analogy. Let us further assume that whereas big guns fire bullets that can blow away heads and holsters (with or without guns still in them), little "anti-guns" can knock out guns as they are drawn from holsters and before they fire. Finally, imagine that drawing and firing big guns is slow, while drawing and firing little "anti-guns" is fast; little "anti-guns" are fast, let us assume, because they are lightweight and thus can only destroy small things like gun barrels rather than such big things as holsters and hearts.

What happens if one party has a big gun and a little "anti-gun" and the other only has a big gun? The big gun of the party with both appears to be an offensive weapon, even if that party claims that its big gun is for defense. That party's little "anti-gun" would appear to be a defensive weapon. (The big gun of the party with no "anti-gun" would appear to have both offensive and defensive uses, although the other's "anti-gun" could nullify either use of its big gun.)

Star Wars is like a little "anti-gun" and *appears* to be *only defensive* and like a *shield* because, as a response to a launched ICBM, it is re-active. But there is a decisive difference in the way shields and anti-guns like Star Wars move to block a blow. Shields absorb and Star Wars disarms. So, *in reality*, Star Wars is more like a *sword*. Relative to big guns, little "anti-guns" function like swords; they are forms of active defense that knock the sword out of the other's hand. Star Wars is an active defense against ICBM's. But Star Wars is more like a sword than a shield for another reason as well. We already know swords and big guns are offensive weapons. The same is, of course, true of little anti-guns. While the little anti-gun we imagined could not be used against holsters or hearts, it might be quite effective against other small and soft targets—like eyes. Star Wars could quite easily be used offensively against such small and soft targets as satellites. Since communications satellites do not make strikes, their destruction would appear to be offensive, rather than defensive. At the least, a weapon used to destroy them *initiates* an attack on them and does not defend against a strike from them. Of course, since satellites, like eyes, can aid offense, one can claim that an attack on them is for defense. Turning off or blowing out the lights someone else is using so as to darken a room can frustrate them in their attack (or retaliation) on you.

Despite this and other potential offensive uses of Star Wars, it *appears* to primarily be a defensive system *when* viewed myopically as merely an "anti-gun" to a big gun. When we recall that anti-guns are still guns, we can broaden our vision. Difference in appearance and size does not always make for a difference in kind. Guns, even little ones, have offensive uses. So just as whether Star Wars would be preventing countervalue or counterforce strikes is indeterminate, even so whether Star Wars would be used for only defensive or also offensive purposes is equally indeterminate. At some point, we reach the limits of analogy and abstraction. Whether no party, one party or both parties have "anti-guns" is not an abstract question, although we can carry out the logic of these possibilities. Many analysts would turn to such considerations at this point in order to assess whether the Star Wars system is stabilizing or destabilizing or whether it is justified or unjustified. However, such logical exercises will not eliminate the ambiguities we have exposed concerning the relation of Star Wars to civil and military defense and to defensive and offensive use. Given these ambiguities, the analysis of Star Wars should not be abstracted from its relation to other defensive systems and strategic plans.

2. Star Wars and the Demise of Deterrence. The United States and the Soviet Union have vast strategic arsenals. This fact is often repeated. Both nations have a TRIAD system, but whereas the US relies more on SLBM's, the Soviets rely primarily on ICBM's. This fact is also well known. Nevertheless, both sides have also taken measures to protect these delivery systems. The relation of Star Wars to these efforts is often neglected. In this section, I will discuss Star Wars in relation to the protection of the TRIAD (i.e., what Star Wars adds to other defensive systems) and in relation to goals of nuclear fighters (i.e., how Star Wars fosters strategic plans which end deterrence).

a. Protection of the TRIAD as Military Defense. Missiles are one type of weapon which a nation may wish to protect or destroy. ABM and Star Wars systems are efforts at missile defense. Even ASAT weapons fit into this picture. While ASAT's, as an aid to protecting or destroying C^3I, are a broader effort at military defense, I will treat them in relation to Star Wars as part of the shift toward developing and countering space weapons. Of course, missile defense systems can aim to protect or destroy only two legs of the TRIAD. Not surprisingly, there are also military defenses to the planes that can drop or launch nuclear bombs. "Air defense," as currently developed, is both "air-to-air" (a "defensive" plane fires on an "offensive" plane that is carrying bombs) and "ground-to-air" (ground-based missiles or artillery fire against aircraft carrying bombs). Together, missile defense and air defense cover the TRIAD. Insofar as these efforts protect one's own systems, they guarantee survivable nuclear deterrent forces. However, insofar as these efforts threaten the "penetration capability" of the other's nuclear forces, they end self-deterrence.

Missile defense, as part of military defense, aims to protect or destroy ICBM's and SLBM's. Over the years a wide-range of systems have been developed or projected for missile defense. ABM systems provide ground-based, last-second attempts at destruction of incoming warheads from ICBM's and SLBM's. An ABM system can aim to protect ICBM's or cities. The original US effort at ABM's was for missile defense rather than for civil defense. In 1967, the year after the Soviet Union developed a modest ABM system around Moscow, the US announced it would construct a "thin" ABM system which would protect our missile fields, supposedly from Chinese ICBM's which were under development. Soviet ABM's around Moscow might appear to be for civil defense. However, given the highly centralized Soviet governmental bureaucracy which is located in Moscow, their ABM system also, perhaps primarily, serves to protect key leadership of C^3I. So, Soviet ABM's, like the developed but now mothballed US ABM's, function for military defense. However, until recently ABM efforts were not taken very seriously from a technical point of view and were viewed suspiciously from a strategic point of view.

During the 70's, the nuclear deterrers' argument prevailed. Arms control aimed to reinforce *mutual* deterrence by enhancing the prospects for retaliation and undercutting the development of effective first-strike capability. Limits on ABM systems were designed to guarantee for each a survivable nuclear deterrent. Without limits on ABM and other military defenses, effective damage limitation (especially from retaliation) might be possible. Neither side would be likely to start a nuclear war if it knew it could not do much to defend itself against retaliation. Those who now argue that Star Wars should primarily function as a "point defense," that is, for the protection of missile fields, are actually returning to the argument of the nuclear deterrers. Insofar as they favor terminal defenses, they may be seeking to guarantee a survivable nuclear deterrent, but insofar as they favor boost-phase defenses their intent is more ambiguous (given the indeterminacy of ICBM targeting until deployment of MIRV's during mid-phase) and may be part of a war fighting strategy.

While ABM's offer a late response to ICBM's and SLBM's, what was once termed BMD (ballistic missile defense) offers an early response. BMD is usually associated with Star Wars and is termed SDI, i.e., the Strategic Defense Initiative is presented as a BMD against ICBM's. Nevertheless, it is illuminating to see how "anti-submarine warfare" can also be viewed as part of BMD. This area of "defense" is often as neglected as air defense in the public debate, but it receives a very high level of defense spending.

Anti-submarine warfare is a response to SLBM's. This form of military defense is oriented toward destruction of the other's strategic submarines. While Star Wars is like a little "anti-gun" that is aimed at a raised gun, since it tries to destroy ICBM's after they are launched, ASW (anti-submarine warfare) is more like a big gun that is aimed at a holster, since it tries to destroy SLBM's before they are launched. ASW is more like a big gun because it has clear offensive first-use possibilities. As an anti-gun, Star Wars reacts to ICBM launches. While ASW can be reactive, it can also initiate action against SLBM's. In this sense, ASW is to SLBM's what counterforce, first-strike, strategic nuclear weapons (whether ICBM or SLBM) are to ICBM's: both are big guns that can knock out the holsters that carry other big guns. Although such uses of big guns make them anti-guns, they are unlike the little anti-guns we discussed earlier. Our little anti-guns could not initiate a strike against big guns. Big guns are most effective as anti-guns when they initiate a strike against other big guns. To the extent that offense is initiative and defense is reactive, ASW is more offense than defensive.

The US has numerous fast-attack submarines that track and can destroy by torpedo Soviet strategic submarines. While fast-attack submarines can help guarantee a survivable nuclear deterrent and can function as a defense against an SLBM-gun, they—unlike SDI—cannot stop their missiles once they are launched. While they can destroy a strategic submarine that has launched some of its missiles, they are most effective when they destroy the fully loaded "gun" in its "holster." However, an analysis of fast attack submarines and the many other components of ASW is not my focus here.

Star Wars is the type of missile defense currently receiving greatest attention. Despite any aid they could give to civil defense, ASW and Star Wars—unlike ABM systems—are hardly last-second responses to missiles. While we have seen that Star Wars—unlike ASW—is both more like an "anti-gun" than a "gun" and more like a "defensive" than an "offensive" weapon, it would complete development of military defense in relation to the TRIAD.

Star Wars is an appropriate umbrella term under which to consider a whole new generation of space weapons and military systems. The militarization of space is not new; the placing of weapons in space would be. For years, the US and USSR have relied on satellites for communications. They play key roles in C^3I. From their function for early warning to their role in long-distance military communication, satellites are viewed as indispensable. Satellite systems would also be essential for the operation of Star Wars and could even be targets of Star Wars. For this reason, discussion of Star Wars needs to include consideration of ASAT's.

Both the US and Soviet Union have developed ASAT's that can function as countermeasures to intelligence-gathering and war-fighting satellites. ASAT's often get presented as forms of active military defense. In this regard, the question to consider is whether their use constitutes an initiative strike or whether, as responses to such a strike, they are directed against the attacking system. Currently, the Soviets can use SS-9 missiles to launch killer satellites that intercept targets in one to three orbits, and the US can launch ASAT's from F-15 jets eighteen miles in the atmosphere. Whether these and related systems will be restricted as a result of arms control is still in question, but their potential offensive use is not.

Ironically, on July 4, 1982 Reagan presented ASAT's for what they really could be. He said we would proceed with development of the F-15 ASAT to deter Soviet attack on US satellites and "to deny any adversary the use of space-based systems that provide support to hostile military forces."[1]   In other words, ASAT's could be countermeasures to not only current intelligence-gathering but also projected war-fighting satellites: ASAT's could be used to protect or destroy space-based components of Star Wars.

When an ASAT is aimed at intelligence-gathering satellites, it is like shooting at the "eyes." When aimed at war-fighting satellites, it is like shooting at a "gun." Reagan's characterization of ASAT's covers both the "eyes" of intelligence-gathering satellites and the "guns" of war-fighting satellites. In either case, a military target is destroyed and ASAT use is clearly active. While their use can be for active military defense, their use can also be for offense. How they will be used is indeterminate; so, it is deceptive to characterize ASAT's as merely defensive systems. In fact, like ASW, ASAT's appear to be more offensive than Star Wars because their use does not require that one even wait until the adversary prepares to fire a weapon. ASAT's appear to be weapons designed to deliver offensive strikes.

When Star Wars is related to ABM's and ASAT's, its role in military defense is clear. When Star Wars is also related to air defense and ASW, its contribution to undercutting self-deterrence can be seen. Beyond certain limits, the development of military defenses for the protection of the TRIAD ceases to insure mutual deterrence. Once military defenses are developed to the point that one can destroy an adversary's strategic forces, the door is open to use one's own strategic forces. Or, so goes the myth of protection.

b. The Shift from MAD to NUTS in Strategic Planning. In relation to strategy, those who support nuclear weapons only as second-strike or retaliatory weapons are advocates of MAD (Mutual Assured Destruction), and those who support nuclear weapons also as first-strike or initiative weapons are advocates of NUTS (Nuclear Use Theorists). Nuclear deterrers are MAD, while nuclear fighters are NUTS. Under MAD, mutual population vulnerability is viewed as insuring deterrence. If you are MAD (a committed nuclear deterrer) and your adversary takes steps to end its vulnerability, you have some analysis to do. If their steps are ones for civil defense,

---

[1]Ronald Reagan, speech, July 4, 1982. Quoted in Union of Concerned Scientists, *The Fallacy of Star Wars* (New York: Vintage Books), p. vii.

you would not develop Star Wars. Remember, you aim to leave your population vulnerable. Instead, you would again make their population vulnerable by targeting more or larger weapons on their shelters. If their steps are ones strictly for military defense of their TRIAD, you again would not need Star Wars. After all, you do not plan a counterforce strike. You plan to destroy their population following an attack. Their pursuit of a survivable nuclear deterrent is not a threat in a MAD world. However, if their steps are toward a counterforce first-strike capability, you do have a problem. Such steps, unlike the previous ones, are offensive. You would need to protect your retaliatory strike capacity in order for you to destroy their population in a second-strike . Such a response would be for military defense even if it included Star Wars. So, in a nuclear world, if you are MAD but your adversary appears to be going NUTS by developing a counterforce first-strike capability, Star Wars would be for military defense. The question concerns who is going NUTS. If you are going NUTS, Star Wars is for offense. Star Wars itself may appear to be defensive, but since it can also be part of an offensive strategy it needs to be related to the actual currents in strategic nuclear planning.

In the language of strategists, deterrence can be obtained either by punishment or denial. (Generally, the former relies on a second-strike, while the latter relies on a first-strike.) The ability to retaliate supposedly deters because one promises to so severely punish an aggressor that there will be no gain from an attack. The ability to pre-empt or absorb supposedly deters because one can deny the adversary use or effectiveness of its weapons. Use can be denied before a strike is initiated or completed, and effectiveness can be denied by absorbing the strike of weapons that reach their targets.

The pursuit of deterrence by punishment is MAD; it threatens massive retaliation. The pursuit of deterrence by denial is NUTS; it threatens nullification of an adversary's forces either before or after they are set in motion. The military thinking of every US President since Truman has been either MAD or NUTS. Moreover, actual strategic plans have always included options for the offensive, first-use of nuclear weapons. Increasingly, counterforce weapons have been developed and counterforce targets have been given greater stress. Star Wars has to be situated in this context. We are not talking about abstract possibilities concerning how it could be used for defense or for offense. In reality, we are talking about the actual strategic struggle between nuclear deterrers (the President's advisors who are MAD) and nuclear fighters (the President's advisors who are NUTS). Nuclear deterrers want to maintain mutual deterrence and oppose Star Wars. Nuclear fighters want to end self-deterrence and support Star Wars.

In light of the factual and linguistic points that I have made, Reagan's "Star Wars" speech becomes open to more than one interpretation. Speaking of the steps taken by his predecessors to respond to the purported Soviet threat, he states:

> those steps have been directed toward deterrence of
> aggression through the promise of retaliation—the
> notion that no rational nation would launch an
> attack that would inevitably result in unacceptable
> losses to themselves.[1]

Is the intent of Star Wars to render both side's nuclear weapons impotent and obsolete or to make mutual nuclear deterrence impotent and obsolete? Is the demise of deterrence by punishment called for by Reagan the form of deterrence Star Wars will end or will it actually only end self-deterrence? The demise of self-deterrence does not require the elimination of nuclear weapons but rather the deployment of effective defensive systems across the TRIAD. In fact, when he made his call for the eventual elimination of nuclear weapons, Reagan also stressed "negotiating from a position of strength" which entailed "modernizing our strategic forces."[2] Such modernization includes the deployment of MX, Trident II and cruise missiles which are so accurate that they could function as counterforce, first-strike offensive weapons. As a result, Reagan's remark on the ambiguity of Star Wars is telling. He stated "If paired with offensive systems, they can be viewed as fostering an aggressive policy and no one wants that."[3] He seems to be correct about what makes for an aggressive policy, but he seems to be

---

[1] Ronald Reagan, speech, March 23, 1983. Reprinted as "President Reagan's 'Star Wars' Speech." In Robert M. Bowman, *Star Wars: Defense or Death Star?* (Chesapeake Beach, MD: Institute for Space and Security Studies, 1985), p. 105.
[2] *Ibid.*, p. 106.
[3] *Ibid.*

subject to a misconception if he believes no one (including those who advised him on Star Wars) wants an aggressive policy. To fight and win, you must have superiority, not parity; you must be able to initiate conflict and not be checked by the self-deterrence.

Of course regardless of how well Reagan understood efforts to manipulate him to shift US nuclear strategy more from a deterrent to war fighting posture, the public has largely understood Star Wars as an effort to protect populations. The public, it would seem, has misunderstood the Myth of Protection. Such a misunderstanding may even have been orchestrated. In statements to the public, advocates of Star Wars often stress more the supposed humanitarian concern to protect population than their actual strategic concerns to aid warfighting. Such deception is a political or ideological use of the Myth of Protection. Star Wars is for military defense, if not offense—despite any marginal humanitarian contribution it might make for civil defense.

For the nuclear deterrer and fighter, the absence of Star Wars on both sides would be the most stable situation—a situation desired by deterrers but not fighters. For nuclear deterrers and fighters, the presence of Star Wars on both sides would represent an intermediate situation. For nuclear deterrers and fighters, possession of Star Wars by only one side would be the least stable situation. As one that might bring about the demise of deterrence, one-sided possession is desired by nuclear fighters and feared by nuclear deterrers who see that it is the fighters' belief in the Myth of Protection that leads them to reject self-deterrence.

If you really believed in mutual deterrence you would either not pursue Star Wars or share Star Wars. Yet, it would seem strange not to share Star Wars until you had the capability to deploy it, because to do so would make vacuous to your adversary the contrast between Star Wars as the least stable situation and Star Wars as an intermediate situation. The adversary could fear that Star Wars is designed to end your self-deterrence. The adversary may fear a first-strike. These fears would not be assuaged if both sides are independently developing Star Wars. Each would fear the other is seeking to nullify its forces. Such a situation could even be doubly destabilizing. However, to the extent that one has already pursued military defenses for two of the legs the TRIAD, one may conjure up the courage to complete the quest for Protection in the Nuclear Age. Star Wars, as a weapon in the arsenal of those who believe in the Myth of Protection, is no invisible shield; it is a sword which may be used in a misguided campaign that could slaughter millions.

University of North Carolina at Charlotte

Deterrence Discourse in
the Post-Deterrence World

Lyle Anderson

In his first meeting with Western media in the
five-month gulf crisis, [King] Fahd also said there
is no need for outside forces on Saudi soil once the
crisis is solved, countering past U.S. government
statements that a Western military presence might
be necessary in the area for some time after an Iraqi
withdrawal.—*Associate Press*, 1/7/91

Introduction

Despite a degree of residual demagoguery on both sides of the
former superpower standoff, most pundits concur that the Cold War
is now dead. We now live in the post-deterrence world (PDW). If we
were to conceive this death in dramatic terms, our temptation might
be to categorize the death of its main character (whether pro- or
antagonist) as the climax, followed (now) by the denouement, or
PDW. Although this drama metaphor may be valid for conceiving
the history of cold war actions, the demise of the *bilateral* deterrence
apologetic that licensed such action ought to be understood not as
the climax but as part of the rising action of a post-WWII drama.

In this essay, I shall argue that: (1) the PDW is not the end or
climax of a script, with the "peace dividend" of post-military
production to be pacifically distributed to more urgent and/or worthy
projects; (2) the larger (U.S.) script for the postwar world is the
"Grand Strategy" in which *any* other major contestants would need
to be deterred lest they should vie for dominance after reconstructing
the rubble of postwar Europe; *but*, (3) the tragic (if you will) *flaw*
of this script is that it archaically identifies, in Hobbesian fashion,
military/ economic with "moral" dominance—hence it is
continually motivated by practical success to perpetual justification
of new ventures. The climax is yet to come; while the other PDW
principals are busily turning inward, either establishing or

expanding their economic programs as a real dividend of shrinking-
to-nonexistent military budgets, the U.S. is symbolically stuck in
the Saudi sand. King Fahd, quoted above, has belatedly captured the
salient details. Although one hates to label the looming war with
Iraq as epiphenomenal (as my concluding quotation will), we need to
study its real causes. I shall begin with the notion of a sponsoring
structure for the U.S. script.

Method: Deterrence Discourse
and Sponsoring Structures

Noam Chomsky notes that "[a] principle familiar to
propagandists is that the doctrines to be instilled in the target
audience should not be articulated; that would expose them to
reflection, inquiry, and, very likely, ridicule. The proper procedure is
to drill them home by constantly presupposing them, so that they
become the very conditions for discourse." He continues, "The
basic doctrine [for U.S. state propagandists] is that the state can do
no wrong (apart from tactical misjudgment, the excess of
benevolence, personal failings, and the like); it is the [external and
internal] enemies of the state who are fundamentally evil."[1]
Simply to explicate this notion of presupposition, the obvious
subtext of a fictitious drama may provide a necessary link here for
our hermeneutic task. The nominal text of the Hollywood fantasy
Pretty Woman is about a leveraged-buyout artist who is forced to
confront his pathological drive to control—all a response to an
emotionally battered childhood—by the hooker whom he picks up
during the consummation of his biggest deal ever. The subtext is
that the deal is for the takeover and dismemberment of a Long Beach
Navy contractor, soon to go bankrupt during the demise of DoD
sponsorship, for the sake of some Los Angeles real estate
speculators. The hooker's query: "Isn't that like stealing a car, and
selling the stripped parts?" Jolted into reality by such a blunt
analogy from his unlikely critic, Mr. Takeover undergoes a
conversion experience: he instead promises his target to help
refinance the boatbuilding operation, re-reasons with the Senator
who has been paid to stop a large appropriation in his Arms
Appropriations subcommittee, and gets back into Real Business.

---

[1] "Letter from Lexington," in *Lies of Our Times*, May 1990, p. 9.

That is: the end of the immoral era of leveraged buyout (presupposed in the previous Hollywood morality tale *Working Girl* as a totally acceptable mode of business); beginning anew with the (legitimate) business of building mega-destroyers.

My aim here is to apply this notion of presupposition to the analysis of the U.S. state doctrine of deterrence. There is obviously a deep structural need for justifying U.S. state policies in the PDW, especially as other nation-states seem more preoccupied with their proper business. I will argue that, with the recent if slow death of "primary" deterrence discourse vs. the Soviet Union, the term is now being applied very generically as the (presupposed) *explanans* of everything in geopolitics that goes "our way." What goes our way, moreover, is right; what goes their way (concerning either external or internal affairs) is wrong. That is: there could not be any internal or independent explanation of such recent events as the changes in the Soviet economic or political maps; such could happen only, ultimately, because of our deterrence posture. Hence, for sheer reasons of efficiency, deterrence discourse has served so well in the past that it ought to be stretched for all possible purposes of justifying future U.S. policy. Specifically *nuclear* deterrence is demonstrably presupposed by state apologists as the cause of the recent breakup of Soviet geopolitical hegemonies; *ergo,* "conventional" deterrence is *still performing* its role of making the rest of the world go our way. Chomsky's point above is that there is no serious process of theory confirmation here; policy apologists simply believe that you can fool all the people all the time. We will ultimately see whether this assessment is overly pessimistic.

Edward Schiappa supplies the methodological corollary needed to apply Chomsky's notion of political presupposition to the specific case of deterrence. "Political language is an important form of symbolic action which plays a major role in constructing social 'reality.' The 'facts' of political life are not 'given,' they must be made meaningful through the use of symbols. Language creates 'terministic screens' which *select* some aspects of 'reality' and *deflect* others."[1] Thus, political language is itself "a part of events. . .

---

[1]Edward Schiappa, "The Rhetoric of Nukespeak," *Communication Monographs* Vol. 56 (Sept. 1989), p. 254.

helping to shape the roles officials and the general public play,"[1]
functioning ideologically as a reality-building strategy even if its
use is not intentional. Any political discourse is not merely the
product of individuals, or politicians, but more generally of the
political interests and/or sponsoring structures that give individuals
licenses to speak. Hence, "something of the rhetorical motive comes
to lurk in every 'meaning,' however purely 'scientific' its
pretensions,"[2] insofar as officials act as the producers of political
discourse and the public as its consumers and transducers.

   Deterrence discourse is ultimately our case in point.
Rhetorically, it has supplied the required terministic screen for
communications from its sponsoring structure, the military-
industrial complex (or MIC). Chomsky genetically traces this
structural discrepancy, between the real (Hobbesian) and the
rhetorical (moralistic) statements of U.S. geopolitical purposes, to
the War and Peace Studies Project of the Council of Foreign
Relations that proffered our (pre-Pearl Harbor) rationale for U.S.
entry into WWII. Noting that "formulation of a statement of war
aims for propaganda purposes is very different from formulation of
one defining the true national interest," Project authors
recommended that:

> if war aims are stated, which seem to be concerned
> solely with Anglo-American imperialism, they
> will offer little to people in the rest of the world,
> and will be vulnerable to Nazi counter-promises.
> Such aims would also strengthen the most
> reactionary [sic] elements in the U.S. and the
> British Empire. The interests of other peoples
> should be stressed, not only those of Europe, but
> also of Asia, Africa and Latin America. This
> would have a better propaganda effect.[3]

Roughly, then, the British empire spread Christian culture; the
American, democracy—in terms of official propaganda. More

---

[1]M . Edelman, *Political Language: Words that Succeed and Policies that
Fail* (New York: Academic Press, 1977), p. 4.

[2]K. Burke, *A Rhetoric of Motives* (Berkeley: UC Press, 1969), p. 172.

[3]Chomsky, *op. cit.*, p. 47.

germane to our attempt to reconstruct the original political context of "deterrence": Why did U.S. war planners even need to employ such propaganda? A revealing (and Top Secret) document by latter-day nuclear saint George Kennan explains why:

> We have about 50% of the world's wealth, but only 6.3% of its population. In this situation, we cannot fail to be the object of envy and resentment. Our real task in the coming period is to devise a pattern of relationships [esp. NATO!] which will permit us to maintain this position of disparity without positive detriment to our national security. To do so, we will have to dispense with all sentimentality and daydreaming; and our attention will have to be concentrated everywhere on our immediate national objectives. We need not deceive ourselves that we can afford today the luxury of altruism and world-benefaction . . .—unreal objectives such as human rights, the raising of the living standards, and democratization. The day is not far off when we are going to have to deal in straight power concepts. The less we are hampered by idealistic slogans, the better.[1]

As Chomsky notes, finally, Kennan was not considered hardline enough and was replaced by Paul Nitze, who proceeded to graft nuclear deterrence discourse onto Kennan's containment doctrine. Policy critics themselves could not have provided such admirable clarity for legitimizing our above motivational distinction between the real (policy-guiding) and rhetorical (public-persuading) levels of political discourse.

Discourse and Discourse Analysis: Two Different Abductions

C. S. Peirce's concept of abduction states basically that, if some hypothesis H predicts different sets of observational data DI,

---

[1] Policy Planning Study (PPS) 23, Feb. 24, 1948, *FRUS 1948*, I (part 2). Quoted in Chomsky, *op. cit.*, p. 48.

D2, etc., then the longer the D-list, the more likely that H is true. Hence, in our case in question: anything of note that happens between the superpowers (or their proxies) happens *because* the deterrence hypothesis is true. But, as Robert Holmes (most recently) has shown,[1] this abduction is decidedly unsound: many U.S. threats failed to deter our adversaries, hence requiring some other explanatory hypothesis for their behavior. There is a related but sound abduction, however, which has a second order status: precisely *because* deterrence is perennially invoked to fill all explanatory space regarding U.S. relations to its rivals, one can say that where hypothesis H concerns not the "facts" but the *discourse* of deterrence, every notable political event is *taken to* confirm it. Not the facts, but what Schiappa calls the "terministic screens" that "select some aspects of 'reality' and deflect others," are at issue. Not the world, but the production and consumption of pictures of the world, such that both producers and consumers must presuppose isomorphic "world maps" as structures in which those pictures can have meaning. This structural isomorphism is what Chomsky intends in our opening quotation: by constantly presupposing the deterrence hypothesis, it has become "the very condition for discourse" about U.S. interests and intentions.

Hence, we can study the rather astounding latitude that deterrence theorists allow themselves in "explaining" events that have supposedly occurred since the collapse of the Warsaw Pact as a functional military entity—in effect, since its being deterred *out of existence*. There is, of course, no argument for this; instead, there is only definition. The post-deterrence world (PDW) has been brought about *by* the deterrence world. *Q.E.D.* Hence, the discourse has truly magical powers of production—as we will see in our concluding case.

The Chomsky/Schiappa hermeneutic can be applied to the post-Cold War status of Germany itself, as in this retrospectively interesting exchange on a PBS news segment, right after the dismantling of the Berlin Wall:

---

[1] "Nuclear Deterrence: The Illusion of Security," Chapter 7 of Robert L. Holmes, *On War and Morality* (Princeton University Press, 1989).

George Bush: Our strategy of deterrence requires
land, air and sea, including ground-based missiles,
for as far as we can foresee. . . .
Charles Krause [PBS reporter]: . . . the Lance
dispute [over whether West Germany is "safe" with
INF missiles aimed at its partner-to-be] has raised
larger questions about the nature of the threat
in Europe. . . .
Steven Szabo [National War College]: Many
members of NATO are   in NATO not simply to
balance the Soviets but also to contain [sic] this
dynamo that is called Germany in the center of
Europe. And it is very clear that no one, with the
possible exception of the Germans, wants a
reunified Germany. . ., the European superpower,
in economic terms.
Cristoph Bertram [*Die Zeit*]: The issue is not so
much German reunification. It's German power.
It's this realization that West Germany is the
largest export nation in the world, the
Deutschmark zone is the dominant financial zone
all over Europe. . ..
Krause: For now. . . the Soviet Union is still
perceived by most Europeans to be a potential
threat. But most analysts believe that. . . the Cold
War has come to an end.
Szabo: I think we have a long-term national
security interest in maintaining our presence in
West Europe, *even apart from the Soviet threat*
[my emphasis], and that is because, after Japan,
West Europe is the area of the greatest economic
and political dynamism. It is where the great
game is being played. So, from that point of view,
I don't see why the U.S. would want to get out of
Europe — voluntarily.[1]

In short, that is, NATO is a useful (military) tool for deterring
Germany from becoming too powerful: "Bush's prescription [with

---

[1]*McNeil/Lehrer Newshour*, PBS television, 5/30/89.

or without Lance missiles] is to anchor [a unified] Germany in NATO as a protection against any unilateral move by the Germans."[1] The Soviet Union has been deterred; now, Germany must be. The Chomskyan analysis actually predicts how the *current* "German question" could have become that of a united Germany *as* NATO member, as *per* the U.S. demand: *how else* could they be deterred? George Kennan's attempted praise of Bush, vis-a-vis the German anti-NATO sentiment voiced in their anti-missile modernization slogan, "The shorter the missiles, the more German the dead," is instructive here: "What Bush did, fundamentally, was to change the subject from the modernization of Lance to the prospect of a new kind of peace in Europe."[2] Reality must occasionally be made *to fit* the presupposed terministic screen. As for the recent past, so for the near future: quoting (now) President Bush again, "The issue in Kuwait is not democracy" but "a new world order," etc.

Georgi Arbatov had remarked (in the above PBS segment) that "We [Soviets] are going to take your enemy away." Well, not quite. Deterrence, in the last analysis, requires an enemy; its identity has simply changed, according to the needs of U.S. hegemony. This structural need, from the viewpoint of moral psychology, is perhaps not so surprising: self-justified policies look all too much like those of aggressors. When "pragmatic" U.S. politicians speak of the "utility" of deterrence theory, accordingly, they are *not* speaking of any process of theory confirmation, in the above sense of our first-order (and unsound) deterrence abduction; they are speaking of a useful tool of intellectual crowd control, in the sense of the second-order (and—so far—sound) abduction. *What* works is not the military hardware, but merely the discourse of deterrence, whether that discourse be used to threaten the enemy or to justify policies to the domestic audience of the state. Hence, what it works *upon* is no longer the external enemy, but the domestic mind. Only by presupposing its truth, all actual counter-examples to the contrary notwithstanding, can it be used as a *justification for* any and all future applications. The only problem is not moral but strategic: when deterrence is disinvited to one party, as in the above remark by

---

[1] "Potential to Break Deadlock on Germany Seen in Soviet Plan," *AP*, 6/7/90.

[2] "The Emperor's Clothes," *New York Review of Books*, 7/20/89.

Arbatov on the redrawn European theater, then its declining utility at that party must be offset by crashing another. Political hegemony ought not to *appear* self-justified, hence it always needs enemies—to "deter."

New Territory for Deterrence

Our above allusion to the manifesto of the War and Peace Studies Project, in which the rhetorical requirement that "the interests of other peoples should be stressed" in U.S. war propaganda, quite naturally is global in scope. Let us return, in this context, to our opening quotation from King Fahd, who begs to disagree on the duration of Iraqi deterrence. I have alluded, as part (3) of my argument, to the "tragically flawed" nature of the U.S. script for the PDW. Here, in Christopher Hitchens' nutshell, is a rendition of the official U.S. text for our presence in Saudi Arabia:

> I'm trying to make sense of what I have just heard, the latest in a long series of justifications. First there was the defense of Saudi Arabia, which nobody believes was Saddam's target anyway. Then came the restoration of Kuwaiti sovereignty. Then came strategic raw materials [to which, *pace* Chomsky, we have the inalienable right], sometimes known as oil. Then came "jobs" (James Baker's explanation of what is certainly, at 400,000 troops, a labor-intensive operation). Now it seems that we are embarking on a war to uphold—at last—the Nuclear Non-Proliferation Treaty. But if that means anything, it must mean a strike against Iraq itself. To push Saddam out of Kuwait would not be to destroy his plant and infrastructure. So there arises the question: If Saddam believes that Iraq is the real target, what incentive does he have to undo his crime in Kuwait?

Answer: none, obviously. And U.S. planners know this. When it appeared that Iraq was willing to compromise, State Department

officials labeled as a "nightmare scenario"[1] Iraq's possible offer to
withdraw from Kuwait and to call elections regarding its political
future. But that, in terms of our presuppositional analysis, only
shows what our occupation of Saudi Arabia is really about. As
Hitchens continues, the subtext:

> [The Kuwaiti-Saudi border area] is filling up quite
> rapidly now. A network of American bases and
> airstrips [sic; actually, the world's largest air base]
> is extending all the way across the peninsula.
> According to [the] dean of Islamic studies at Umm
> al-Qura University in Mecca, this mega-
> deployment represents the vindication of a long-
> meditated American ambition to occupy Saudi
> Arabia, an ambition that long predates Saddam's
> exorbitance and expansionism. [He] points to
> speeches and writings from past American Pres-
> idents and generals expressing [this] desire. . ..
> Here is another "sensitivity," and one that is shared
> by many average Saudi citizens. ... [2]

Hitchens concludes that this sensitivity "is one that neither the
President nor his legions of Orientalists seem to register," a
somewhat fatuous inference in light of our foregoing analysis.
Unless the short-term windfall profits of the Fahd Family bank, an
estimated $1.5 million/day on the "Sabah surcharge" for post-
Kuwati oil, is gratefully contrasted with the estimated $1 to $2
billion/day cost to the U.S. for a real shooting war with Iraq, I
would not deem the word "sensitivity" quite relevant to the longterm
gains apparently being assumed by U.S. war planners.

Whereas the economic price is something that those planners
are quite willing to pay, however, the moral or blood-price is still a
topic about which philosophers can feel relevant in speculating.
After all, this is the first-ever U.S. military venture that has
spawned public and congressional protest *before* the event. Essentially, this moral-price possibility boils down to the question

---

[1]*New York Times*, 10/8/90: A6
[2]"Minority Report", *Nation* 12/24/90, p. 794.

whether the presumed "terministic screen" of the related discourse has any large conceptual holes.

I will approach this topic indirectly, using an analogy that is unwelcome to perpetrators of deterrence discourse. In an article entitled "General learned Vietnam's political lesson," written before Bush's post-election doubling of the troop commitment, Colin Powell's "lesson" is summarized succinctly: "Throw enough firepower on the ground right away to keep military commanders from being crippled if a paralysis of civilian will follows."[1] Logically parsed, this argument runs: if there is no civilian mandate, one ought to throw all the firepower possible at the problem. Quite aside from the niceties of interpreting "civilian will," democracy and related constitutional and moral notions of "legitimate authority" for declaring war, etc., Powell seems to have drawn an exactly contradictory inference to that of other Vietnam analysts. Namely, one cannot throw all that firepower at a potential target *unless* there is a civilian mandate. Again, logically: if there is no civilian mandate, one ought *not* throw that firepower at the problem.

Being a mere philosopher, I cannot speculate which of these two contradictory inferences will prevail regarding the current Saudi/Iraqi scenario. I can only point out the contradiction, and/or voice my own prejudice for a two-valued logic. But, the mere fact that even the U.S. public is able to do the same (if perchance without the same degree of hermeneutic mien) shows that a few items—quite unwelcomed by U.S. state apologists and/or planners—have leaked through their terministic screen. I will conclude, by way of an illustrative quotation from Daniel Singer, that only the foregoing "presuppositional" status of deterrence can explain how U.S. foreign policy elites are *emboldened* by the "success" (political utility) of deterrence in one theater to use it as a justification for playing in others.

> The end of the Cold War makes the U.S. presence in Europe very precarious. . .. For nearly half a century the West's economic progress and its "miracles" have been dependent on a system that rests on military output. But will it now be able to function properly without such wasteful

---

[1] *New York Times*, 8/17/90.

production? Miraculously, as if in a tale from the
Thousand and One Nights, the Iraqi expedition . . .
has give the armorers a new lease on life and a
renewed feeling of confidence. It has provided the
United States with an opportunity to gain a firmer
foothold in the Middle East and a stronger control
over oil prices. And finally, it has allowed
Washington to claim that a military alliance is
still badly needed, with special treatment required
for its leader. All of this seems so convenient that
when Europe learned of U.S. Ambassador April
Glaspie's message to Baghdad—warning of the dire
consequences of an invasion of Saudi Arabia,
though not of Kuwai—this was interpreted [by
Europeans] less as a misunderstanding than as an
invitation. As far as the White House was
concerned, the argument ran, if Saddam Hussein
didn't exist, he would have had to be invented.[1]

University of San Diego

[1]*The Nation,* 1/7-14/91, p. 11.

Afterword: Gulf War Commentaries

CPP Presidents

Bush's Abuse of Just War Theory

Douglas P. Lackey

CPP President, 1989

Baruch College, CUNY

The President's invocation last February of Plato, Augustine, and Aquinas in defense of his Gulf War policies should warm the hearts of old-style philosophy teachers like myself. But I must be excused if I do not sign on. Does the Just War theory developed by these and later philosophers declare that the war against Saddam Hussein was just? I think not.

The Just War theory as we now have it asserts that a war is just if and only if it is fought with just cause, with just intention, with competent authority, with just means, with proportionate damage, and as a last resort.

I think that most authorities will agree that this war was fought with just cause, in response to an act of naked aggression. I also think that many authorities would agree that the allies fought with just intention. You should believe this provided that you believe that when Saddam withdrew from Kuwait, allied military operations ceased, demonstrating that the primary allied objective was the liberation of Kuwait. But if you do not believe this, the President's argument is lost. And when we turn to the remaining conditions for just war, all of them necessary, the allied case is even less compelling.

The three articles contained in the afterword first appeared in *Concerned Philosophers for Peace Newsletter*, Vol 11, No 1 (Spring, 1991), pp. 3-6.

The question of competent authority falls heavily on President Bush. The President made some attempts to internationalize his initiative, but the crucial UN resolution did not so much require the use of force as acquiesce in it. On the domestic scene, the President sought and obtained Congressional blessing, but he got it only after dispatching enough troops to make war unavoidable. Congress became philosophical and accepted the inevitable, beaten down by a blizzard of yellow ribbons. Historians may judge that Bush's manipulation of Congress in 1990 mimics Lyndon Johnson's maneuvers in the Tonkin Gulf in 1964.

Strategic bombing was the principal means by which the war was fought, and about strategic bombing St. Thomas Aquinas has little to say. But if you can believe that blowing up every bridge in Iraq is an attack on military capacity, and not an assault on Iraqi society at large, you can believe anything. Just war theorists have always had qualms about strategic bombing, and the many conflicting moral rationales for such bombings developed over the years are as ingenious as they are unconvincing.

The scale of the allied bombardment runs the President into trouble with the rule of proportionality, which requires that the damage caused by allied action be less than the damage it prevents. Since the damage to Iraq was nearly total, and Iraq is considerably larger than Kuwait, the restoration of Kuwait cannot counterbalance the destruction of Iraq. If Saddam is evil because he has brought so much death and destruction into the world, the moral remedy can hardly be to cause even more destruction and death.

But it is the "last resort" requirement that is the weakest link in the Presidential chain. The speed and size of American deployments, the limited time allowed for sanctions to take effect, the inflexibility of the Administration's negotiating stance, all point to a decision to use force sooner rather than later. I agree that Saddam Hussein should not profit from his crimes, but he cannot profit from oil he cannot sell. Many experts believe that, given the destabilizing effect of sanctions, Saddam might have settled for a minor change in the border and two small islands in the Persian Gulf. True, he had no right to those islands, but the United States had no right to the lives of children in Iraq. On the scales of justice, two small children should count for more than two small islands. The President, of course, did not heed Just War Theory; once again, emotion drowned out ethics.

War with Iraq: Just Another Unjust War

James P. Sterba

CPP President 1990

University of Notre Dame

The U.S. led war against Iraq has resulted in a popular victory for President Bush and his administration. For many in the U.S., the President's ability to cope with a myriad of social problems, such as a deepening budget crunch, trade deficits, a $3 trillion national debt, inadequate health care, drug problems, homelessness, deteriorating highways and bridges and a $500 billion savings and loan bailout, seems less important than his ability to triumph over the military forces of Saddam Hussein.

The morality of a war, however, is never determined by whether it produces victory or whether it distracts people from the social problems they face. The morality of the war against Iraq is determined by whether it satisfies the requirements of just war theory, specifically the requirement of just cause that nonbelligerent correctives must be either hopeless or too costly, and the requirement of just means that the harm resulting from the use of belligerent means must be neither directly inflicted on innocents nor disproportionate to the military objectives to be attained. Unfortunately, neither of these basic requirements of just war theory was met in the U.S. led war against Iraq.

First, going to war against Iraq was not the last resort because there was strong evidence that economic sanctions would have worked. In a comparative study of 115 cases where economic sanctions were employed since the beginning of World War I, economic sanctions were effective 34% of the time. In the case of Iraq, the estimated cost of the economic sanctions was 48% of its gross national product, which was three times higher than the cost imposed on any country where sanctions had been successful, So the likelihood that economic sanctions would be successful in the case of Iraq was near 100% if the sanctions were kept in place for about a year. The results of this study were also clearly available to the Bush administration as they were reported in *The New York Times* two days before Desert Storm began.

Second, war with Iraq also violated the proportionality requirement of just means. Intelligence sources estimated that as many as 150,000 Iraqi soldiers were killed during the war, and the number of civilian deaths could equal that number. A recent United Nations survey of civilian damage caused by allied bombing of Iraq calls the results "near apocalyptic" and claims that the bombing has relegated Iraq to "a pre-industrial age," warning that the nation could face "epidemic and famine if massive life-supporting needs are not rapidly met." During the war, we were shown precision attacks with smart bombs, But after the war was over, we were told that only 7% of the explosives dropped on Iraq and Kuwait were smart bombs and that 70% of the 88,500 tons of bombs dropped on Iraq and Kuwait actually missed their targets, thereby causing extensive collateral damage. There were also a number of opportunities during the war when military action could have been halted or slowed down to allow for a diplomatic solution to develop, which would have meant less damage and fewer casualties, but these opportunities were ignored in the rush to achieve a military victory.

But why do so many people approve of the U.S. led war against Iraq? It is that they reject the moral requirements of just war theory? Not necessarily. First of all, it may be that they are simply misinformed about the likelihood that an economic blockade would have been successful, although the close vote in the U. S. Senate suggests that many U.S. political leaders were well aware of that likelihood. Note also that those who favored staying with the economic blockade included such well known moderates and conservatives as Sam Nunn, Lloyd Bensen, Casper Weinberger, and two former Chairs of the Joint Chiefs of Staff, Admiral William Crowe and General David Jones. Secondly, so much attention was devoted to the limited damage and the small number of casualties suffered by the U.S. and its allies, that many people failed to appreciate to widespread damage and the large number of causalities suffered by Iraq. But the proportionality requirements of both just cause and just means demand that we take both types of harm into account. Thirdly, once it appeared that the casualties to the U.S. and its allies could be minimized, many people were attracted to the idea of winning this war with Iraq as though it were like winning a game. After to debacle of Vietnam, many in the U.S. wanted to show the world that their military forces could be victorious again in a large scale war. All of these simply lost sight of the fact that only justifiable goal of any war is peace with justice.

The irony of it all is that once the full costs of this war for the U.S. and its allies are known, it may turn out that even this war with Iraq, like so many other unjust wars in the past, has only losers.

Personal Reflections on the Persian Gulf War

Duane Cady

CPP President 1991

Hamline University

"War is a test of might and is, therefore, inherently
incapable of settling questions of right."
—Jenny Teichman
Pacifism and the Just War

1991 has been a hard year for philosophers concerned for peace.
War critics have been silenced or marginalized as Americans
celebrate the US coalition's destruction of Iraq after Saddam's
takeover of Kuwait. American euphoria and gloating have left me
feeling increasingly estranged from the dominant culture. We have
finally put Vietnam behind us as war returns to its WWII glory.
(Never mind that 57,000 American deaths in a decade was our
tragedy while 100,000 Iraqi deaths in six weeks, most from aerial
bombing and many from strafing as they retreated, was just "kicking
butt.") Jingoistic patriotism is rife; flags and desert camouflage
form the marketing motif for virtually all consumer good. All of
this has given me new appreciation for Plato's observation that
"practically never does anyone act sanely in public affairs" and that
genuine philosophers, "being unwilling to join in wrongdoing and
not being strong enough to hold out against the fury alone" are
advised to "take refuge under a small wall" (*Republic* 496cd). But
questioning what is usually taken for granted is doing philosophy,
and CPP offers us company in holding out against the fury.

    This war has left me alternately depressed and angry, challenged
and discouraged, hopeful and beaten. I have found it hard to work
and I have felt both invigorated and overwhelmed by a variety of
concerns, many with interesting and significant philosophic aspects.
I look forward to the work of colleagues applying philosophic skills
to a myriad of related problems. What does the future hold for
diplomacy now that the war option has been resurrected? What are

the implications for the arms race, first, for replacing spent weapons supplies, second, for marketing high-tech weaponry showcased worldwide, and third, for nuclear proliferation, now that conventional weapons have proven insufficient to deter superpowers? How will developing nations position themselves to preserve independence from major-power dominations? Will peace be anything more than the absence of open hostilities? To all the unsolved problems in the Middle East left over from before the war we must add many new problems created by the war: refugees, reconstruction costs, environmental disaster, military occupation and others. What institutions can solve these problems and minimize future wars? What are sources of hope for peace, for those in developing nations as well as in dominant nations.

All of these concerns reinforce my inclination to think that modern Western culture is itself trapped in what I have called a warist system: we simply accept war morally. A few do so through careful deliberations, but most just take war for granted as the normal thing for nations to do when sufficiently at odds with other nations. Little or no thought is required. The system itself provides the conceptual framework or paradigm within which we operate; so few in the culture have recognized and distanced themselves from the dominate conceptual framework that they tend to be considered crackpots and are usually relegated to the margins of society. Trying to expose and begin dismantling this warist structure has kept me out of or into mischief, depending on your perspective. As insignificant as it is, this activity has saved me from deep despair over what Rick Werner has called the moral surd of our culture: a fifth of the world's children quietly starve while we spend trillions preparing for civilizational death in the name of peace.[1]

This conceptual situation, being caught in a system which restricts understanding is familiar to philosophers. It is the point of Plato's allegory of the cave (*Republic* Book VII). It is also the situation of feminist philosophers, philosophers of color, critics from the underclass and others as they work in our profession.

---

[1] Richard Werner, "Nuclear Deterrence and the Limits of Moral Theory," in *Issues in War and Peace: Philosophical Inquiries*, eds. Joseph C. Kunkel and Kenneth H. Klein (Wolfeboro, NH: Longwood Academic, 1989), p. 136.

Genuine philosophers have always found themselves questioning what is usually taken from granted, and have generally found it exciting work, albeit underappreciated and sometimes dangerous. (This danger comes in more forms than hemlock, as department chairs, deans and tenure committees can attest; I wish I meant to be joking.)

There is important and difficult work to do in applying our professional training and our teaching skills to the range of issues involved in the Persian Gulf War. Perhaps the most difficult step is in claiming the legitimacy of our doing so. Professors are not expected to profess much of anything anymore, and we are invited to articulate and defend the status quo. Our professional lives would be much easier if we stuck with Copi's *Logic*, the ontological argument, Bishop Berkeley and G. E. Moore. But many of us cannot accept the given.

The Persian Gulf War is (sort of) over. The war option has new vitality. War itself is what we need to get over. Understanding our situation and finding our way out may be beyond each and every one of us, but that doesn't excuse endorsing might where only right will do.

Star Wars Bibliography

William C. Gay

The Star Wars Bibliography was compiled for this volume by William C. Gay. For useful bibliographies on the broader philosophical issues of just war, nonviolence and nuclear deterrence we suggest that the interested reader consult William C. Gay, "Philosophical Bibliography on War and Peace in The Nuclear Age," *Issues in War and Peace: Philosophical Inquiries*, eds. Joseph C. Kunkel and Kenneth H. Klein (Wolfeboro, NH: Longwood Academic, 1989), pp. 299-318 and "Bibliography of Cited and Selected Works," *In the Interest of Peace*, eds. Kenneth H. Klein and Joseph C. Kunkel (Wakefield, NH: Longwood Academic, 1990), pp. 325-345. For a continuing bibliography see *Concerned Philosophers for Peace Newsletter*, available through its editor William C. Gay, Department of Philosophy, UNC at Charlotte, Charlotte, NC

The following was written by Professor Gay to explain the relationship between his paper in this volume and the Star Wars Bibliography.

My analysis of Star Wars was written after I researched the technical and political, as well as philosophical, literature. In order to convey my own position and for the sake of readability, I kept the text of my essay as free from notes as possible. Many of my factual observations and argumentative points are based on my assimilation of this literature. For convenience to readers, I offer the following bibliography. I provide the most comprehensive listing available of philosophical writings on Star Wars and a highly selective listing of technical and political sources. Titles with an asterisk (*) to the left are ones that I particularly recommend.

Philosophical Writings on Star Wars

Allen, Paul. "Does Star Wars Depend on Contradiction and Deception?" In Inquiries Into Values. Ed. Sander H. Lee (Lewiston: Mellon Press, 1988): 429-440. Graybosch, Anthony. "SDI: Tactics and Ethics." *Philosophy in Context* 15 (1985): 62-72.* — -."Star Wars: Close Encounters of the Worst Kind." *Cogito* (Dec. 1985): 1-20.

*Hockema, David. "The Man in the Teflon Suit: A Flaw in the Argument for Strategic Defense." In *Issues in War and Peace: Philosophical Inquiries.* Ed. Joseph C. Kunkel and Kenneth H. Klein (Wolfeboro, NH: Longwood Press, 1989): 159-69.

Kavka, Gregory S. "Critique of Pure Defense." *Journal of Philosophy* 83, 11 (1986): 625-33.

* _____."Sweethearts of SDI: A Response to Woodward." *Ethics* 99   (April 1989): 572-573.

* _____."Space War *Ethics.*" *Ethics* 95, 3 (1985): 673-91.

*Lackey, Douglas. "Moral Principles and Strategic Defense,*Philosophical Forum* 18 (Fall 1986): 1-7.

_____."Taking Risk Seriously." *Journal of Philosophy* 83, 11 (1986): 633-40.

_____. ed. *Ethics and Strategic Defense: American Philosophers Debate Star Wars and the Future of Nuclear Deterrence.* Belmont, CA: Wadsworth, 1989.

*Lee, Steven. "Moral Vision of Strategic Defense." *Philosophical Forum* 18 (Fall 1986): 15-20.

_____."Morality, the SDI, and Limited Nuclear War." *Philosophy and Public Affairs* 17, 1 (1988): 15-43.

McMahan, Jefferson. "A Note on 'Pure Defense.'" *Journal of Philosophy* 83, 11 (1986): 640-41.

Myers, David B. "Understanding and Evaluating Strategic Defense." *Public Affairs Quarterly* 1, 1 (1987): 43-60.

Schonsheck, Jonathan. "Confusion and False Advertising of the Strategic 'Defense' Initiatives." *International Journal of World Peace* 3 (1988): 69-107.* _____."Philosophical Scrutiny of the Strategic 'Defense' Initiatives." *Journal of Applied Philosophy* 3, 2 (1986): 151-66.

Shue, Henry. "Morality of Offense Determines the Morality of Defense." *Philosophical Forum* 18 (Fall 1986): 8-14.

*Sterba, James. "Legitimate Defense and Strategic Defense." In *Issues in War and Peace: Philosophical Inquiries.* Ed. Joseph C. Kunkel and Kenneth H. Klein (Wolfeboro, NH: Longwood Press, 1989): 147-58.

Woodward, P. A. "The 'Game' of Nuclear Strategy: Kavka on Strategic Defense." *Ethics* 99 (April 1989): 563-571.

Technical and Political Writings on Star Wars

*Bowman, Robert M. *Star Wars: Defense or Death Star?* Chesapeake Beach, MD: Institute for Space and Security Studies, 1985.

Broad, William J. *Star Warriors: The Young Scientists Who are Inventing the Weaponry of Space.* New York: Simon and Schuster, 1985.

*Bundy, McGeorge, George Kennan, Robert McNamara, and Gerard Smith. "The President's Choice: Star Wars or Arms Control." *Foreign Affairs* 63, 2 (1984/85): 277-92.

Canan, James. *War in Space.* New York: Harper & Row, 1982.

Carter, Ashton B. and David N. Schwartz, eds. *Ballistic Missile Defense.* Washington, D.C.: Brookings, 1984.

*Center for Defense Information. "Star Wars: Vision and Reality." *The Defense Monitor* 15, 2 (1986).

Council on Economic Priorities. *Star Wars: The Economic Fallout.* Cambridge, MA: Ballinger, 1987.

Davis, Jacquelyn K. et al. *The Soviet Union and Ballistic Missile Defense.* Cambridge, MA: Institute for Foreign Policy Analysis, 1980.

DeLauer, Richard D. *The Strategic Defense Initiative: Defensive Technologies Study.* Washington, D.C.: Department of Defense, 1984.

Graham, Daniel. *High Frontier: A New National Strategy.* Washington, D.C.: Heritage Foundation, 1983.

Graham, Daniel and Gregory A. Fossedal. *A Defense That Defends: Blocking Nuclear Attack.* Old Greenwich, CT: Devin-Adair, 1983.

Gray, Colin. "Strategic Defense, Deterrence, and the Prospects for Peace." *Ethics* 95, 3 (1985): 659-72.

Hoffman, Fred S. *Ballistic Missile Defenses and U.S. National Security, Summary Report.* Washington, D.C.: Department of Defense, 1983.

*Jasani, Bhupendra. *Outer Space: A New Dimension of the Arms Race.* Stockholm: Oelgeschlager, Gunn, & Hain, 1982.

Karas, Thomas. *The New High Ground: Strategies and Weapons of Space-Age War.* New York: Simon & Schuster, 1983.

Manno, Jack. *Arming the Heavens: The Hidden Military Agenda for Space, 1945-1995.* New York: Dodd, Mead, and Company, 1984.

*Miller, Steven and Stephen Van Evera, eds. *The Star Wars Controversy: An International Security Reader.* Princeton, NJ: Princeton University Press, 1986.

Parnas, David. "Software Aspects of Strategic Defense Systems." *American Scientist* 13 (1985): 432-44.

Pournelle, Jerry and Dean Ing. *Mutual Assured Survival.* New York: Baen Books, 1984.

Ritchie, David. *Spacewar.* New York: Atheneum, 1983.

Stein, Jonathan B. *From H-Bomb to Star Wars: The Politics of Strategic Decision Making.* Lexington, MA: Heath, 1984.

Stine, G. Harry. *Confrontation in Space: Wars of the Future Will be Fought in Space.* New York: Prentice-Hall, 1981.

Stores, Paul B. *The Militarization of Space: U.S. Policy, 1945-84.* Ithaca, NY: Cornell University Press, 1985.

Teller, Edward. *Better a Shield Than a Sword: Perspectives on Defense and Technology.* New York: Free Press, 1987.

Thompson, E. P., ed. *Star Wars: Science Fiction, Fantasy or Serious Probability.* New York: Pantheon, 1985.

Tirman, John, ed. *Empty Promise: The Growing Case Against Star Wars.* Boston: Beacon, 1986.

Union of Concerned Scientists. *Anti-Satellite Weapons: Arms Control or Arms Race?* Cambridge, MA: Union of Concerned Scientists, 1983.

* _____.*The Fallacy of Star Wars.* New York: Vintage Books, 1984.

* _____.U.S. Congress. House Committee on Armed Services. Subcommittee on Research and Development. *Hearings on the Strategic Defense Initiative.* Washington, D.C.: Government Printing Office, 1984.

Weinberger, Caspar W. *Defense Against Ballistic Missiles; An Assessment of Technologies and Policy Implications.* Washington, D.C.: Department of Defense, 1984.

Zuckerman, Solly. *Star Wars in a Nuclear World.* London: William Kimber, 1986.

Index of Proper Names